Machine Learning for the Web

Explore the web and make smarter predictions
using Python

Andrea Isoni

BIRMINGHAM - MUMBAI

Machine Learning for the Web

First published: July 2016

Production reference: 1250716

Published by Packt Publishing Ltd.
Livery Place
35 Livery Street
Birmingham B3 2PB, UK.

ISBN 978-1-78588-660-7

www.packtpub.com

Credits

Author
Andrea Isoni

Reviewers
Chetan Khatri
Pavan Kumar Kolluru
Dipanjan Sarkar

Commissioning Editor
Akram Hussain

Acquisition Editor
Sonali Vernekar

Content Development Editor
Arun Nadar

Technical Editor
Sushant S Nadkar

Copy Editor
Vikrant Phadkay

Project Coordinator
Ritika Manoj

Proofreader
Safis Editing

Indexer
Mariammal Chettiyar

Graphics
Disha Haria
Kirk D'Penha
Abhinash Sahu

Production Coordinator
Arvindkumar Gupta

Cover Work
Arvindkumar Gupta

Foreword

What is machine learning? In the past year, whether it was during a conference, a seminar or an interview, a lot of people have asked me to define machine learning. There is a lot of curiosity around what it is, as human nature requires us to define something before we begin to understand what its potential impact on our lives may be, what this *new thing* may mean for us in the future.

Similar to other disciplines that become suddenly popular, machine learning is not new. A lot of people in the scientific community have been working with algorithms to automate repetitive activities over time for several years now. An algorithm where the parameters are fixed is called static algorithm and its output is predictable and function only of the input variables. On the other hand, when the parameters of the algorithm are dynamic and function of external factors (most frequently, the previous outputs of the same algorithm), then it is called dynamic. Its output is no longer a function only of the input variables and that is the founding pillar of machine learning: a set of instructions that can learn from the data generated during the previous iterations to make a better output the following time.

Scientists, developers, and engineers have been dealing with fuzzy logic, neural networks, and other kinds of machine learning techniques for years, but it is only now that this discipline is becoming popular, as its applications have left the lab and are now used in marketing, sales, and finance — basically, every activity that requires the repetition of the same operation over and over again could benefit from machine learning.

The implications are easy to grasp and will have a deep impact on our society. The best way I can think of to describe what will likely happen in the next 5 to 10 years with machine learning is recalling what happened during the industrial revolution. Before the advent of the steam engine, lots of people were performing highly repetitive physical tasks, often risking their lives or their health for minimum wages; thanks to the industrial revolution, society evolved and machines took over the relevant parts of manufacturing processes, leading to improved yields, more predictable and stable outputs, improved quality of the products and new kinds of jobs, controlling the machines that were replacing physical labor. This was the first time in the history of mankind where man had delegated the responsibility for the creation of something else to a thing we had designed and invented. In the same way, machine learning will change the way data operations are performed, reducing the need of human intervention and leaving optimization to machines and algorithms. Operators will no longer have a direct control over data, but they will control algorithms that, in turn, will control data. This will allow faster execution of operations, larger datasets will be manageable by fewer people, errors will be reduced, and more stable and predictable outcomes will be guaranteed. As many things that have a deep impact on our society, it is easy to love it as it is to hate it. Lovers will praise the benefits that machine learning will drive to their lives, haters will be criticizing the fact that, in order to be effective, machine learning needs lots of iterations, hence, lots of data. Usually, the data we feed algorithms with is our own personal information.

In fact, the main applications where machine learning is taking off as a tool to improve productivity are marketing and customer support, where a deep knowledge of the customer is required to give him/her the personal service that will make the difference between a purchase or a visit or between a happy and an unhappy customer.

In marketing, for example, marketers are starting to take into consideration information, such as location, device, past purchases, what websites one has visited, weather conditions, to name just a few of the parameters that determine whether a company would decide to display its ads to a specific set of customers.

Long gone are the days of broadcasting marketing messages through untraceable media, such as TV or newspapers. Today's marketers want to know everything about who clicks and buys their products so that they can optimize creatives, spend, and allocate budget to make the best possible use of the resources at their disposal. This leads to unprecedented levels of personalization that, when exploited properly, make customers feel valued as individuals and not part of a socio-demographic group.

It is intriguing and challenging at the same time, but there is no doubt that the winners of the next decade will be those companies or individuals who can understand unstructured data and make decisions based on them in a scalable way: I see no other way than machine learning to achieve such a feat.

Andrea Isoni's book is a step into this world; reading it will be like a peek down the rabbit hole, where you'll be able to see a few applications of these techniques, mostly applied to web development, where machine learning serves to create customized websites and allow customers to see their own, optimized version of a service.

If you want to futureproof your career, this is a must read; anyone dealing with data in the next decade will need to be proficient in these techniques to succeed.

Davide Cervellin, @ingdave
Head of EU Analytics at eBay

About the Author

Andrea Isoni is a data scientist, PhD, and physicist professional with extensive experience in software developer positions. He has an extensive knowledge of machine learning algorithms and techniques. He also has experience with multiple languages, such as Python, C/C++, Java, JavaScript, C#, SQL, HTML, and Hadoop.

About the Reviewers

Chetan Khatri is a data science researcher who has a total of 4.6 years of experience in research and development. He works as a principal engineer, data and machine learning, at Nazara Technologies Pvt. Ltd, where he leads data science practice in the gaming business and the subscription telecom business. He has worked with a leading data company and a Big 4 company, where he managed the Data Science Practice Platform and one of the Big 4 company's resources team. Previously, he was worked with R & D Lab and Eccella Corporation. He completed his master's degree in computer science and minor data science at KSKV Kachchh University as a gold medalist.

He contributes to society in various ways, including giving talks to sophomore students at universities and giving talks on the various fields of data science in academia and at various conferences, thus helping the community by providing a data science platform. He has excellent correlative knowledge of both academic research and industry best practices. He loves to participate in Data Science Hackathons. He is one of the founding members of PyKutch—A Python Community. Currently, he is exploring deep neural networks and reinforcement learning with parallel and distributed computing for government data.

I would like to thanks Prof. Devji Chhanga, Head of the Computer Science Department, University of Kachchh, for routing me to the correct path and for his valuable guidance in the field of data science research. I would also like to thank my beloved family.

Pavan Kumar Kolluru is an interdisciplinary engineer with expertise in Big Data; digital images and processing; remote sensing (hyperspectral data and images); and programming in Python, R, and MATLAB. His major emphasis is on Big Data, using machine learning techniques, and its algorithm development.

His quest is to find a link between different disciplines so as to make their processes much easier computationally and automatic.

As a data (image and signal) processing professional/trainer, he has worked on multi/hyper spectral data, which gave him expertise in processing, information extraction, and segmentation with advanced processing using OOA, random sets, and Markov random fields.

As a programmer/trainer, he concentrates on Python and R languages, serving both the corporate and educational fraternities. He also trained various batches in Python and packages (signal, image, data analytics, and so on).

As a machine learning researcher/trainer, he has expertise in classifications (Sup and Unsup), modeling and data understanding, regressions, and data dimensionality reduction (DR). This lead him to develop a novel machine learning algorithm on Big Data (images or signals) that performs DR and classifications in a single framework in his M.Sc. research, fetching distinction marks for it. He trained engineers from various corporate giants on Big Data analysis using Hadoop and MapReduce. His expertise in Big Data analysis is in HDFS, Pig, Hive, and Spark.

Dipanjan Sarkar is an Data Scientist at Intel, the world's largest silicon company which is on a mission to make the world more connected and productive. He primarily works on analytics, business intelligence, application development, and building large scale intelligent systems. He received his Master's degree in Information Technology from the International Institute of Information Technology, Bangalore. His area of specialization includes software engineering, data science, machine learning, and text analytics.

Dipanjan's interests include learning about new technology, disruptive start-ups, data science, and more recently deep learning. In his spare time he loves reading, writing, gaming, and watching popular sitcoms. He has authored a book on Machine Learning titled *R Machine Learning by Example*, Packt Publishing and also acted as a technical reviewer for several books on machine learning and Data Science from Packt Publishing.

www.PacktPub.com

eBooks, discount offers, and more

Did you know that Packt offers eBook versions of every book published, with PDF and ePub files available? You can upgrade to the eBook version at www.PacktPub.com and as a print book customer, you are entitled to a discount on the eBook copy. Get in touch with us at customercare@packtpub.com for more details.

At www.PacktPub.com, you can also read a collection of free technical articles, sign up for a range of free newsletters and receive exclusive discounts and offers on Packt books and eBooks.

https://www2.packtpub.com/books/subscription/packtlib

Do you need instant solutions to your IT questions? PacktLib is Packt's online digital book library. Here, you can search, access, and read Packt's entire library of books.

Why subscribe?

- Fully searchable across every book published by Packt
- Copy and paste, print, and bookmark content
- On demand and accessible via a web browser

Table of Contents

Preface

Data science and machine learning in particular are emerging as leading topics in the tech commercial environment to evaluate the always increasing amount of data generated by the users. This book will explain how to use Python to develop a web commercial application using Django and how to employ some specific libraries (sklearn, scipy, nltk, Django, and some others) to manipulate and analyze (through machine learning techniques) data that is generated or used in the application.

What this book covers

Chapter 1, *Introduction to Practical Machine Learning Using Python*, discusses the main machine learning concepts together with the libraries used by data science professionals to handle the data in Python.

Chapter 2, *Machine Learning Techniques – Unsupervised Learning*, describes the algorithms used to cluster datasets and to extract the main features from the data.

Chapter 3, *Supervised Machine Learning*, presents the most relevant supervised algorithms to predict the labels of a dataset.

Chapter 4, *Web Mining Techniques*, discusses the main techniques to organize, analyze, and extract information from web data

Chapter 5, *Recommendation Systems*, covers the most popular recommendation systems used in a commercial environment to date in detail.

Chapter 6, *Getting Started with Django*, introduces the main Django features and characteristics to develop a web application.

Chapter 7, Movie Recommendation System Web Application, describes an example to put in practice the machine learning concepts developed in *Chapter 5, Recommendation Systems* and *Chapter 6, Getting Started with Django*, recommending movies to final web users.

Chapter 8, Sentiment Analyser Application on Movie Reviews, covers another example to use the knowledge explained in *Chapter 3, Supervised Machine Learning, Chapter 4, Web Mining Techniques*, and *Chapter 6, Getting Started with Django*, analyzing the sentiment of the movies' reviews online and their importance.

What you need for this book

The reader should have a computer with Python 2.7 installed to be able to run (and modify) the code discussed throughout the chapters.

Who this book is for

Any person with some programming (in Python) and statistics background who is curious about machine learning and/or pursuing a career in data science will benefit from reading this book.

Conventions

In this book, you will find a number of text styles that distinguish between different kinds of information. Here are some examples of these styles and an explanation of their meaning.

Code words in text, database table names, folder names, filenames, file extensions, pathnames, dummy URLs, user input, and Twitter handles are shown as follows: "The Django library is installed by typing the following command in the Terminal: `sudo pip install django`."

A block of code is set as follows:

```
INSTALLED_APPS = (
...
'rest_framework',
'rest_framework_swagger',
'nameapp',
)
```

Any command-line input or output is written as follows:

```
python manage.py migrate
```

New terms and **important words** are shown in bold. Words that you see on the screen, for example, in menus or dialog boxes, appear in the text like this: "As you can see, the body of the page is specified by two boxes to be filled in with the person's name and their e-mail address, pressing **Add** to add them to the database."

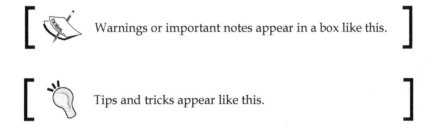

Warnings or important notes appear in a box like this.

Tips and tricks appear like this.

Reader feedback

Feedback from our readers is always welcome. Let us know what you think about this book—what you liked or disliked. Reader feedback is important for us as it helps us develop titles that you will really get the most out of.

To send us general feedback, simply e-mail feedback@packtpub.com, and mention the book's title in the subject of your message.

If there is a topic that you have expertise in and you are interested in either writing or contributing to a book, see our author guide at www.packtpub.com/authors.

Customer support

Now that you are the proud owner of a Packt book, we have a number of things to help you to get the most from your purchase.

Downloading the example code

You can download the example code files for this book from your account at http://www.packtpub.com. If you purchased this book elsewhere, you can visit http://www.packtpub.com/support and register to have the files e-mailed directly to you.

You can download the code files by following these steps:

1. Log in or register to our website using your e-mail address and password.
2. Hover the mouse pointer on the **SUPPORT** tab at the top.
3. Click on **Code Downloads & Errata**.
4. Enter the name of the book in the **Search** box.
5. Select the book for which you're looking to download the code files.
6. Choose from the drop-down menu where you purchased this book from.
7. Click on **Code Download**.

You can also download the code files by clicking on the **Code Files** button on the book's webpage at the Packt Publishing website. This page can be accessed by entering the book's name in the **Search** box. Please note that you need to be logged in to your Packt account.

Once the file is downloaded, please make sure that you unzip or extract the folder using the latest version of:

*   WinRAR / 7-Zip for Windows
*   Zipeg / iZip / UnRarX for Mac
*   7-Zip / PeaZip for Linux

The code bundle for the book is also hosted on GitHub at `https://github.com/PacktPublishing/Machine-Learning-for-the-Web`. We also have other code bundles from our rich catalog of books and videos available at `https://github.com/PacktPublishing/`. Check them out!

Downloading the color images of this book

We also provide you with a PDF file that has color images of the screenshots/diagrams used in this book. The color images will help you better understand the changes in the output. You can download this file from `http://www.packtpub.com/sites/default/files/downloads/Machine-Learning-for-the-Web_ColorImages.pdf`.

Errata

Although we have taken every care to ensure the accuracy of our content, mistakes do happen. If you find a mistake in one of our books—maybe a mistake in the text or the code—we would be grateful if you could report this to us. By doing so, you can save other readers from frustration and help us improve subsequent versions of this book. If you find any errata, please report them by visiting http://www.packtpub.com/submit-errata, selecting your book, clicking on the **Errata Submission Form** link, and entering the details of your errata. Once your errata are verified, your submission will be accepted and the errata will be uploaded to our website or added to any list of existing errata under the Errata section of that title.

To view the previously submitted errata, go to https://www.packtpub.com/books/content/support and enter the name of the book in the search field. The required information will appear under the **Errata** section.

Piracy

Piracy of copyrighted material on the Internet is an ongoing problem across all media. At Packt, we take the protection of our copyright and licenses very seriously. If you come across any illegal copies of our works in any form on the Internet, please provide us with the location address or website name immediately so that we can pursue a remedy.

Please contact us at copyright@packtpub.com with a link to the suspected pirated material.

We appreciate your help in protecting our authors and our ability to bring you valuable content.

Questions

If you have a problem with any aspect of this book, you can contact us at questions@packtpub.com, and we will do our best to address the problem.

1
Introduction to Practical Machine Learning Using Python

In the technology industry, the skill of analyzing and mining commercial data is becoming more and more important. All the companies that are related to the online world generate data that can be exploited to improve their business, or can be sold to other companies. This huge amount of information, which can be commercially useful, needs to be restructured and analyzed using the expertise of data science (or data mining) professionals. Data science employs techniques known as machine learning algorithms to transform the data in models, which are able to predict the behavior of certain entities that are highly considered by the business environment. This book is about these algorithms and techniques that are so crucial in today's technology business world, and how to efficiently deploy them in a real commercial environment. You will learn the most relevant machine-learning techniques and will have the chance to employ them in a series of exercises and applications designed to enhance commercial awareness and, with the skills learned in this book, these can be used in your professional experience. You are expected to already be familiar with the Python programming language, linear algebra, and statistics methodologies to fully acquire the topics discussed in this book.

- There are many tutorials and classes available online on these subjects, but we recommend you read the official Python documentation (`https://docs.python.org/`), the books *Elementary Statistics* by A. Bluman and *Statistical Inference* by G. Casella and R. L. Berger to understand the statistical main concepts and methods and *Linear Algebra and Its Applications* by G. Strang to learn about linear algebra.

The purpose of this introductory chapter is to familiarize you with the more advanced libraries and tools used by machine-learning professionals in Python, such as **NumPy**, **pandas,** and **matplotlib,** which will help you to grasp the necessary technical knowledge to implement the techniques presented in the following chapters. Before continuing with the tutorials and description of the libraries used in this book, we would like to clarify the main concepts of the machine-learning field, and give a practical example of how a machine-learning algorithm can predict useful information in a real context.

General machine-learning concepts

In this book, the most relevant machine-learning algorithms are going to be discussed and used in exercises to make you familiar with them. In order to explain these algorithms and to understand the content of this book, there are a few general concepts we need to visit that are going to be described hereafter.

First of all, a good definition of machine learning is the subfield of computer science that has been developed from the fields of pattern recognition, artificial intelligence, and computational learning theory. Machine learning can also be seen as a data-mining tool, which focuses more on the data analysis aspects to understand the data provided. The purpose of this discipline is the development of programs, which are able to *learn* from previously seen data, through tunable parameters (usually arrays of double precision values), that are designed to be adjusted automatically to improve the resulting predictions. In this way, computers can predict a behavior, *generalizing* the underlying structure of the data, instead of just storing (or retrieving) the values like usual database systems. For this reason, machine learning is associated with computational statics, which also attempt to predict a behavior based on previous data. Common industrial applications of machine-learning algorithms are spam filtering, search engines, optical character recognition, and computer vision. Now that we have defined the discipline, we can describe the terminology used in each machine-learning problem, in more detail.

Any learning problem starts with a data set of *n* samples, which are used to predict the properties of the future unknown data. Each sample is typically composed of more than a single value so it is a vector. The components of this vector are called *features*. For example, imagine predicting the price of a second-hand car based on its characteristics: year of fabrication, color, engine size, and so on. Each car *i* in the dataset will be a vector of features *x(i)* that corresponds to its color, engine size, and many others. In this case, there is also a *target* (or label) variable associated with each car *i*, *y(i)* which is the second-hand car price. A *training example* is formed by a pair *(x(i), y(i))* and therefore the complete set of *N* data points used to learn is called a *training dataset {(x(i), y(i));i=1,...,N}*. The symbol *x* will denote the space of feature (input) values, and *y* the space of target (output) values. The machine-learning algorithm chosen to solve the problem will be described by a mathematical model, with some parameters to tune in the training set. After the training phase is completed, the performance of the prediction is evaluated using another two sets: validation and testing sets. The validation set is used to choose, among multiple models, the one that returns the best results, while the testing set is usually used to determine the actual precision of the chosen model. Typically the dataset is divided into 50% training set, 25% validation set, and 25% testing set.

The learning problems can be divided in two main categories (both of which are extensively covered in this book):

- **Unsupervised learning**: The training dataset is given by input feature vectors *x* without any corresponding label values. The usual objective is to find similar examples within the data using clustering algorithms, or to project the data from a high-dimensional space down to a few dimensions (blind signal separations algorithms such as principal component analysis). Since there is usually no target value for each training example, it is not possible to evaluate errors of the model directly from the data; you need to use a technique that evaluates how the elements within each cluster are similar to each other and different from the other cluster's members. This is one of the major differences between unsupervised learning and supervised learning.

- **Supervised learning**: Each data sample is given in a pair consisting of an input feature vector and a label value. The task is to infer the parameters to predict the target values of the test data. These types of problems can be further divided into:

    ° **Classification**: The data targets belong to two or more classes, and the goal is to learn how to predict the class of unlabeled data from the training set. Classification is a discrete (as opposed to continuous) form of supervised learning, where the label has a limited number of categories. A practical example of the classification problem is the handwritten digit recognition example, in which the objective is to match each feature vector to one of a finite number of discrete categories.

    ° **Regression**: The label is a continuous variable. For example, the prediction of the height of a child based on his age and weight is a regression problem.

We are going to focus on unsupervised learning methods in *Chapter 2, Machine Learning Techniques: Unsupervised Learning,* while the most relevant supervised learning algorithms are discussed in *Chapter 3, Supervised Machine Learning. Chapter 4, Web Mining Techniques* will approach the field of web-mining techniques that can also be considered as both supervised and unsupervised methods. The recommendation systems, which are again part of the supervised learning category, are described in *Chapter 5, Recommendation Systems*. The **Django** web framework is then introduced in *Chapter 6, Getting Started with Django,* and then an example of the recommendation system (using both the Django framework and the algorithms explained in *Chapter 5, Recommendation Systems*) is detailed in *Chapter 7, Movie Recommendation System Web Application*. We finish the book with an example of a Django web-mining application, using some of the techniques learned in *Chapter 4, Web Mining Techniques*. By the end of the book you should be able to understand the different machine-learning methods and be able to deploy them in a real working web application using Django.

We continue the chapter by giving an example of how machine learning can be used in real business problems and in tutorials for Python libraries (NumPy, pandas, and matplotlib), which are essential for putting the algorithms learned in each of the following chapters into practice.

Machine-learning example

To explain further what machine learning can do with real data, we consider the following example (the following code is available in the author's GitHub book folder `https://github.com/ai2010/machine_learning_for_the_web/tree/master/chapter_1/`). We have taken the *Internet Advertisements Data Set* from the *UC Irvine Machine Learning Repository* (`http://archive.ics.uci.edu`). Web advertisements have been collected from various web pages, and each of them has been transformed into a numeric feature's vector. From the `ad.names` file we can see that the first three features represent the image size in the page, and the other features are related to the presence of specific words or phrases on the URL of the image or in the text (1558 features in total). The labels values are either `ad` or `nonad`, depending on whether the page has an advert or not. As an example, a web page in `ad.data` is given by:

```
125, 125, ...., 1. 0, 1, 0, ad.
```

Based on this data, a classical machine-learning task is to find a model to predict which pages are adverts and which are not (classification). To start with, we consider the data file `ad.data` which contains the full feature's vectors and labels, but it has also missing values indicated with a `?`. We can use the pandas Python library to transform the `?` to `-1` (see next paragraph for a full tutorial on the pandas library):

```python
import pandas as pd
df = pd.read_csv('ad-dataset/ad.data',header=None)
df=df.replace({'?': np.nan})
df=df.replace({' ?': np.nan})
df=df.replace({'  ?': np.nan})
df=df.replace({'   ?': np.nan})
df=df.replace({'    ?': np.nan})
df=df.fillna(-1)
```

A **DataFrame** is created with the data from the `ad.data` file, and each `?` is first replaced with the an value (`replace` function), then with `-1` (the `fillna` function). Now each label has to be transformed into a numerical value (and so do all the other values in the data):

```python
adindices = df[df.columns[-1]]== 'ad.'
df.loc[adindices,df.columns[-1]]=1
nonadindices = df[df.columns[-1]]=='nonad.'
df.loc[nonadindices,df.columns[-1]]=0
df[df.columns[-1]]=df[df.columns[-1]].astype(float)
df.apply(lambda x: pd.to_numeric(x))
```

Each `ad.` label has been transformed into `1` while the `nonad.` values have been replaced by `0`. All the columns (features) need to be numeric and float types (using the `astype` function and the `to_numeric` function through a `lambda` function).

We want to use the **Support Vector Machine (SVM)** algorithm provided by the `scikit-learn` library (see *Chapter 3, Supervised Machine Learning*) to predict 20% of the labels in the data. First, we split the data into two sets: a training set (80%) and a test set (20%):

```
import numpy as np
dataset = df.values[:,:]
np.random.shuffle(dataset)
data = dataset[:,:-1]
labels = dataset[:,-1].astype(float)
ntrainrows = int(len(data)*.8)
train = data[:ntrainrows,:]
trainlabels = labels[:ntrainrows]
test = data[ntrainrows:,:]
testlabels = labels[ntrainrows:]
```

Using the libraries provided by Numpy (a tutorial is provided in the next paragraph), the data are shuffled (function `random.shuffle`) before being split to assure the rows in the two sets are randomly selected. The `-1` notation indicates the last column of the array is not considered.

Now we train our SVM model using the training data:

```
from sklearn.svm import SVC
clf = SVC(gamma=0.001, C=100.)
clf.fit(train, trainlabels)
```

We have defined our `clf` variable that declares the SVM model with the values of the parameters. Then the function `fit` is called to fit the model with the training data (see *Chapter 3, Supervised Machine Learning* for further details). The mean accuracy in predicting the 20% test cases is performed as follows, using the score function:

```
score=clf.score(test,testlabels)
print 'score:',score
```

Running the preceding code (the full code is available in the `chapter_1` folder of the author's GitHub account) gives a result of 92% accuracy, which means 92% of the test cases of the predicted label agree with the true label. This is the power of machine learning: from previous data, we are able to infer if a page will contain an advert or not. To achieve that, we have essentially prepared and manipulated the data using the NumPy and pandas libraries, and then applied the SVM algorithm on the cleaned data using the `scikit-learn` library. Since this book will largely employ the `numpy` and `pandas` (and some `matplotlib`) libraries, the following paragraphs will discuss how to install the libraries and how the data can be manipulated (or even created) using these libraries.

Installing and importing a module (library)

Before continuing with the discussion on the libraries, we need to clarify how to install each module we want to use in Python. The usual way to install a module is through the `pip` command using the terminal:

```
>>> sudo pip install modulename
```

The module is then usually imported into the code using the statement:

```
import numpy as np
```

Here, `numpy` is the library name and `np` is the reference name from which any function X in the library can be accessed using `np.X` instead of `numpy.X`. We are going to assume that all the libraries (`scipy`, `scikit-learn`, `pandas`, `scrapy`, `nltk`, and all others) have been be installed and imported in this way.

Preparing, manipulating and visualizing data – NumPy, pandas and matplotlib tutorials

Most of the data comes in a very unpractical form for applying machine-learning algorithms. As we have seen in the example (in the preceding paragraph), the data can have missing values or non-numeric columns, which are not ready to be fed into any machine-learning technique. Therefore, a machine-learning professional usually spends a large amount of time cleaning and preparing the data to transform it into a form suitable for further analysis or visualization. This section will teach how to use numpy and pandas to create, prepare, and manipulate data in Python while the matplotlib paragraph will provide the basis of plotting a graph in Python. The Python shell has been used to discuss the NumPy tutorial, although all versions of the code in the IPython notebook, and plain Python script, are available in the chapter_1 folder of the author's GitHub. pandas and matplotlib are discussed using the IPython notebook.

Using NumPy

Numerical Python or NumPy, is an open source extension library for Python, and is a fundamental module required for data analysis and high performance scientific computing. The library features support Python for large, multi-dimensional arrays and matrices, and it provides precompiled functions for numerical routines. Furthermore, it provides a large library of mathematical functions to manipulate these arrays.

The library provides the following functionalities:

- Fast multi-dimensional array for vector arithmetic operations
- Standard mathematical functions for fast operations on entire arrays of data
- Linear algebra
- Sorting, unique, and set operations
- Statistics and aggregating data

The main advantage of NumPy is the speed of the usual array operations compared to standard Python operations. For instance, a traditional summation of 10000000 elements:

```
>>> def sum_trad():
>>>     start = time.time()
```

```
>>>    X = range(10000000)
>>>    Y = range(10000000)
>>>    Z = []
>>>    for i in range(len(X)):
>>>        Z.append(X[i] + Y[i])
>>>    return time.time() - start
```

Compare this to the Numpy function:

```
>>> def sum_numpy():
>>>    start = time.time()
>>>    X = np.arange(10000000)
>>>    Y = np.arange(10000000)
>>>    Z=X+Y
>>>    return time.time() - start
>>> print 'time sum:',sum_trad(),' time sum numpy:',sum_numpy()
time sum: 2.1142539978   time sum numpy: 0.0807049274445
```

The time used is `2.1142539978` and `0.0807049274445` respectively.

Arrays creation

The array object is the main feature provided by the NumPy library. Arrays are the equivalent of Python lists, but each element of an array has the same numerical type (typically float or int). It is possible to define an array casting from a list using the function array by using the following code. Two arguments are passed to it: the list to be converted and the type of the new generated array:

```
>>> arr = np.array([2, 6, 5, 9], float)
>>> arr
array([ 2., 6., 5., 9.])
>>> type(arr)
<type 'numpy.ndarray'>
```

And vice versa, an array can be transformed into a list by the following code:

```
>>> arr = np.array([1, 2, 3], float)
>>> arr.tolist()
[1.0, 2.0, 3.0]
>>> list(arr)
[1.0, 2.0, 3.0]
```

Assigning an array to a new one will not create a new copy in memory, it will just link the new name to the same original object.

To create a new object from an existing one, the copy function needs to be used:

```
>>> arr = np.array([1, 2, 3], float)
>>> arr1 = arr
>>> arr2 = arr.copy()
>>> arr[0] = 0
>>> arr
array([0., 2., 3.])
>>> arr1
array([0., 2., 3.])
>>> arr2
array([1., 2., 3.])
```

Alternatively an array can be filled with a single value in the following way:

```
>>> arr = np.array([10, 20, 33], float)
>>> arr
array([ 10., 20., 33.])
>>> arr.fill(1)
>>> arr
array([ 1., 1., 1.])
```

Arrays can also be created randomly using the random submodule. For example, giving the length of an array as an input of the function, permutation will find a random sequence of integers:

```
>>> np.random.permutation(3)
array([0, 1, 2])
```

Another method, normal, will draw a sequence of numbers from a normal distribution:

```
>>> np.random.normal(0,1,5)
array([-0.66494912, 0.7198794 , -0.29025382, 0.24577752, 0.23736908])
```

0 is the mean of the distribution while 1 is the standard deviation and 5 is the number of array's elements to draw. To use a uniform distribution, the random function will return numbers between 0 and 1 (not included):

```
>>> np.random.random(5)
array([ 0.48241564,  0.24382627,  0.25457204,  0.9775729 ,  0.61793725])
```

NumPy also provides a number of functions for creating two-dimensional arrays (matrices). For instance, to create an identity matrix of a given dimension, the following code can be used:

```
>>> np.identity(5, dtype=float)
array([[ 1.,  0.,  0.,  0.,  0.],
       [ 0.,  1.,  0.,  0.,  0.],
       [ 0.,  0.,  1.,  0.,  0.],
       [ 0.,  0.,  0.,  1.,  0.],
       [ 0.,  0.,  0.,  0.,  1.]])
```

The eye function returns matrices with ones along the kth diagonal:

```
>>> np.eye(3, k=1, dtype=float)
array([[ 0.,  1.,  0.],
       [ 0.,  0.,  1.],
       [ 0.,  0.,  0.]])
```

The most commonly used functions to create new arrays (1 or 2 dimensional) are zeros and ones which create new arrays of specified dimensions filled with these values. These are:

```
>>> np.ones((2,3), dtype=float)
array([[ 1.,  1.,  1.],
       [ 1.,  1.,  1.]])
>>> np.zeros(6, dtype=int)
array([0, 0, 0, 0, 0, 0])
```

The zeros_like and ones_like functions instead create a new array with the same type as an existing one, with the same dimensions:

```
>>> arr = np.array([[13, 32, 31], [64, 25, 76]], float)
>>> np.zeros_like(arr)
array([[ 0.,  0.,  0.],
       [ 0.,  0.,  0.]])
```

```
>>> np.ones_like(arr)
array([[ 1.,   1.,   1.],
       [ 1.,   1.,   1.]])
```

Another way to create two-dimensional arrays is to merge one-dimensional arrays using `vstack` (vertical merge):

```
>>> arr1 = np.array([1,3,2])
>>> arr2 = np.array([3,4,6])
>>> np.vstack([arr1,arr2])
array([[1, 3, 2],
       [3, 4, 6]])
```

The creation using distributions are also possible for two-dimensional arrays, using the `random` submodule. For example, a random matrix 2x3 from a uniform distribution between 0 and 1 is created by the following command:

```
>>> np.random.rand(2,3)
array([[ 0.36152029,  0.10663414,  0.64622729],
       [ 0.49498724,  0.59443518,  0.31257493]])
```

Another often used distribution is the multivariate normal distribution:

```
>>> np.random.multivariate_normal([10, 0], [[3, 1], [1, 4]], size=[5,])
array([[ 11.8696466 ,  -0.99505689],
       [ 10.50905208,   1.47187705],
       [  9.55350138,   0.48654548],
       [ 10.35759256,  -3.72591054],
       [ 11.31376171,   2.15576512]])
```

The list [10,0] is the mean vector, [[3, 1], [1, 4]] is the covariance matrix and 5 is the number of samples to draw.

Method	Description
tolist	Function to transform NumPy array to list
copy	Function to copy NumPy array values
ones, zeros	Functions to create an array of zeros or ones
zeros_like, ones_like	Functions to create two-dimensional arrays with same shape of the input list
fill	Function to replace an array entries with a certain value
identity	Function to create identity matrix

Method	Description
eye	Function to create a matrix with one entry along a kth diagonal
vstack	Function to merge arrays into two-dimensional arrays
random submodule: random, permutation, normal, rand, multivariate_ normal, and others	Random submodule create arrays drawing samples from distributions

Array manipulations

All the usual operations to access, slice, and manipulate a Python list can be applied in the same way, or in a similar way to an array:

```
>>> arr = np.array([2., 6., 5., 5.])
>>> arr[:3]
array([ 2., 6., 5.])
>>> arr[3]
5.0
>>> arr[0] = 5.
>>> arr
array([ 5., 6., 5., 5.])
```

The unique value can be also selected using unique:

```
>>> np.unique(arr)
array([ 5., 6., 5.])
```

The values of the array can also be sorted using sort and its indices with argsort:

```
>>> np.sort(arr)
array([ 2., 5., 5., 6.])
>>> np.argsort(arr)
array([0, 2, 3, 1])
```

It is also possible to randomly rearrange the order of the array's elements using the shuffle function:

```
>>> np.random.shuffle(arr)
>>> arr
array([ 2., 5., 6., 5.])
```

NumPy also has a built-in function to compare arrays array_equal:

```
>>> np.array_equal(arr,np.array([1,3,2]))
False
```

Multi-dimensional arrays, however, differ from the list. In fact, a list of dimensions is specified using the comma (instead of a bracket for list). For example, the elements of a two-dimensional array (that is a matrix) are accessed in the following way:

```
>>> matrix = np.array([[ 4., 5., 6.], [2, 3, 6]], float)
>>> matrix
array([[ 4., 5., 6.],
       [ 2., 3., 6.]])
>>> matrix[0,0]
4.0
>>> matrix[0,2]
6.0
```

Slicing is applied on each dimension using the colon : symbol between the initial value and the end value of the slice:

```
>>> arr = np.array([[ 4., 5., 6.], [ 2., 3., 6.]], float)
>>> arr[1:2,2:3]
array([[ 6.]])
```

While a single : means all the elements along that axis are considered:

```
>>> arr[1,:]
array([2, 3, 6])
>>> arr[:,2]
array([ 6., 6.])
>>> arr[-1:,-2:]
array([[ 3., 6.]])
```

One-dimensional arrays can be obtained from multi-dimensional arrays using the flatten function:

```
>>> arr = np.array([[10, 29, 23], [24, 25, 46]], float)
>>> arr
array([[ 10., 29., 23.],
       [ 24., 25., 46.]])
>>> arr.flatten()
array([ 10., 29., 23., 24., 25., 46.])
```

It is also possible to inspect an array object to obtain information about its content. The size of an array is found using the attribute shape:

```
>>> arr.shape
(2, 3)
```

In this case, `arr` is a matrix of two rows and three columns. The `dtype` property returns the type of values are stored within the array:

```
>>> arr.dtype
dtype('float64')
```

`float64` is a numeric type to store double-precision (8-byte) real numbers (similar to `float` type in regular Python). There are also other data types such as `int64`, `int32`, `string`, and an array can be converted from one type to another. For example:

```
>>>int_arr = matrix.astype(np.int32)
>>>int_arr.dtype
dtype('int32')
```

The `len` function returns the length of the first dimension when used on an array:

```
>>>arr = np.array([[ 4., 5., 6.], [ 2., 3., 6.]], float)
>>> len(arr)
2
```

Like in Python for loop, the `in` word can be used to check if a value is contained in an array:

```
>>> arr = np.array([[ 4., 5., 6.], [ 2., 3., 6.]], float)
>>> 2 in arr
True
>>> 0 in arr
False
```

An array can be manipulated in such a way that its elements are rearranged in different dimensions using the function `reshape`. For example, a matrix with eight rows and one column can be reshaped to a matrix with four rows and two columns:

```
>>> arr = np.array(range(8), float)
>>> arr
array([ 0., 1., 2., 3., 4., 5., 6., 7.])
>>> arr = arr.reshape((4,2))
>>> arr
```

```
array([[ 0.,   1.],
       [ 2.,   3.],
       [ 4.,   5.],
       [ 6.,   7.]])
>>> arr.shape
(4, 2)
```

In addition, transposed matrices can be created; that is to say, a new array with the final two dimensions switched can be obtained using the transpose function:

```
>>> arr = np.array(range(6), float).reshape((2, 3))
>>> arr
array([[ 0., 1., 2.],
       [ 3., 4., 5.]])
>>> arr.transpose()
array([[ 0., 3.],
       [ 1., 4.],
       [ 2., 5.]])
```

Arrays can also be transposed using the T attribute:

```
>>> matrix = np.arange(15).reshape((3, 5))
>>> matrix
array([[ 0, 1, 2, 3, 4],
       [ 5, 6, 7, 8, 9],
       [10, 11, 12, 13, 14]])
>>>matrix .T
array([[ 0, 5, 10],
       [ 1, 6, 11],
       [ 2, 6, 12],
       [ 3, 8, 13],
       [ 4, 9, 14]])
```

Another way to reshuffle the elements of an array is to use the newaxis function to increase the dimensionality:

```
>>> arr = np.array([14, 32, 13], float)
>>> arr
array([ 14.,   32.,   13.])
>> arr[:,np.newaxis]
```

```
array([[ 14.],
       [ 32.],
       [ 13.]])
>>> arr[:,np.newaxis].shape
(3,1)
>>> arr[np.newaxis,:]
array([[ 14.,   32.,   13.]])
>>> arr[np.newaxis,:].shape
(1,3)
```

In this example, in each case the new array has two dimensions, the one generated by newaxis has a length of one.

Joining arrays is an operation performed by the concatenate function in NumPy, and the syntax depends on the dimensionality of the array. Multiple one-dimensional arrays can be chained, specifying the arrays to be joined as a tuple:

```
>>> arr1 = np.array([10,22], float)
>>> arr2 = np.array([31,43,54,61], float)
>>> arr3 = np.array([71,82,29], float)
>>> np.concatenate((arr1, arr2, arr3))
array([ 10.,   22.,   31.,   43.,   54.,   61.,   71.,   82.,   29.])
```

Using a multi-dimensional array, the axis along which multiple arrays are concatenated needs to be specified. Otherwise, NumPy concatenates along the first dimension by default:

```
>>> arr1 = np.array([[11, 12], [32, 42]], float)
>>> arr2 = np.array([[54, 26], [27,28]], float)
>>> np.concatenate((arr1,arr2))
array([[ 11.,   12.],
       [ 32.,   42.],
       [ 54.,   26.],
       [ 27.,   28.]])
>>> np.concatenate((arr1,arr2), axis=0)
array([[ 11.,   12.],
       [ 32.,   42.],
       [ 54.,   26.],
       [ 27.,   28.]])
```

```
>>> np.concatenate((arr1,arr2), axis=1)
array([[ 11.,   12.,   54.,   26.],
       [ 32.,   42.,   27.,   28.]])
```

It is common to save a large amount of data as a binary file instead of using the direct format. NumPy provides a function, `tostring`, to convert an array to a binary string. Of course there's also the inverse operation, where a conversion of a binary string to an array is supported using the `fromstring` routine. For example:

```
>>> arr = np.array([10, 20, 30], float)
>>> str = arr.tostring()
>>> str
'\x00\x00\x00\x00\x00\x00$@\x00\x00\x00\x00\x00\x004@\x00\x00\x00\x00\
x00\x00>@'
>>> np.fromstring(str)
array([ 10.,  20.,  30.])
```

Method	Description
`unique`	Function to select only unique values from an array
`random, shuffle`	Function to randomly rearrange the elements of an array
`sort, argsort`	`sort` sorts the order of an array's values in increasing order, while `argsort` orders the array's indices such that the array gets arranged in an increasing order
`array_equal`	Compare two arrays and return a True id (they are equal False otherwise)
`flatten`	Transform a two-dimensional array into a one-dimensional array
`transpose`	Calculate the transpose of a two-dimensional array
`reshape`	Rearrange entries of a two-dimensional array into a different shape
`concatenate`	Concatenate two -dimensional arrays into one matrix
`fromstring, tostring`	Convert an array to a binary string

Array operations

Common mathematical operations are obviously supported in NumPy. For example:

```
>>> arr1 = np.array([1,2,3], float)
>>> arr2 = np.array([1,2,3], float)
>>> arr1 + arr2
array([2.,4., 6.])
```

```
>>> arr1-arr2
array([0., 0., 0.])
>>> arr1 * arr2
array([51, 4., 9.])
>>> arr2 / arr1
array([1., 1., 1.])
>>> arr1 % arr2
array([0., 0., 0.])
>>> arr2**arr1
array([1., 4., 9.])
```

Since any operation is applied element wise, the arrays are required to have the same size. If this condition is not satisfied, an error is returned:

```
>>> arr1 = np.array([1,2,3], float)
>>> arr2 = np.array([1,2], float)
>>> arr1 + arr2
Traceback (most recent call last):
File "<stdin>", line 1, in <module>
ValueError: shape mismatch: objects cannot be broadcast to a single shape
```

The error states that the objects cannot be broadcasted because the only way to perform an operation with arrays of different size is called broadcasting. This means the arrays have a different number of dimensions, and the array with less dimensions will be repeated until it matches the dimensions of the other array. Consider the following:

```
>>> arr1 = np.array([[1, 2], [3, 4], [5, 6]], float)
>>> arr2 = np.array([1, 2], float)
>>> arr1
array([[ 1., 2.],
       [ 3., 4.],
       [ 5., 6.]])
>>> arr2
array([1., 1.])
>>> arr1 + arr2
array([[ 2., 4.],
       [ 4., 6.],
       [ 6., 8.]])
```

The array `arr2` was *broadcasted* to a two-dimensional array that matched the size of `arr1`. Therefore, `arr2` was repeated for each dimension of `arr1`, equivalent to the array:

```
array([[1., 2.],[1., 2.],[1., 2.]])
```

If we want to make the way an array is broadcasted explicit, the `newaxis` constant allows us to specify how we want to broadcast:

```
>>> arr1 = np.zeros((2,2), float)
>>> arr2 = np.array([1., 2.], float)
>>> arr1
array([[ 0., 0.],[ 0., 0.]])
>>> arr2
array([1., 2.])
>>> arr1 + arr2
array([[-1., 3.],[-1., 3.]])
>>> arr1 + arr2[np.newaxis,:]
array([[1., 2.],[1., 2.]])
>>> arr1 + arr2[:,np.newaxis]
array([[1.,1.],[ 2., 2.]])
```

Unlike Python lists, arrays can be queried using conditions. A typical example is to use Boolean arrays to filter the elements:

```
>>> arr = np.array([[1, 2], [5, 9]], float)
>>> arr >= 7
array([[ False, False],
[False, True]], dtype=bool)
>>> arr[arr >= 7]
array([ 9.])
```

Multiple Boolean expressions can be used to subset the array:

```
>>> arr[np.logical_and(arr > 5, arr < 11)]
>>> arr
array([ 9.])
```

Arrays of integers can be used to specify the indices to select the elements of another array. For example:

```
>>> arr1 = np.array([1, 4, 5, 9], float)
>>> arr2 = np.array([0, 1, 1, 3, 1, 1, 1], int)
>>> arr1[arr2]
array([ 1., 4., 4., 9., 4., 4., 4.])
```

The arr2 represents the ordered indices to select elements from array arr1: the zeroth, first, first, third, first, first, and first elements of arr1, in that order have been selected. Also lists can be used for the same purpose:

```
>>> arr = np.array([1, 4, 5, 9], float)
>>> arr[[0, 1, 1, 3, 1]]
array([ 1., 4., 4., 9., 4.])
```

In order to replicate the same operation with multi-dimensional arrays, multiple one-dimensional integer arrays have to be put into the selection bracket, one for each dimension.

The first selection array represents the values of the first index in the matrix entries, while the values on the second selection array represent the column index of the matrix entries. The following example illustrates the idea:

```
>>> arr1 = np.array([[1, 2], [5, 13]], float)
>>> arr2 = np.array([1, 0, 0, 1], int)
>>> arr3 = np.array([1, 1, 0, 1], int)
>>> arr1[arr2,arr3]
array([ 13., 2., 1., 13.])
```

The values on arr2 are the first index (row) on arr1 entries while arr3 are the second index (column) values, so the first chosen entry on arr1 corresponds to row 1 column 1 which is 13.

The function take can be used to apply your selection with integer arrays, and it works in the same way as bracket selection:

```
>>> arr1 = np.array([7, 6, 6, 9], float)
>>> arr2 = np.array([1, 0, 1, 3, 3, 1], int)
>>> arr1.take(arr2)
array([ 6., 7., 6., 9., 9., 6.])
```

Subsets of a multi-dimensional array can be selected along a given dimension specifying the axis argument on the `take` function:

```
>>> arr1 = np.array([[10, 21], [62, 33]], float)
>>> arr2 = np.array([0, 0, 1], int)
>>> arr1.take(arr2, axis=0)
array([[ 10.,   21.],
       [ 10.,   21.],
       [ 62.,   33.]])
>>> arr1.take(arr2, axis=1)
array([[ 10.,   10.,   21.],
       [ 62.,   62.,   33.]])
```

The `put` function is the opposite of the `take` function, and it takes values from an array and puts them at specified indices in the array that calls the `put` method:

```
>>> arr1 = np.array([2, 1, 6, 2, 1, 9], float)
>>> arr2 = np.array([3, 10, 2], float)
>>> arr1.put([1, 4], arr2)
>>> arr1
array([ 2.,   3.,   6.,   2.,   10.,   9.])
```

We finish this section with the note that multiplication also remains element-wise for two-dimensional arrays (and does not correspond to matrix multiplication):

```
>>> arr1 = np.array([[11,22], [23,14]], float)
>>> arr2 = np.array([[25,30], [13,33]], float)
>>> arr1 * arr2
array([[ 275.,   660.],
       [ 299.,   462.]])
```

Method	Description
take	Select values of an array from indices given by a second array
put	Replace the values in an array with values of another array at given positions

Linear algebra operations

The most common operations between matrices is the inner product of a matrix with its transpose, $X^T X$, using `np.dot`:

```
>>> X = np.arange(15).reshape((3, 5))
>>> X
array([[ 0,  1,  2,  3,  4],
       [ 5,  6,  7,  8,  9],
       [10, 11, 12, 13, 14]])
>>> X.T
array([[ 0,  5, 10],
       [ 1,  6, 11],
       [ 2,  6, 12],
       [ 3,  8, 13],
       [ 4,  9, 14]])
>>>np.dot(X .T, X)#X^T X
array([[ 2.584 , 1.8753, 0.8888],
       [ 1.8753, 6.6636, 0.3884],
       [ 0.8888, 0.3884, 3.9781]])
```

There are functions to directly calculate the different types of product (`inner`, `outer`, and `cross`) on arrays (that is matrices or vectors).

For one-dimensional arrays (vectors) the inner product corresponds to the dot product:

```
>>> arr1 = np.array([12, 43, 10], float)
>>> arr2 = np.array([21, 42, 14], float)
>>> np.outer(arr1, arr2)
array([[  252.,   504.,   168.],
       [  903.,  1806.,   602.],
       [  210.,   420.,   140.]])
>>> np.inner(arr1, arr2)
2198.0
>>> np.cross(arr1, arr2)
array([ 182.,   42., -399.])
```

NumPy also contains a sub-module, `linalg` that has a series of functions to perform linear algebra calculations over matrices. The determinant of a matrix can be computed as:

```
>>> matrix = np.array([[74, 22, 10], [92, 31, 17], [21, 22, 12]], float)
>>> matrix
array([[ 74.,   22.,   10.],
       [ 92.,   31.,   17.],
       [ 21.,   22.,   12.]])
>>> np.linalg.det(matrix)
-2852.0000000000032
```

Also the inverse of a matrix can be generated using the function `inv`:

```
>>> inv_matrix = np.linalg.inv(matrix)
>>> inv_matrix
array([[ 0.00070126,  0.01542777, -0.02244039],
       [ 0.26192146, -0.23772791,  0.11851332],
       [-0.48141655,  0.4088359 , -0.09467041]])
>>> np.dot(inv_matrix,matrix)
array([[  1.00000000e+00,   2.22044605e-16,   4.77048956e-17],
       [ -2.22044605e-15,   1.00000000e+00,   0.00000000e+00],
       [ -3.33066907e-15,  -4.44089210e-16,   1.00000000e+00]])
```

It is straightforward to calculate the eigenvalues and eigenvectors of a matrix:

```
>>> vals, vecs = np.linalg.eig(matrix)
>>> vals
array([ 107.99587441,   11.33411853,   -2.32999294])
>>> vecs
array([[-0.57891525, -0.21517959,  0.06319955],
       [-0.75804695,  0.17632618, -0.58635713],
       [-0.30036971,  0.96052424,  0.80758352]])
```

Method	Description
dot	Dot product between two arrays
inner	Inner product between multi-dimensional arrays

Method	Description
`linalg` module with functions such as: `linalg.det`, `linalg.inv`, `linalg.eig`	`linalg` is a module that collects several linear algebra methods among which are the determinant of a matrix (`det`), the inverse of a matrix (`inv`) and the eigenvalues, eigenvectors of a matrix (`eig`)

Statistics and mathematical functions

NumPy provides a set of functions to compute statistics of the data contained in the arrays. Operations of the aggregation type, such as sum, mean, median, and standard deviation are available as an attribute of an array. For example, creating a random array (from a normal distribution), it is possible to calculate the mean in two ways:

```
>>> arr = np.random.rand(8, 4)
>>> arr.mean()
0.45808075801881332
>>> np.mean(arr)
0.45808075801881332
>>> arr.sum()
14.658584256602026
```

The full list of functions is shown in the table below:

Method	Description
`mean`	mean of the elements. If the array is empty, the mean is set to NaN by default.
`std`, `var`	Functions to calculate the standard deviation (`std`) and variance (`var`) of the array. An optional degree of freedom parameter can be specified (default is the length of the array).
`min`, `max`	Functions to determine the minimum (`min`) and maximum (`max`) value contained in the array.
`argmin`, `argmax`	These functions return the index of the smallest element (`argmin`) and largest element (`argmax`).

Understanding the pandas module

pandas is a powerful Python module that contains a wide range of functions to analyze data structures. pandas relies on the NumPy library and it is designed to make data analysis operations easy and fast. This module offers high performance with respect to normal Python functions, especially for reading or writing files or making databases; pandas is the optimal choice to perform data manipulation. The following paragraphs discuss the main methods to explore the information contained in the data, and how to perform manipulations on it. We start by describing how data is stored in pandas and how to load data into it.

Throughout the rest of the book, we use the following import conventions for pandas:

```
import pandas as pd
```

Therefore, whenever code contains the letters pd, it is referring to pandas.

Exploring data

In order to introduce the database structure, called **DataFrame**, into pandas, we need to describe the one-dimensional array-like object containing data of any NumPy data type and an associated array of data label called its index. This structure is called Series and a simple example is:

```
In [8]:  obj = pd.Series([3,5,-2,1])
         obj

Out[8]:  0     3
         1     5
         2    -2
         3     1
         dtype: int64
```

The `obj` object is composed of two values, the index on the left and the associated value on the right. Given that the length of the data is equal to *N*, the default indexing goes from 0 to *N-1*. The array and index objects of the `Series` can be obtained using its values and index attributes, respectively:

```
In [9]:  obj.values
Out[9]:  array([ 3,  5, -2,  1])
In [10]:  obj.index
Out[10]:  Int64Index([0, 1, 2, 3], dtype='int64')
```

The indexing is preserved by applying NumPy array operations (such as scalar multiplication, filtering with a Boolean array, or applying math functions):

```
In [11]:  obj *2
Out[11]:  0      6
          1     10
          2     -4
          3      2
          dtype: int64

In [12]:  obj[obj>2]
Out[12]:  0      3
          1      5
          dtype: int64
```

A Python dictionary can be transformed into a `Series` but the indexing will correspond to the key values:

```
In [19]:  data = {'a': 30, 'b': 70, 'c': 160, 'd': 5}
          obj = pd.Series(data)
          obj
Out[19]:  a       30
          b       70
          c      160
          d        5
          dtype: int64
```

It is possible to specify a separated list as an index:

```
In [20]: index = ['a','b','c','d','g']
         obj = pd.Series(data, index=index)
         obj
Out[20]: a     30
         b     70
         c    160
         d      5
         g    NaN
         dtype: float64
```

In this case, the last index value, g, has not got an associated object value, so by default a **Not a Number (NaN)** is inserted.

The terms of *missing* or *NA* will be used to refer to missing data. To find the missing data the `isnull` and `notnull` functions can be used in pandas:

```
In [16]: pd.isnull(obj)
Out[16]: a    False
         b    False
         c    False
         d    False
         dtype: bool


In [17]: pd.notnull(obj)
Out[17]: a    True
         b    True
         c    True
         d    True
         dtype: bool
```

We can now start loading a CSV file into a DataFrame structure. A DataFrame represents a data structure containing an ordered set of columns, each of which can be a different value type (numeric, string, Boolean, and others). The DataFrame has two indices (a row and column index) and it can be thought of as a dictionary of `Series` that share the same index (column). For the purpose of this tutorial, we are using the data contained in the `ad.data` file stored in the `http://archive.ics.uci.edu` website (at `http://archive.ics.uci.edu/ml/datasets/Internet+Advertisements`) as already explained in the preceding machine-learning example.

The data is loaded in the following way using the terminal (in this case the path is data_example/ad-dataset/ad-data):

```
In [4]:  data = pd.read_csv("data_example/ad-dataset/ad.data",header=None)
```

This file does not have a header (set to none) so the column's names are numbers and we can get a summary of the DataFrame by using the describe function on the object data:

```
In [5]:  data.describe()
```

Out[5]:		4	5	6	7	8	9	10	11	12	13	...
	count	3279.000000	3279.000000	3279.000000	3279.000000	3279.000000	3279.000000	3279.000000	3279.000000	3279.000000	3279.000000	...
	mean	0.004270	0.011589	0.004575	0.003355	0.003965	0.011589	0.003355	0.004880	0.009149	0.004575	...
	std	0.065212	0.107042	0.067491	0.057831	0.062850	0.107042	0.057831	0.069694	0.095227	0.067491	...
	min	0.000000	0.000000	0.000000	0.000000	0.000000	0.000000	0.000000	0.000000	0.000000	0.000000	...
	25%	0.000000	0.000000	0.000000	0.000000	0.000000	0.000000	0.000000	0.000000	0.000000	0.000000	...
	50%	0.000000	0.000000	0.000000	0.000000	0.000000	0.000000	0.000000	0.000000	0.000000	0.000000	...
	75%	0.000000	0.000000	0.000000	0.000000	0.000000	0.000000	0.000000	0.000000	0.000000	0.000000	...
	max	1.000000	1.000000	1.000000	1.000000	1.000000	1.000000	1.000000	1.000000	1.000000	1.000000	...

8 rows × 1554 columns

This summarizes quantitative information. We can see that there are 1554 numeric columns (indicated by numbers since there is no header) and 3279 rows (called count for each column). Each of the columns has a list of statistical parameters (mean, standard deviation, min, max, and percentiles) that helps to obtain an initial estimate of the quantitative information contained in the data.

It is possible to obtain the column names using the columns property:

```
In [25]:  data.columns
Out[25]:  Int64Index([   0,    1,    2,    3,    4,    5,    6,    7,    8,    9,
                       ...
                    1549, 1550, 1551, 1552, 1553, 1554, 1555, 1556, 1557, 1558],
                   dtype='int64', length=1559)
```

So all the columns names are of type `int64` and the following command returns the actual types of all the columns:

```
In [26]:  data.dtypes
Out[26]:  0          object
          1          object
          2          object
          3          object
          4           int64
          5           int64
                    ...
          1557        int64
          1558       object
          dtype: object
```

The first four columns and the label (last column) are of the type `object`, while the others are of the type `int64`. Columns can be accessed in two ways. The first method is by specifying the column name like the key in a dictionary:

```
In [6]:  data[1]
Out[6]:  0          125
         1          468
         29         234
                  ...
         3277         ?
         3278        40
         Name: 1, dtype: object
```

Multiple columns can be obtained by specifying a list of them with the column names:

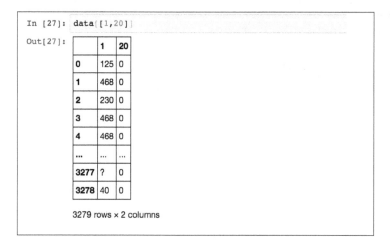

```
In [27]:  data[[1,20]]
Out[27]:
```

	1	20
0	125	0
1	468	0
2	230	0
3	468	0
4	468	0
...	...	...
3277	?	0
3278	40	0

3279 rows × 2 columns

The other way to access columns is by using the *dot* syntax, but it will only work if the column name could also be a Python variable name (that is no spaces), if it is not the same as the DataFrame property or function name (such as count or sum), and the name is of the string type (not `int64` like in this example).

To briefly gain an insight into the content of a DataFrame, the function `head()` can be used. The first five items in a column (or the first five rows in the DataFrame) are returned by default:

```
In [28]: data[1].head()
Out[28]: 0    125
         1    468
         2    230
         3    468
         4    468
         Name: 1, dtype: object
```

The opposite method is `tail()`, which returns the last five items or rows by default. Specifying a number on the `tail()` or `head()` function, will return the first *n* items in the chosen column:

```
In [29]: data[1].head(10)
Out[29]: 0    125
         1    468
         2    230
         3    468
         4    468
         5    468
         6    460
         7    234
         8    468
         9    468
         Name: 1, dtype: object
```

It is also possible to use the Python's regular slicing syntax to obtain a certain number of rows of the DataFrame:

```
In [7]: data[1:3]
```

	0	1	2	3	4	5	6	7	8	9	...	1549	1550	1551	1552	1553	1554	1555	1556	1557	1558
1	57	468	8.2105	1	0	0	0	0	0	0	...	0	0	0	0	0	0	0	0	0	ad.
2	33	230	6.9696	1	0	0	0	0	0	0	...	0	0	0	0	0	0	0	0	0	ad.

2 rows × 1559 columns

This example shows only rows from 1 to 3.

Manipulate data

It is possible to select row(s) in different ways, such as specifying the index or the condition as follows:

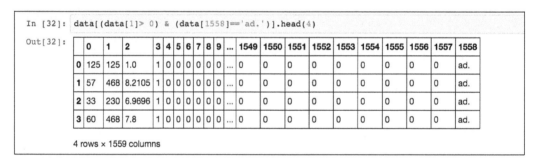

Or specifying multiple conditions:

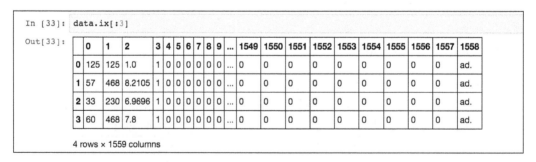

The data returned are web pages with feature 1 greater than 0 and containing an advert.

The ix method allows us to select rows specifying the desired index:

```
In [33]: data.ix[:3]
```

Out[33]:

	0	1	2	3	4	5	6	7	8	9	...	1549	1550	1551	1552	1553	1554	1555	1556	1557	1558
0	125	125	1.0	1	0	0	0	0	0	0	...	0	0	0	0	0	0	0	0	0	ad.
1	57	468	8.2105	1	0	0	0	0	0	0	...	0	0	0	0	0	0	0	0	0	ad.
2	33	230	6.9696	1	0	0	0	0	0	0	...	0	0	0	0	0	0	0	0	0	ad.
3	60	468	7.8	1	0	0	0	0	0	0	...	0	0	0	0	0	0	0	0	0	ad.

4 rows × 1559 columns

Alternatively the function `iloc` can be used:

```
In [34]:  data.iloc[:3]
```

Out[34]:

	0	1	2	3	4	5	6	7	8	9	...	1549	1550	1551	1552	1553	1554	1555	1556	1557	1558
0	125	125	1.0	1	0	0	0	0	0	0	...	0	0	0	0	0	0	0	0	0	ad.
1	57	468	8.2105	1	0	0	0	0	0	0	...	0	0	0	0	0	0	0	0	0	ad.
2	33	230	6.9696	1	0	0	0	0	0	0	...	0	0	0	0	0	0	0	0	0	ad.

3 rows × 1559 columns

The difference is that `ix` works on labels in the index column and `iloc` works on the positions in the index (so it only takes integers). Therefore, in this example, `ix` finds all the rows from 0 until the label 3 appears, while the `iloc` function returns the rows in the first 3 positions in the data frame. There is a third function to access data in a DataFrame, `loc`. This function looks at the index names associated with the rows and it returns their values. For example:

```
In [35]:  data.loc[:3]
```

Out[35]:

	0	1	2	3	4	5	6	7	8	9	...	1549	1550	1551	1552	1553	1554	1555	1556	1557	1558
0	125	125	1.0	1	0	0	0	0	0	0	...	0	0	0	0	0	0	0	0	0	ad.
1	57	468	8.2105	1	0	0	0	0	0	0	...	0	0	0	0	0	0	0	0	0	ad.
2	33	230	6.9696	1	0	0	0	0	0	0	...	0	0	0	0	0	0	0	0	0	ad.
3	60	468	7.8	1	0	0	0	0	0	0	...	0	0	0	0	0	0	0	0	0	ad.

4 rows × 1559 columns

Note that this function behaves differently with respect to the normal slicing in Python because both starting and ending rows are included in the result (the row with index 3 is included in the output).

It is possible to set an entire column to a value:

```
In [36]:  data[1547] = 0
```

To also set a specific cell value to the desired values:

```
In [37]:  data.ix[3,1]=0
```

Or the entire row to a set of values (random values between 0 and 1 and ad. label in this example):

```
In [38]:  import random
          data.ix[0] = [random.randint(0,1) for r in xrange(1558)]+['ad.']
```

After transforming an array of values in a Series object, it is possible to append a row at the end of the DataFrame:

```
In [40]:  row = [random.randint(0,1) for r in xrange(1558)]+['ad.']
          data = data.append(pd.Series(row,index = data.columns),ignore_index=True)
```

Alternatively, the loc function (as in NumPy) can be used to add a row at the last line:

```
In [70]:  data.loc[len(data)] = row
```

It is easy to add a column in the DataFrame by simply assigning the new column name to a value:

```
In [41]:  data['newcolumn'] = 'test value'
          data.columns
Out[41]:  Index([          0,            1,           2,          3,           4,
                           5,            6,           7,          8,           9,
                 ...
                        1550,         1551,        1552,       1553,        1554,
                        1555,         1556,        1557,       1558, u'newcolumn'],
                 dtype='object', length=1560)
```

In this case, the new column has all the entries assigned to *test value*. Similarly, the column can be deleted using the drop function:

```
In [56]:  data = data.drop('newcolumn', 1)
          data.columns
Out[56]:  Index([   0,    1,    2,    3,    4,    5,    6,    7,    8,    9,
                 ...
                    1549, 1550, 1551, 1552, 1553, 1554, 1555, 1556, 1557, 1558],
                 dtype='object', length=1559)
```

A dataset may contain duplicates for various reasons, so pandas provides the method `duplicated` to indicate whether each row is a repetition or not:

```
In [42]: data.duplicated()
Out[42]: 0          False
         1          False
         2          False
         3          False
         4          False
                    ...
         3279       False
         dtype: bool
```

More usefully, though, the `drop_duplicates` function returns a DataFrame with only the unique values. For example, for the label the unique values are:

```
In [43]: data[1558].drop_duplicates()
Out[43]: 0            ad.
         459       nonad.
         Name: 1558, dtype: object
```

It is possible to transform the result into a list:

```
In [44]: data[1558].drop_duplicates().tolist()
Out[44]: ['ad.', 'nonad.']
```

As we did in the machine-learning example, these labels can be transformed into numeric values using the methods explained in the preceding example:

```
In [46]: adindices = data[data .columns[-1]]== 'ad.'
         data.loc[adindices,data .columns[-1]]=1
         nonadindices = data[data .columns[-1]]=='nonad.'
         data.loc[nonadindices,data .columns[-1]]=0
```

The label column is still the `object` type:

```
In [47]:  data[1558].dtypes

Out[47]:  dtype('O')
```

So the column now can be converted into the float type:

```
In [63]:  data[data.columns[-1]]=data[data.columns[-1]].astype(float)
```

The first four columns contain mixed values (strings, ?, and float numbers), so we need to remove the string values to convert the columns into a numeric type. We can use the function `replace` to substitute all the instances of ? (missing values) with NaN:

```
In [71]:  data=data.replace({'?': np.nan})
          data=data.replace({'  ?': np.nan})
          data=data.replace({'   ?': np.nan})
          data=data.replace({'    ?': np.nan})
          data=data.replace({'     ?': np.nan})
```

Now we can handle these rows with missing data in two ways. The first method is just to remove the lines with missing values using `dropna`:

```
In [73]:  data=data.dropna()
```

Instead of removing the rows with missing data (which may lead to deleting important information), the empty entries can be filled. For most purposes, a constant value can be inserted in the empty cells with the `fillna` method:

```
In [74]:  data=data.fillna(-1)
```

Now that all the values are numeric the columns can be set to type `float`, applying the `astype` function. Alternatively, we can apply a `lambda` function to convert each column in the DataFrame to a numeric type:

```
In [82]:  data=data.apply(lambda x: pd.to_numeric(x))
```

Each *x* instance is a column and the `to_numeric` function converts it to the closest numeric type (`float` in this case).

For the sake of completeness of this tutorial, we want to show how two DataFrames can be concatenated since this operation can be useful in real applications. Let's create another small DataFrame with random values:

```
In [83]: data1 = pd.DataFrame(columns=[i for i in xrange(1559)])
         data1.loc[len(data1)] = [random.randint(0,1) for r in xrange(1558)]+[1]
         data1.loc[len(data1)] = [random.randint(0,1) for r in xrange(1558)]+[1]
```

This new table with two rows can be merged with the original DataFrame using the `concat` function placing the rows of `data1` at the bottom of the `data`:

```
In [85]: print len(data)
         datatot = pd.concat([data[:],data1[:]])
         len(datatot)

         2362

Out[85]: 2364
```

The number of rows of `datatot` is now increased by two rows with respect to `data` (note that the number of rows is different from the beginning because we dropped the rows with `NaN`).

Matplotlib tutorial

`matplotlib.pyplot` is a library that collects a series of methods to plot data similar to **MATLAB**. Since the following chapters will employ this library to visualize some results, a simple example here will explain all the `matplotlib` code you will see as you continue in this book:

```
In [1]: import matplotlib.pyplot as plt

In [2]: plt.plot([10,5,2,4],color='green',label='line 1', linewidth=5)
        plt.ylabel('y',fontsize=40)
        plt.xlabel('x',fontsize=40)
        plt.axis([0,3, 0,15])
        plt.show()

In [5]: fig = plt.figure(figsize=(10,10))
        ax = fig.add_subplot(111)
        ax.set_xlabel('x',fontsize=40)
        ax.set_ylabel('y',fontsize=40)
        fig.suptitle('figure',fontsize=40)
        ax.plot([10,5,2,4],color='green',label='line 1', linewidth=5)
        fig.savefig('figure.png')
```

After importing the library (as `plt`), the `figure` object is initialized (`fig`) and an `axis` object is added (`ax`). Each line plotted into the `ax` object through the command `ax.plot()` is called a handle. All the following instructions are then recorded by `matplotlib.pyplot` and plotted in the `figure` object. In this case, the line in green has been shown from the terminal and saved as a `figure.png` file, using the commands `plt.show()` and `fig.savefig()` respectively. The result is equal to:

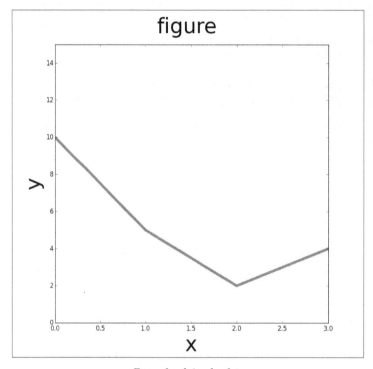

Example of simple plot

The next example illustrates a plot of several lines with different format styles in one command using Numpy arrays:

```
In [8]:  import numpy as np
         fig = plt.figure(figsize=(10,10))
         ax = fig.add_subplot(111)
         r = np.arange(0., 10., 0.3)
         p1, = ax.plot(r, r, 'r--',label='line 1', linewidth=10)
         p2, = ax.plot(r, r**0.5, 'bs',label='line 2', linewidth=10)
         p3, = ax.plot(r,np.sin(r),'g^', label='line 3', markersize=10)
         handles, labels = ax.get_legend_handles_labels()
         ax.legend(handles, labels,fontsize=40)
         ax.set_xlabel('x',fontsize=40)
         ax.set_ylabel('y',fontsize=40)
         fig.suptitle('figure 1',fontsize=40)
         fig.savefig('figure_multiplelines.png')
```

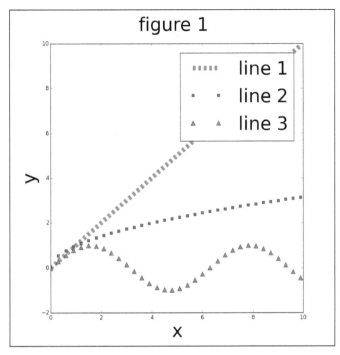

Example of plot with multiple lines

Note that the function get_legend_handles_labels() returns the list of handles and labels stored in the object ax and they are passed to the function legend to be plotted. The symbols 'r--', 'bs', and 'g^' refer to the shape of the points and their color (red rectangles, blue squares, and green triangles respectively). The linewidth parameter sets the thickness of the line while markersize sets the size of the dots.

Another useful plot to visualize the results is the scatter plot in which values for typically two variables of a set of data (data generated using NumPy random submodule) are displayed:

```
In [10]: colors = ['b', 'c', 'y', 'm', 'r']
         fig = plt.figure(figsize=(10,10))
         ax = fig.add_subplot(111)
         ax.scatter(np.random.random(10), np.random.random(10), marker='x', color=colors[0])
         p1 = ax.scatter(np.random.random(10), np.random.random(10), marker='x', color=colors[0],s=50)
         p2 = ax.scatter(np.random.random(10), np.random.random(10), marker='o', color=colors[1],s=50)
         p3 = ax.scatter(np.random.random(10), np.random.random(10), marker='o', color=colors[2],s=50)
         ax.legend((p1,p2,p3),('points 1','points 2','points 3'),fontsize=20)
         ax.set_xlabel('x',fontsize=40)
         ax.set_ylabel('y',fontsize=40)
         fig.savefig('figure_scatterplot.png')
```

The s option represents the size of the points and colors are the colors that correspond to each set of points and the handles are passed directly into the legend function (p1, p2, p3):

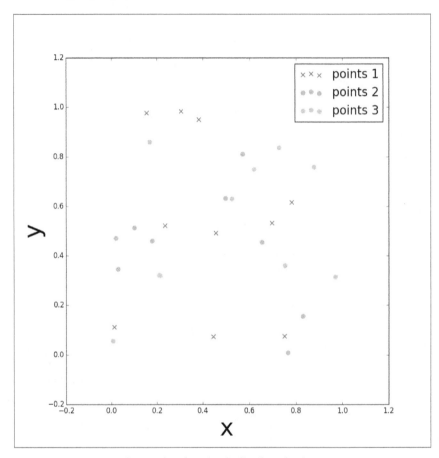

Scatter plot of randomly distributed points

For further details on how to use matplotlib we advise the reader to read online material and tutorials such as http://matplotlib.org/users/pyplot_tutorial.html.

Scientific libraries used in the book

Throughout this book, certain libraries are necessary to implement the machine-learning techniques discussed in each chapter. We are going to briefly describe the most relevant libraries employed hereafter:

- **SciPy** is a collection of mathematical methods based on the NumPy array objects. It is an open source project so it takes advantage of additional methods continuously written from developers around the world. Python software that employs a SciPy routine is part of advanced projects or applications comparable to similar frameworks such as MATLAB, **Octave** or **RLab**. There are a wide range of methods available from manipulating and visualizing data functions to parallel computing routines that enhance the versatility and potentiality of the Python language.

- **scikit-learn** (**sklearn**) is an open source machine learning module for Python programming language. It implements various algorithms such as clustering, classification, and regression including support vector machines, **Naive Bayes**, **Decision Trees**, **Random Forests**, **k-means**, and **Density Based Spatial Clustering of Applications with Noise** (**DBSCAN**) and it interacts natively with numerical Python libraries such as NumPy and SciPy. Although most of the routines are written in Python, some functions are implemented in **Cython** to achieve better performance. For instance, support vector machines and logistic regression are written in Cython wrapping other external libraries (**LIBSVM**, **LIBLINEAR**).

- **The Natural Language Toolkit** (**NLTK**), is a collection of libraries and functions for **Natural Language Processing** (**NLP**) for Python language processing. NLTK is designed to support research and teaching on NLP and related topics including artificial intelligence, cognitive science, information retrieval, linguistics, and machine learning. It also features a series of text processing routines for tokenization, stemming, tagging, parsing, semantic reasoning, and classification. NLTK includes sample codes and sample data and interfaces to more than 50 corpora and lexical databases.

- **Scrapy** is an open source web crawling framework for the Python programming language. Originally designed for scraping websites, and as a general purpose crawler, it is also suitable for extracting data through APIs. The Scrapy project is written around *spiders* that act by providing a set of instructions. It also features a web crawling shell that allows the developers to test their concepts before actually implementing them. Scrapy is currently maintained by Scrapinghub Ltd., a web scraping development and services Company.

- **Django** is a free and open source web application framework implemented in Python following the *model view controller* architectural pattern. Django is designed for creation of complex, database-oriented websites. It also allows us to manage the application through an administrative interface, which can create, read, delete, or update data used in the application. There are a series of established websites that currently use Django, such as Pinterest, Instagram, Mozilla, The Washington Times, and Bitbucket.

When to use machine learning

Machine learning is not magic and it may be not be beneficial to all data-related problems. It is important at the end of this introduction to clarify when machine-learning techniques are extremely useful:

- It is not possible to code the rules: a series of human tasks (to determine if an e-mail is spam or not, for example) cannot be solved effectively using simple rules methods. In fact, multiple factors can affect the solution and if rules depend on a large number of factors it becomes hard for humans to manually implement these rules.

- A solution is not scalable: whenever it is time consuming to manually take decisions on certain data, the machine-learning techniques can scale adequately. For example, a machine-learning algorithm can efficiently go through millions of e-mails and determine if they are spam or not.

However, if it is possible to find a good target prediction, by simply using mathematical rules, computations, or predetermined schemas that can be implemented without needing any data-driven learning, these advanced machine-learning techniques are not necessary (and you should not use them).

Summary

In this chapter we introduced the basic machine-learning concepts and terminology that will be used in the rest of the book. Tutorials of the most relevant libraries (NumPy, pandas, and matplotlib) used by machine-learning professionals to prepare, t manipulate, and visualize data have been also presented. A general introduction of all the other Python libraries that will be used in the following chapters has been also provided.

You should have a general knowledge of what the machine-learning field can practically do, and you should now be familiar with the methods employed to transform the data into a usable format, so that a machine-learning algorithm can be applied. In the next chapter we will explain the main unsupervised learning algorithms and how to implement them using the `sklearn` library.

2
Unsupervised Machine Learning

As we have seen in the *Chapter 1, Introduction to Practical Machine Learning Using Python*, unsupervised learning is designed to provide insightful information on data unlabeled date. In many cases, a large dataset (both in terms of number of points and number of features) is unstructured and does not present any information at first sight, so these techniques are used to highlight hidden structures on data (clustering) or to reduce its complexity without losing relevant information (dimensionality reduction). This chapter will focus on the main clustering algorithms (the first part of the chapter) and dimensionality reduction methods (the second part of the chapter). The differences and advantages of the methods will be highlighted by providing a practical example using Python libraries. All of the code will be available on the author's GitHub profile, in the `https://github.com/ai2010/machine_learning_for_the_web/tree/master/chapter_2/` folder. We will now start describing clustering algorithms.

Clustering algorithms

Clustering algorithms are employed to restructure data in somehow ordered subsets so that a meaningful structure can be inferred. A cluster can be defined as a group of data points with some similar features. The way to quantify the similarity of data points is what determines the different categories of clustering.

Clustering algorithms can be divided into different categories based on different metrics or assumptions in which data has been manipulated. We are going to discuss the most relevant categories used nowadays, which are distribution methods, centroid methods, density methods, and hierarchical methods. For each category, a particular algorithm is going to be presented in detail, and we will begin by discussing distribution methods. An example to compare the different algorithms will be discussed, and both the IPython notebook and script are available in the my GitHub book folder at `https://github.com/ai2010/machine_learning_for_the_web/tree/master/chapter_2/`.

Distribution methods

These methods assume that the data comes from a certain distribution, and the expectation maximization algorithm is used to find the optimal values for the distribution parameters. Expectation maximization and the mixture of **Gaussian** clustering are discussed hereafter.

Expectation maximization

This algorithm is used to find the maximum likelihood estimates of parameter distribution models that depend on hidden (unobserved) variables. Expectation maximization consists of iterating two steps: the **E-step**, which creates the **log-likelihood** function evaluated using the current values of the parameters, and the **M-step**, where the new parameters' values are computed, maximizing the log-likelihood of the E-step.

Consider a set of N elements, $\{x^{(i)}\}i = 1,...,N$, and a log-likelihood on the data as follows:

$$l(\theta) = \sum_{i=1}^{N} \log p\left(x^{(i)}; \theta\right) = \sum_{i=1}^{N} \log \sum_{z} p\left(x^{(i)}, z^{(i)}; \theta\right)$$

Here, θ represents the set of parameters and $z^{(i)}$ are the so-called hidden variables.

We want to find the values of the parameters that maximize the log-likelihood without knowing the values of the $z^{(i)}$ (unobserved variables). Consider a distribution over the $z^{(i)}$, and $Q(z^{(i)})$, such as $\sum_{i=1} \underset{\sim}{Q}\left(z^{(i)}\right) = 1$. Therefore:

$$Q\left(z^{(i)}\right) = \frac{p\left(x^{(i)}, z^{(i)}; \theta\right)}{p\left(x^{(i)}; \theta\right)} = p\left(z^{(i)} \mid x^{(i)}; \theta\right)$$

This means $Q(z^{(i)})$ is the posterior distribution of the hidden variable, $z^{(i)}$, given $x^{(i)}$ parameterized by θ. The expectation maximization algorithm comes from the use of Jensen's inequality and it ensures that carrying out these two steps:

1. $Q\left(z^{(i)}\right) = p\left(z^{(i)} \mid z^{(i)}; \theta\right)$

2. $\sum_i \sum_{z^{(i)}} Q\left(z^{(i)}\right) \log \dfrac{p\left(x^{(i)}, z^{(i)}; \theta\right)}{Q\left(z^{(i)}\right)}$

The log-likelihood converges to the maximum, and so the associated θ values are found.

Mixture of Gaussians

This method models the entire dataset using a mixture of Gaussian distributions. Therefore, the number of clusters will be given as the number of Gaussians considered in the mixture. Given a dataset of N elements, {x(i)}i = 1,...,N, where each $x^{(i)} \in R^d$ is a vector of d-features modeled by a mixture of Gaussian such as the following:

$$p\left(x^{(i)} \mid \bar{\mu}, \bar{\Sigma}\right) = \sum_{k=1}^{K} p\left(x^{(i)} \bar{\mu}, \bar{\Sigma}, z^{(i)} = k\right) p\left(z^{(i)} = k, \phi\right) = \sum_{k=1}^{K} p\left(x^{(i)} \mid \mu_k, \Sigma_k\right) \phi_k$$

Where:

- $z^{(i)} \in 1,...,K$ is a hidden variable that represents the Gaussian component each $x^{(i)}$ is generated from
- $\mu = \{\mu_{1,...}, \mu_K\}$ represents the set of mean parameters of the Gaussian components
- $\Sigma = \{\Sigma_1,...,\Sigma_K\}$ represents the set of variance parameters of the Gaussian components
- ϕ_k is the mixture weight, representing the probability that a randomly selected $x^{(i)}$ was generated by the Gaussian component k, where $\sum_{k=1}^{K} \phi_k = 1$, and $\phi = \{\phi_{1,...}, \phi_K\}$ is the set of weights

- $p\left(x^{(i)} \mid \mu_k, \Sigma_k\right) = \dfrac{1}{(2\pi)^{d/2} \mid \Sigma_k^{1/2}} e^{-\frac{1}{2}\left(x^{(i)}-\mu_k\right)^T \Sigma_k^{-1}\left(x^{(i)}-\mu_k\right)}$ is the Gaussian

   component k with parameters $\left(\mu_k, \Sigma_k\right)$ associated with the point $x^{(i)}$

The parameters of our model are thus φ, μ and Σ. To estimate them, we can write down the log-likelihood of the dataset:

$$l\left(\phi, \bar{\mu}, \bar{\Sigma}\right) = \sum_{i=1}^{N} \log\left(p\left(x^{(i)} \mid \bar{\mu}, \bar{\Sigma}\right)\right) = \sum_{i=1}^{N} \log \sum_{i=1}^{N} p\left(x^{(i)}\bar{\mu}, \bar{\Sigma}, z^{(i)} = k\right) p\left(z^{(i)} = k, \phi\right)$$

In order to find the values of the parameters, we apply the expectation maximization algorithm explained in the previous section where $\theta = \left(\mu, \Sigma\right)$ and $Q\left(z^{(i)}\right) = p\left(z^{(i)}, \phi\right)$.

After choosing a first guess of the parameters, we iterate the following steps until convergence:

1. **E- step**: The weights $W_k^{(i)} = p\left(z^{(i)} = k \mid x^{(i)}, \phi, \bar{\mu}, \bar{\Sigma}\right)$ are updated by following the rule obtained by applying Bayes' theorem:

$$p\left(z^{(i)} = k \mid x^{(i)}, \phi, \bar{\mu}, \bar{\Sigma}\right) = \frac{p\left(x^{(i)} \mid \mu_k, \Sigma_k\right)\phi_k}{\sum_{l=1}^{K} p\left(x^{(i)} \mid \mu_l, \Sigma_l\right)\phi_l}$$

2. **M-step**: The parameters are updated to the following (these formulas come from solving the maximization problem, which means setting the derivatives of the log-likelihood to zero):

$$\mu_k = \frac{\sum_{i=1}^{N} w_k^{(i)} x^{(i)}}{\sum_{i=1}^{N} w_k^{(i)}}$$

$$\Sigma_k = \frac{\sum_{i=1}^{N} w_k^{(i)} \left(x^{(i)} - \mu_k \right) \left(x^{(i)} - \mu_k \right)^T}{\sum_{i=1}^{N} w_k^{(i)}}$$

$$\phi_k = \frac{\sum_{i=1}^{N} w_k^{(i)}}{N}$$

Note that the expectation maximization algorithm is needed because the hidden variables $z^{(i)}$ are unknown. Otherwise, it would have been a supervised learning problem, where $z^{(i)}$ is the label of each point of the training set (and the supervised algorithm used would be the Gaussian discriminant analysis). Therefore, this is an unsupervised algorithm and the goal is also to find $z^{(i)}$, that is, which of the K Gaussian components each point $x^{(i)}$ is associated with. In fact, by calculating the posterior probability $p\left(z^{(i)} = k \mid x^{(i)}, \phi, \overline{\mu}, \overline{\Sigma} \right)$ for each of the K classes, it is possible to assign each $x(i)$ to the class k with the highest posterior probability. There are several cases in which this algorithm can be successfully used to cluster (label) the data.

A possible practical example is the case of a professor with student grades for two different classes but not labeled per class. He wants to split the grades into the original two classes assuming that the distribution of grades in each class is Gaussian. Another example solvable with the mixture of the Gaussian approach is to determine the country of each person based on a set of people's height values coming from two different countries and assuming that the distribution of height in each country follows Gaussian distribution.

Centroid methods

This class collects all the techniques that find the centers of the clusters, assigning the data points to the nearest cluster center and minimizing the distances between the centers and the assigned points. This is an optimization problem and the final centers are vectors; they may not be the points in the original dataset. The number of clusters is a parameter to be specified a priori and the generated clusters tend to have similar sizes so that the border lines are not necessarily well defined. This optimization problem may lead to a local optimal solution, which means that different initialization values can result in slightly different clusters. The most common method is known as **k-means (Lloyd's algorithm)**, in which the distance minimized is the **Euclidean norm**. Other techniques find the centers as the medians of the clusters (**k-medians clustering**) or impose the center's values to be the actual data points. Furthermore, other variations of these methods differ in the choice that the initial centers are defined (**k-means++** or **fuzzy c-means**).

k-means

This algorithm tries to find the center of each cluster as the mean of all the members that minimize the distance between the center and the assigned points themselves. It can be associated with the k-nearest-neighbor algorithm in classification problems, and the resulting set of clusters can be represented as a **Voronoi diagram** (a method of partitioning the space in regions based on the distance from a set of points, in this case, the clusters' centers). Consider the usual dataset, $x^{(i)}, i \in 1, \ldots, N$. The algorithm prescribes to choose a number of centers K, assign the initial mean cluster centers $\mu_j, j \in 1, \ldots, K$ to random values, and then iterate the following steps until convergence:

1. For each data point i, calculate the Euclidean square distances between each point i and each center j and find the center index $d_{i'}$ which corresponds to the minimum of these distances: $|\mu_j - x^{(i)}|, j \in 1, \ldots, K$.

2. For each center j, recalculate its mean value as the mean of the points that have $d\_i j$ equal to j (that is, points belonging to the cluster with mean μ_j):

$$\mu_j = \frac{\sum_{i=1}^{N} \delta_{d,j} x(i)}{\sum_{i=1}^{N} \delta_{d\_ij}}$$

It is possible to show that this algorithm converges with respect to the function given by the following function:

$$F = \sum_{i=1}^{N} \left| x^{(i)} - \mu_{d\_i} \right|$$

It decreases monotonically with the number of iterations. Since F is a nonconvex function, it is not guaranteed that the final minimum will be the global minimum. In order to avoid the problem of a clustering result associated with the local minima, the k-means algorithm is usually run multiple times with different random initial center's means. Then the result associated with the lower F value is chosen as the optimal clustering solution.

Density methods

These methods are based on the idea that sparse areas have to be considered borders (or noise) and high-density zones should be related to the cluster's centers. The common method is called **density-based spatial clustering of applications with noise (DBSCAN)**, which defines the connection between two points through a certain distance threshold (for this reason, it is similar to hierarchical algorithms; see *Chapter 3*, *Supervised Machine Learning*). Two points are considered linked (belonging to the same cluster) only if a certain density criterion is satisfied — the number of neighboring points has to be higher than a threshold value within a certain radius. Another popular method is mean-shift, in which each data point is assigned to the cluster that has the highest density in its neighborhood. Due to the time-consuming calculations of the density through a kernel density estimation, mean-shift is usually slower than DBSCAN or centroid methods. The main advantages of this class of algorithms are the ability to define clusters with arbitrary shapes and the ability to determine the best number of clusters instead of setting this number a priori as a parameter, making these methods suitable to cluster datasets in which it is not known.

Mean – shift

Mean-shift is nonparametric algorithm that finds the positions of the local maxima in a density kernel function defined on a dataset. The local maxima found can be considered the centers of clusters in a dataset $x^{(i)}, i \in 1,..,N$, and the number of maxima is the number of clusters. In order to be applied as a clustering algorithm, each point $x^{(l)} \in R^d$ has to be associated with the density of its neighborhood:

$$f\left(x^{(l)}\right) = \frac{1}{Nh^d} \sum_{i=1}^{N} K\left(\frac{x^{(l)} - x^{(i)}}{h}\right)$$

Here, h is the so-called bandwidth; it estimates the radius of the neighborhood in which the points affect the density value $f(x^{(l)})$ (that is, the other points have negligible effect on $f\left(x^{(l)}\right)$). K is the kernel function that satisfies these conditions:

- $\int_{R \wedge d} K\left(x^{(i)}\right) = 1$

- $K\left(x^{(i)}\right) \geq 0, i \in 1, \ldots, N$

Typical examples of $K(x^{(i)})$ are the following functions:

- $K\left(x^{(i)}\right) = e^{\frac{-\left(x^{(i)}\right)^2}{2\sigma^2}}$: Gaussian kernel

- $K\left(x^{(i)}\right) = \begin{cases} \frac{3}{4}\left(1 - \left(x^{(i)}\right)^2\right) if \left|x^{(i)}\right| \leq 1 \\ 0 \quad else \end{cases}$: Epanechnikov kernel

The mean-shift algorithm imposes the maximization of $f(x^{(l)})$, which translates into the mathematical equation (remember that in function analysis, the maximum is found by imposing the derivative to 0):

$$\nabla f\left(x^{(l)}\right) = 0 \rightarrow x^{(l)} = \frac{\sum_{i=1}^{N} K'\left(\frac{x^{(l)} - x^{(i)}}{h}\right) x^{(i)}}{K'\left(\frac{x^{(l)} - x^{(i)}}{h}\right)}$$

Here, K' is derivative of the kernel density function K.

Therefore, to find the local maxima position associated with the feature vector $x^{(l)}$, the following iterative equation can be computed:

$$x_{t+1}^{(l)} = x_t^{(l)} + \frac{\sum_{i=1}^{N} K' \left(\frac{x_t^{(l)} - x^{(i)}}{h} \right) x^{(i)}}{K' \left(\frac{x_t^{(l)} - x^{(i)}}{h} \right)} - x_t^{(l)} = x_t^{(l)} + m \left(x_t^{(l)} \right)$$

Here, $m\left(x_t^{(l)}\right)$ is called the mean-shift vector. The algorithm will converge when at iteration $t=a$, the condition $\nabla f\left(x_a^{(l)}\right) = 0 \to m\left(x_a^{(l)}\right) = 0$ is satisfied.

Supported by the equation, we can now explain the algorithm with the help of the following figure. At the first iteration $t=0$, the original points $x^{(l)}, l \in 1, ..., N$ (red) are spread on the data space, the mean shift vector $m\left(x_0^{(l)}\right) = m\left(x^{(l)}\right), l \in 1, ..., N$ is calculated, and the same points are marked with a cross (x) to track their evolution with the algorithm. At iteration 1, the dataset will be obtained using the aforementioned equation, and the resulting points $x_1^{(l)}, l \in 1, .., N$ are shown in the following figure with the (+) symbol:

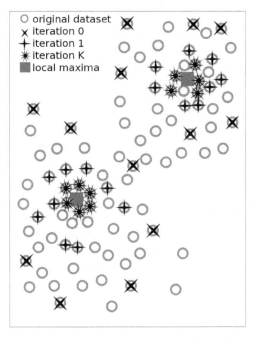

Sketch of the mean-shift evolution through iterations

In the preceding figure, at iteration *0* the original points are shown in red (cross), at iteration *1* and *K* the sample points (symbols + and * respectively) move towards the local density maxima indicated by blue squares.

Again, at iteration K, the new data points $x_K^{(l)}, l \in 1,.., N$ are computed and they are shown with the * symbol in the preceding figure. The density function values $f\left(x_K^{(l)}\right)$ associated with $x_K^{(l)}$ are larger than the values in the previous iterations since the algorithm aims to maximize them. The original dataset is now clearly associated with points $x_K^{(l)}, l \in 1,.., N$, and they converge to the locations plotted in blue squares in the preceding figure. The feature vectors $x^{(l)}, l \in 1,\ldots,N$ are now collapsing to two different local maxima, which represent the centers of the two clusters.

In order to properly use the method, some considerations are necessary.

The only parameter required, the bandwidth h, needs to be tuned cleverly to achieve good results. In fact, too low value of h may result in a large number of clusters, while a large value of h may merge multiple distinct clusters. Note also that if the number d of feature vector dimensions is large, the mean-shift method may lead to poor results. This is because in a very-high-dimensional space, the number of local maxima is accordingly large and the iterative equation can easily converge too soon.

Hierarchical methods

The class of hierarchical methods, also called connectivity-based clustering, forms clusters by collecting elements on a similarity criteria based on a distance metric: close elements gather in the same partition while far elements are separated into different clusters. This category of algorithms is divided in two types: **divisive clustering** and **agglomerative clustering**. The divisive approach starts by assigning the entire dataset to a cluster, which is then divided in two less similar (distant) clusters. Each partition is further divided until each data point is itself a cluster. The agglomerative method, which is the most often employed method, starts from the data points, each of them representing a cluster. Then these clusters are merged by similarity until a single cluster containing all the data points remains. These methods are called **hierarchical** because both categories create a hierarchy of clusters iteratively, as the following figure shows. This hierarchical representation is called a **dendrogram**. On the horizontal axis, there are the elements of the dataset, and on the vertical axis, the distance values are plotted. Each horizontal line represents a cluster and the vertical axis indicates which element/cluster forms the related cluster:

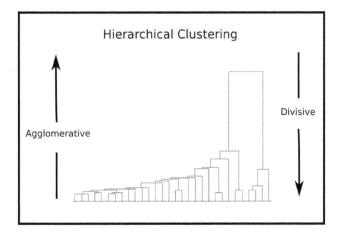

In the preceding figure, agglomerative clustering starts from many clusters as dataset points and ends up with a single cluster that contains the entire dataset. Vice versa, the divisive method starts from a single cluster and finishes when all clusters contain a single data point each.

The final clusters are then formed by applying criteria to stop the agglomeration/division strategy. The distance criteria sets the maximum distance above which two clusters are too far away to be merged, and the *number of clusters* criteria sets the maximum number of clusters to stop the hierarchy from continuing to merge or split the partitions.

An example of agglomeration is given by the following algorithm:

1. Assign each element i of the dataset $x^{(i)}, i \in 1,..,N$ to a different cluster.
2. Calculate the distances between each pair of clusters and merge the closest pair into a single cluster, reducing the total number of clusters by 1.
3. Calculate the distances of the new cluster from the others.
4. Repeat steps 2 and 3 until only a single cluster remains with all N elements.

Since the distance $d(C1,C2)$ between two clusters $C1$, $C2$, is computed by definition between two points $c1 \in C1, c2 \in C2$ and each cluster contains multiple points, a criteria to decide which elements have to be considered to calculate the distance is necessary (linkage criteria). The common linkage criteria of two clusters $C1$ and $C2$ are as follows:

- **Single linkage**: The minimum distance among the distances between any element of $C1$ and any element of $C2$ is given by the following:

$$d(C1, C2) = \min\{d(c1, c2) : c1 \in C1, c2 \in C2\}$$

- **Complete linkage**: The maximum distance among the distances between any element of $C1$ and any element of $C2$ is given by the following:

$$d(C1, C2) = \max\{d(c1, c2) : c1 \in C1, c2 \in C2\}$$

- **Unweighted pair group method with arithmetic mean (UPGMA) or average linkage**: The average distance among the distances between any element of $C1$ and any element of $C2$ is $d(C1, C2) = \dfrac{1}{|N_{c1}||N_{c2}|} \sum_{c1 \in C1} \sum_{c2 \in C2} d(c1, c2)$, where $|N_{c1}|, |N_{c2}|$ are the numbers of elements of $C1$ and $C2$, respectively.

- **Ward algorithm**: This merges partitions that do not increase a certain measure of heterogeneity. It aims to join two clusters $C1$ and $C2$ that have the minimum increase of a variation measure, called the merging cost $\Delta(C1, C2)$, due to their combination. The distance in this case is replaced by the merging cost, which is given by the following formula:

$$\Delta(C1, C2) = \frac{N_{c1} N_{c2}}{N_{c1} + N_{c2}} |\mu_{c1} - \mu_{c2}|^2 \quad \mu_{c1} = \frac{1}{N_{c1}} \sum_{c1 \in C1} c1, \mu_{c2} = \frac{1}{N_{c2}} \sum_{c2 \in C2} c2$$

Here, $|N_{c1}|, |N_{c2}|$ are the numbers of elements of C1 and C2, respectively.

There are different metrics $d(c1,c2)$ that can be chosen to implement a hierarchical algorithm. The most common is the Euclidean distance:

$$d(c1, c2) = \sqrt{\sum_i (c1_i - c2_i)^2}$$

Note that this class of method is not particularly time-efficient, so it is not suitable for clustering large datasets. It is also not very robust towards erroneously clustered data points (outliers), which may lead to incorrect merging of clusters.

Training and comparison of the clustering methods

To compare the clustering methods just presented, we need to generate a dataset. We choose the two dataset classes given by the two two-dimensional multivariate normal distributions with means and covariance equal to $\mu_1 = [10,0], \mu_2 = [0,10]$ and $\sigma_1 = \sigma_2 = \begin{bmatrix} 3 & 1 \\ 1 & 4 \end{bmatrix}$, respectively.

The data points are generated using the NumPy library and plotted with matplotlib:

```
from matplotlib import pyplot as plt
import numpy as np
np.random.seed(4711)  # for repeatability
c1 = np.random.multivariate_normal([10, 0], [[3, 1], [1, 4]],
size=[100,])
l1 = np.zeros(100)
l2 = np.ones(100)
c2 = np.random.multivariate_normal([0, 10], [[3, 1], [1, 4]],
size=[100,])
#add noise:
np.random.seed(1)  # for repeatability
noise1x = np.random.normal(0,2,100)
noise1y = np.random.normal(0,8,100)
noise2 = np.random.normal(0,8,100)
c1[:,0] += noise1x
c1[:,1] += noise1y
c2[:,1] += noise2

fig = plt.figure(figsize=(20,15))
ax = fig.add_subplot(111)
ax.set_xlabel('x',fontsize=30)
ax.set_ylabel('y',fontsize=30)
fig.suptitle('classes',fontsize=30)
labels = np.concatenate((l1,l2),)
X = np.concatenate((c1, c2),)
```

```
pp1= ax.scatter(c1[:,0], c1[:,1],cmap='prism',s=50,color='r')
pp2= ax.scatter(c2[:,0], c2[:,1],cmap='prism',s=50,color='g')
ax.legend((pp1,pp2),('class 1', 'class2'),fontsize=35)
fig.savefig('classes.png')
```

A normally distributed noise has been added to both classes to make the example more realistic. The result is shown in the following figure:

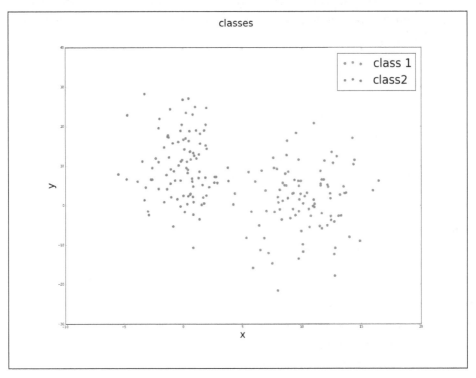

Two multivariate normal classes with noise

The clustering methods have been implemented using the sklearn and scipy libraries and again plotted with matplotlib:

```
import numpy as np
from sklearn import mixture
from scipy.cluster.hierarchy import linkage
from scipy.cluster.hierarchy import fcluster
from sklearn.cluster import KMeans
from sklearn.cluster import MeanShift
```

```
from matplotlib import pyplot as plt

fig.clf()#reset plt
fig, ((axis1, axis2), (axis3, axis4)) = plt.subplots(2, 2, sharex='col',
sharey='row')

#k-means
kmeans = KMeans(n_clusters=2)
kmeans.fit(X)
pred_kmeans = kmeans.labels_
plt.scatter(X[:,0], X[:,1], c=kmeans.labels_, cmap='prism')  # plot
points with cluster dependent colors
axis1.scatter(X[:,0], X[:,1], c=kmeans.labels_, cmap='prism')
axis1.set_ylabel('y',fontsize=40)
axis1.set_title('k-means',fontsize=20)

#mean-shift
ms = MeanShift(bandwidth=7)
ms.fit(X)
pred_ms = ms.labels_
axis2.scatter(X[:,0], X[:,1], c=pred_ms, cmap='prism')
axis2.set_title('mean-shift',fontsize=20)

#gaussian mixture
g = mixture.GMM(n_components=2)
g.fit(X)
pred_gmm = g.predict(X)
axis3.scatter(X[:,0], X[:,1], c=pred_gmm, cmap='prism')
axis3.set_xlabel('x',fontsize=40)
axis3.set_ylabel('y',fontsize=40)
axis3.set_title('gaussian mixture',fontsize=20)

#hierarchical
# generate the linkage matrix
```

```
Z = linkage(X, 'ward')
max_d = 110
pred_h = fcluster(Z, max_d, criterion='distance')
axis4.scatter(X[:,0], X[:,1], c=pred_h, cmap='prism')
axis4.set_xlabel('x',fontsize=40)
axis4.set_title('hierarchical ward',fontsize=20)
fig.set_size_inches(18.5,10.5)
fig.savefig('comp_clustering.png', dpi=100)
```

The k-means function and Gaussian mixture model have a specified number of clusters (n_clusters =2,n_components=2), while the mean-shift algorithm has the bandwidth value bandwidth=7. The hierarchical algorithm is implemented using the ward linkage and the maximum (ward) distance, max_d, is set to 110 to stop the hierarchy. The fcluster function is used to obtain the predicted class for each data point. The predicted classes for the k-means and the mean-shift method are accessed using the labels_ attribute, while the Gaussian mixture model needs to employ the predict function. The k -means, mean-shift, and Gaussian mixture methods have been trained using the fit function, while the hierarchical method has been trained using the linkage function. The output of the preceding code is shown in the following figure:

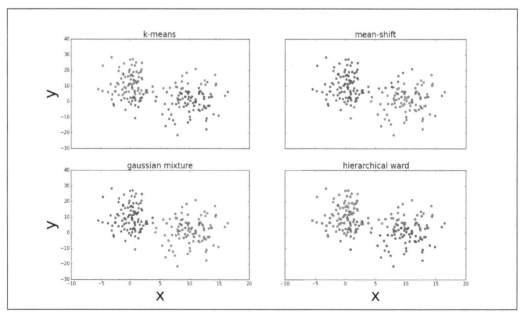

IClustering of the two multivariate classes using k-means, mean-shift, Gaussian mixture model, and hierarchical ward method

The mean-shift and hierarchical methods show two classes, so the choice of parameters (bandwidth and maximum distance) is appropriate. Note that the maximum distance value for the hierarchical method has been chosen looking at the dendrogram (the following figure) generated by the following code:

```
from scipy.cluster.hierarchy import dendrogram
fig = plt.figure(figsize=(20,15))
plt.title('Hierarchical Clustering Dendrogram',fontsize=30)
plt.xlabel('data point index (or cluster index)',fontsize=30)
plt.ylabel('distance (ward)',fontsize=30)
dendrogram(
    Z,
    truncate_mode='lastp',  # show only the last p merged clusters
    p=12,
    leaf_rotation=90.,
    leaf_font_size=12.,
    show_contracted=True,
)
fig.savefig('dendrogram.png')
```

The `truncate_mode='lastp'` flag allows us to specify the number of last merges to show in the plot (in this case, p=12). The preceding figure clearly shows that when the distance is between `100` and `135`, there are only two clusters left:

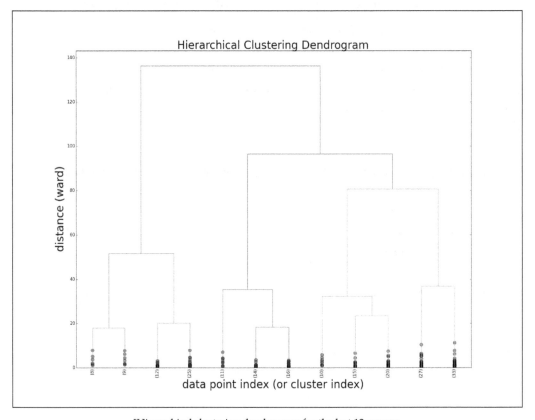

IHierarchical clustering dendrogram for the last 12 merges

In the preceding figure on the horizontal axis, the number of data points belonging to each cluster before the last *12* merges is shown in brackets ().

Apart from the Gaussian mixture model, the other three algorithms misclassify some data points, especially k-means and hierarchical methods. This result proves that the Gaussian mixture model is the most robust method, as expected, since the dataset comes from the same distribution assumption. To evaluate the quality of the clustering, scikit-learn provides methods to quantify the correctness of the partitions: v-measure, completeness, and homogeneity. These methods require the real value of the class for each data point, so they are referred to as external validation procedures. This is because they require additional information not used while applying the clustering methods. Homogeneity, *h*, is a score between *0* and *1* that measures whether each cluster contains only elements of a single class. Completeness, *c*, quantifies with a score between *0* and *1* whether all the elements of a class are assigned to the same cluster. Consider a clustering that assigns each data point to a different cluster. In this way, each cluster will contains only one class and the homogeneity is *1*, but unless each class contains only one element, the completeness is very low because the class elements are spread around many clusters. Vice versa, if a clustering results in assigning all the data points of multiple classes to the same cluster, certainly the completeness is *1* but homogeneity is poor. These two scores have a similar formula, as follows:

$$h = 1 - \frac{H(C_l|C)}{H(C_l)}, \quad c = 1 - \frac{H(C|C_l)}{H(C)}$$

Here:

- $H(C_l|C)$ is the conditional entropy of the classes C_l, given the cluster assignments $H(C_l|C) = -\sum_{p=1}^{|C_l|}\sum_{c=1}^{|C|} \frac{N_{pc}}{N} \log\left(\frac{N_{pc}}{N_c}\right)$

- $H(C|C_l)$ is the conditional entropy of the clusters, given the class membership $H(C|C_l) = -\sum_{p=1}^{|C_l|}\sum_{c=1}^{|C|} \frac{N_{pc}}{N} \log\left(\frac{N_{pc}}{N_p}\right)$

- $H(C_l)$ is the entropy of the classes: $H(C_l) = -\sum_{p=1}^{|C_l|} \frac{N_p}{N} \log\left(\frac{N_p}{N}\right)$

- $H(C)$ is the entropy of the clusters: $H(C) = -\sum \frac{N_c}{N} \log\left(\frac{N_c}{N}\right)$

- N_{pc} is the number of elements of class *p* in cluster *c*, N_p is the number of elements of class *p*, and N_c is the number of elements of cluster *c*

The v-measure is simply the harmonic mean of the homogeneity and the completeness:

$$v = 2\frac{hc}{h+c}$$

These measures require the true labels to evaluate the quality of the clustering, and often this is not real-case scenario. Another method only employs data from the clustering itself, called **silhouette**, which calculates the similarities of each data point with the members of the cluster it belongs to and with the members of the other clusters. If on average each point is more similar to the points of its own cluster than the rest of the points, then the clusters are well defined and the score is close to *1* (it is close to *-1*, otherwise). For the formula, consider each point *i* and the following quantities:

- $d_s(i)$ is the average distance of the point *i* from the points of the same cluster
- $d_{rest}(i)$ is the minimum distance of point *i* from the rest of the points in all other clusters

The silhouette can be defined as

$$s(i) = \frac{d_{rest}(i) - d_s(i)}{max(d_s(i), d_{rest}(i))}$$, and the silhouette score is the average of *s(i)* for all

data points.

The four clustering algorithms we covered are associated with the following values of these four measures calculated using `sklearn` (scikit-learn):

```
from sklearn.metrics import homogeneity_completeness_v_measure
from sklearn.metrics import silhouette_score
res = homogeneity_completeness_v_measure(labels,pred_kmeans)
print 'kmeans measures, homogeneity:',res[0],' completeness:',res[1],'
v-measure:',res[2],' silhouette score:',silhouette_score(X,pred_kmeans)
res = homogeneity_completeness_v_measure(labels,pred_ms)
print 'mean-shift measures, homogeneity:',res[0],'
completeness:',res[1],' v-measure:',res[2],' silhouette
score:',silhouette_score(X,pred_ms)
res = homogeneity_completeness_v_measure(labels,pred_gmm)
print 'gaussian mixture model measures, homogeneity:',res[0],'
completeness:',res[1],' v-measure:',res[2],' silhouette
score:',silhouette_score(X,pred_gmm)
res = homogeneity_completeness_v_measure(labels,pred_h)
```

```
print 'hierarchical (ward) measures, homogeneity:',res[0],'
completeness:',res[1],' v-measure:',res[2],' silhouette
score:',silhouette_score(X,pred_h)
```

The preceding code produces the following output:

kmeans measures, homogeneity: 0.25910415428 completeness: 0.259403626429
v-measure: 0.259253803872 silhouette score: 0.409469791511

mean-shift measures, homogeneity: 0.657373750073 completeness:
0.662158204648 v-measure: 0.65975730345 silhouette score: 0.40117810244

gaussian mixture model measures, homogeneity: 0.959531296098
completeness: 0.959600517797 v-measure: 0.959565905699 silhouette
score: 0.380255218681

hierarchical (ward) measures, homogeneity: 0.302367273976 completeness:
0.359334499592 v-measure: 0.32839867574 silhouette score:
0.356446705251

As expected from the analysis of the preceding figure, the Gaussian mixture model has the best values of the homogeneity, completeness, and v-measure measures (close to *1*); mean-shift has reasonable values (around *0.5*); while k-means and hierarchical methods result in poor values (around *0.3*). The silhouette score instead is decent for all the methods (between *0.35* and *0.41*), meaning that the clusters are reasonably well defined.

Dimensionality reduction

Dimensionality reduction, which is also called feature extraction, refers to the operation to transform a data space given by a large number of dimensions to a subspace of fewer dimensions. The resulting subspace should contain only the most relevant information of the initial data, and the techniques to perform this operation are categorized as linear or non-linear. Dimensionality reduction is a broad class of techniques that is useful for extracting the most relevant information from a large dataset, decreasing its complexity but keeping the relevant information.

The most famous algorithm, **Principal Component Analysis (PCA)**, is a linear mapping of the original data into a subspace of uncorrelated dimensions, and it will be discussed hereafter. The code shown in this paragraph is available in IPython notebook and script versions at the author's GitHub book folder at https://github.com/ai2010/machine_learning_for_the_web/tree/master/chapter_2/.

Principal Component Analysis (PCA)

The principal component analysis algorithm aims to identify the subspace where the relevant information of a dataset lies. In fact, since the data points can be correlated in some data dimensions, PCA will find the few uncorrelated dimensions in which the data varies. For example, a car trajectory can be described by a series of variables such as velocity in km/h or m/s, position in latitude and longitude, position in meters from a chosen point, and position in miles from a chosen point. Clearly, the dimensions can be reduced because the velocity variables and the position variables give the same information (correlated variables), so the relevant subspace can be composed of two uncorrelated dimensions (a velocity variable and a position variable). PCA finds not only the uncorrelated set of variables but also the dimensions where the variance is maximized. That is, between the velocity in km/h and miles/h, the algorithm will select the variable with the highest variance, which is trivially represented by the line between the two axes given by the function *velocity[km/h]=3.6*velocity[m/s]* (typically closer to the km/h axis because *1 km/h = 3.6 m/s* and the velocity projections are more spread along the km/h axis than the m/s axis):

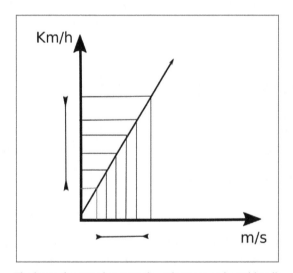

The linear function between the velocity in m/s and km/h

The preceding figure represents the linear function between the velocity in m/s and km/h. The projections of the points along the km/h axis have a large variance, while the projections on the m/s axis have a lower variance. The variance along the linear function *velocity[km/h]=3.6*velocity[m/s]* is larger than both axes.

Now we are ready to discuss the method and its features in detail. It is possible to show that finding the uncorrelated dimensions in which the variance is maximized is equivalent to computing the following steps. As usual, we consider the feature vectors $x^{(i)}, i \in 1,.., N$:

- The average of the dataset: $\mu = \dfrac{1}{N} \sum_{i=1}^{N} x^{(i)}$

- The mean shifted dataset: $u^{(i)} = x^{(i)} - \mu, i \in 1,\ldots, N$

- The rescaled dataset, in which each feature vector component $u_j^{(i)}$ has been divided by the standard deviation, $u_j^{(i)} / \sigma_j \rightarrow u_j^{(i)}$, where

$$\sigma_j = \left(\frac{1}{N} \sum_{i=1}^{N} \left(x_j^{(i)} \right)^2 \right)^{1/2}$$

- The sample covariance matrix: $\sum = \dfrac{1}{N-1} \sum_{i=1}^{N} \left(u^{(i)} \right)^T u^{(i)}$

- The k largest eigenvalues, $\lambda_i i \in 1,\ldots, k$, and their associated eigenvectors, $w^{(i)} i \in 1,\ldots, k$

- Projected feature vectors on the subspace of the k eigenvectors $v^{(i)} = W^T u^{(i)} \in R^k$, where $W = \left[w^1 \ldots w^k \right] \in R^{Nxk}$ is the matrix of the eigenvectors with N rows and k columns

The final feature's vectors (principal components), $v^{(i)}$ lie on a subspace R^k, which still retain the maximum variance (and information) of the original vectors.

Note that this technique is particularly useful when dealing with high-dimensional datasets, such as in face recognition. In this field, an input image has to be compared with a database of other images to find the right person. The PCA application is called **Eigenfaces**, and it exploits the fact that a large number of pixels (variables) in each image are correlated. For instance, the background pixels are all correlated (the same), so a dimensionality reduction can be applied, and comparing images in a smaller subspace is a faster approach that gives accurate results. An example of implementation of Eigenfaces can be found on the author's GitHub profile at `https://github.com/ai2010/eigenfaces`.

PCA example

As an example of the usage of PCA as well as the NumPy library discussed in *Chapter 1, Introduction to Practical Machine Learning using Python* we are going to determine the principal component of a two-dimensional dataset distributed along the line *y=2x*, with random (normally distributed) noise. The dataset and the corresponding figure (see the following figure) have been generated using the following code:

```python
import numpy as np
from matplotlib import pyplot as plt


#line y = 2*x
x = np.arange(1,101,1).astype(float)
y = 2*np.arange(1,101,1).astype(float)
#add noise
noise = np.random.normal(0, 10, 100)
y += noise


fig = plt.figure(figsize=(10,10))
#plot
plt.plot(x,y,'ro')
plt.axis([0,102, -20,220])
plt.quiver(60, 100,10-0, 20-0, scale_units='xy', scale=1)
plt.arrow(60, 100,10-0, 20-0,head_width=2.5, head_length=2.5, fc='k',
ec='k')
plt.text(70, 110, r'$v^1$', fontsize=20)


#save
ax = fig.add_subplot(111)
ax.axis([0,102, -20,220])
ax.set_xlabel('x',fontsize=40)
ax.set_ylabel('y',fontsize=40)
fig.suptitle('2 dimensional dataset',fontsize=40)
fig.savefig('pca_data.png')
```

The following figure shows the resulting dataset. Clearly there is a direction in which the data is distributed and it corresponds to the principal component v^1 that we are going to extract from the data.

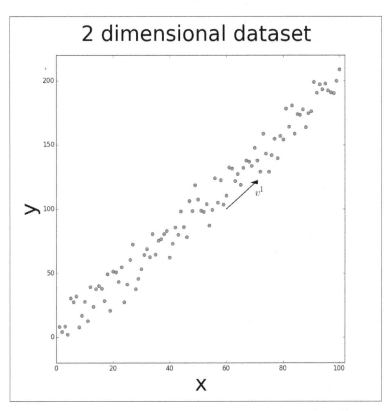

A two-dimensional dataset. The principal component direction v1 is indicated by an arrow.

The algorithm calculates the mean of the two-dimensional dataset and the mean shifted dataset, and then rescales with the corresponding standard deviation:

```
mean_x = np.mean(x)
mean_y = np.mean(y)
u_x = (x- mean_x)/np.std(x)
u_y = (y-mean_y)/np.std(y)
sigma = np.cov([u_x,u_y])
```

To extract the principal component, we have to calculate the eigenvalues and eigenvectors and select the eigenvector associated with the largest eigenvalue:

```
eig_vals, eig_vecs = np.linalg.eig(sigma)
eig_pairs = [(np.abs(eig_vals[i]), eig_vecs[:,i])
             for i in range(len(eig_vals))]

eig_pairs.sort()
eig_pairs.reverse()
v1 = eig_pairs[0][1]
print v1
array([ 0.70710678,  0.70710678]
```

To check whether the principal component lies along the line as expected, we need to rescale back its coordinates:

```
x_v1 = v1[0]*np.std(x)+mean_x
y_v1 = v1[1]*np.std(y)+mean_y
print 'slope:',(y_v1-1)/(x_v1-1)
slope: 2.03082418796
```

The resulting slope is approximately 2, which agrees with the value chosen at the beginning. The `scikit-learn` library provides a possible ready-to-use implementation of the PCA algorithm without applying any rescaling or mean shifting. To use the `sklearn` module, we need to transform the rescaled data into a matrix structure in which each row is a data point with x, y coordinates:

```
X = np.array([u_x,u_y])
X = X.T
print X.shape
(100,2)
```

The PCA module can be started now, specifying the number of principal components we want (1 in this case):

```
from sklearn.decomposition import PCA
pca = PCA(n_components=1)
pca.fit(X)
v1_sklearn = pca.components_[0]
print v1_sklearn
[ 0.70710678  0.70710678]
```

The principal component is exactly the same as the one obtained using the step-by-step approach, `[ 0.70710678   0.70710678]`, so the slope will also be the same. The dataset can now be transformed into the new one-dimensional space with both approaches:

```
#transform in reduced space
X_red_sklearn = pca.fit_transform(X)
W = np.array(v1.reshape(2,1))
X_red = W.T.dot(X.T)
#check the reduced matrices are equal
assert X_red.T.all() == X_red_sklearn.all(), 'problem with the pca
algorithm'
```

The assert exception is not thrown, so the results show a perfect agreement between the two methods.

Singular value decomposition

This method is based on a theorem that states that a matrix $X\ d\ x\ N$ can be decomposed as follows:

$$X = U\sum V^T$$

Here:

- U is a $d\ x\ d$ unitary matrix
- $\sum$ is a $d\ x\ N$ diagonal matrix where the diagonal entries σ_i are called singular values
- V is an $N\ x\ N$ unitary matrix

In our case, X can be composed by the feature's vectors $x^{(i)} i \in 1,\ldots,N$, where each $x^{(i)} \in R^d$ is a column. We can reduce the number of dimensions of each feature vector d, approximating the singular value decomposition. In practice, we consider only the largest singular values $\sigma_1., \sigma_t\ t < d$ so that:

$$X \simeq U_t \sum_t V_t^T, U_t\left(d\ x\ t\right), \sum_t\left(t\ x\ t\right), V^T\left(t\ x\ N\right)$$

t represents the dimension of the new reduced space where the feature vectors are projected. *A* vector $x^{(i)}$ is transformed in the new space using the following formula:

$$x_t^{(i)} = \left(x^{(i)} \right)^T U_t \, \Sigma_t^{-1} \in R^t$$

This means that the matrix $\Sigma_t V_t^T$ (not V_t^T) represents the feature vectors in the *t* dimensional space.

Note that it is possible to show that this method is very similar to the PCA; in fact, the `scikit-learn` library uses SVD to implement PCA.

Summary

In this chapter, the main clustering algorithms were discussed in detail. We implemented them (using scikit-learn) and compared the results. Also, the most relevant dimensionality reduction technique, principal component analysis, was presented and implemented. You should now have the knowledge to use the main unsupervised learning techniques in real scenarios using Python and its libraries.

In the next chapter, the supervised learning algorithms will be discussed, for both classification and regression problems.

Supervised Machine Learning

3

In this chapter, the most relevant regression and classification techniques are discussed. All of these algorithms share the same background procedure, and usually the name of the algorithm refers to both a classification and a regression method. The linear regression algorithms, Naive Bayes, decision tree, and support vector machine are going to be discussed in the following sections. To understand how to employ the techniques, a classification and a regression problem will be solved using the mentioned methods. Essentially, a labeled train dataset will be used to *train the models*, which means to find the values of the parameters, as we discussed in the introduction. As usual, the code is available in my GitHub folder at `https://github.com/ai2010/machine_learning_for_the_web/tree/master/chapter_3/`.

We will conclude the chapter with an extra algorithm that may be used for classification, although it is not specifically designed for this purpose (hidden Markov model). We will now begin to explain the general causes of error in the methods when predicting the true labels associated with a dataset.

Model error estimation

We said that the trained model is used to predict the labels of new data, and the quality of the prediction depends on the ability of the model to *generalize*, that is, the correct prediction of cases not present in the trained data. This is a well-known problem in literature and related to two concepts: bias and variance of the outputs.

The bias is the error due to a wrong assumption in the algorithm. Given a point $x^{(t)}$ with label y_t, the model is biased if it is trained with different training sets, and the predicted label y_t^{pred} will always be different from y_t. The variance error instead refers to the different, wrongly predicted labels of the given point $x^{(t)}$. A classic example to explain the concepts is to consider a circle with the true value at the center (true label), as shown in the following figure. The closer the predicted labels are to the center, the more unbiased the model and the lower the variance (top left in the following figure). The other three cases are also shown here:

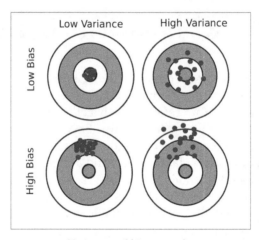

Variance and bias example.

A model with low variance and low bias errors will have the predicted labels that is blue dots (as show in the preceding figure) concentrated on the red center (true label). The high bias error occurs when the predictions are far away from the true label, while high variance appears when the predictions are in a wide range of values.

We have already seen that labels can be continuous or discrete, corresponding to regression classification problems respectively. Most of the models are suitable for solving both problems, and we are going to use word regression and classification referring to the same model. More formally, given a set of N data points and corresponding labels $y_t \, t \in 1, \ldots, N$, a model with a set of parameters $\theta = \theta_0, .., \theta_{M-1}, \theta_j \ j \in 0, .., M-1$ with the true parameter values $\hat{\theta} = \hat{\theta}_0, .., \hat{\theta}_{M-1}, \hat{\theta}_j \ j \in 0, .., M-1$ will have the **mean square error** (**MSE**), equal to:

$$MSE\left(\hat{\theta}\right) = \frac{1}{N}\sum_{t=1}^{N}\left(y_t - y_t^{pred}\right)^2 = E\left[\left(\hat{\theta} - \theta\right)\right] = E\left[\left(\theta - E\left(\theta\right)\right)^2\right] + \left(E\left(\theta\right) - \hat{\theta}\right)^2 = Var\left(\theta\right) + Bias\left(\theta, \hat{\theta}\right)^2$$

We will use the MSE as a measure to evaluate the methods discussed in this chapter. Now we will start describing the generalized linear methods.

Generalized linear models

The generalized linear model is a group of models that try to find the M parameters $\theta_j, j \in 0, \ldots, M-1$ that form a linear relationship between the labels y_i and the feature vector $x^{(i)}$ that is as follows:

$$y_i = \sum_{j=0}^{M-1} \theta_j x_j^{(i)} + \in_i = h_\theta\left(x^{(i)}\right) + \in_i \ \forall i \in 0, \ldots, N-1$$

Here, $\in_i$ are the errors of the model. The algorithm for finding the parameters tries to minimize the total error of the model defined by the cost function J:

$$J = \frac{1}{2} \sum_{i=0}^{N-1} \left(y_i - h_\theta\left(x^{(i)}\right)\right)^2$$

The minimization of J is achieved using an iterative algorithm called **batch gradient descent**:

$$\theta_j \leftarrow \theta_j + \alpha \sum_{i=0}^{N-1} \frac{\partial J}{\partial \theta_j}, \forall j \in 0, \ldots, M-1$$

Here, α is called learning rate, and it is a trade-off between convergence speed and convergence precision. An alternative algorithm that is called **stochastic gradient descent**, that is loop for $i \in 0, \ldots, N-1$:

$$\theta_j \leftarrow \theta_j + \alpha \frac{\partial J}{\partial \theta_j}, \forall j \in 0, \ldots, M-1$$

The θ_j is updated for each training example i instead of waiting to sum over the entire training set. The last algorithm converges near the minimum of J, typically faster than batch gradient descent, but the final solution may oscillate around the real values of the parameters. The following paragraphs describe the most common model $h_\theta\left(x^{(i)}\right)$ and the corresponding cost function, J.

Linear regression

Linear regression is the simplest algorithm and is based on the model:

$$h_\theta\left(x^{(i)}\right)=\theta_0+\theta_1 x_1^{(i)}+\theta_2 x_2^{(i)}+\ldots=\sum_{j=0}^{M-1}\theta_j x_j^{(i)},\forall i\in 0,..,N-1$$

The cost function and update rule are:

$$J=\frac{1}{2}\sum_{i=0}^{N-1}\left(y_i-h_\theta\left(x^{(i)}\right)\right)^2\rightarrow\frac{\partial J}{\partial\theta_j}=\left(y_i-h_\theta\left(x^{(i)}\right)\right)x_j^{(i)}\ \forall j\in 0,..,M-1$$

Ridge regression

Ridge regression, also known as **Tikhonov regularization,** adds a term to the cost function J such that:

$$J=\frac{1}{2}\sum_{i=0}^{N-1}\left(y_i-h_\theta\left(x^{(i)}\right)\right)^2+\frac{\lambda}{2}\sum_{j=0}^{M-1}\theta_j^2\rightarrow\frac{\partial J}{\partial\theta_j}=\left(y_i-h_\theta\left(x^{(i)}\right)\right)x_j^{(i)}+\lambda\theta_j$$

$\forall j\in 0,..,M-1$, where λ is the regularization parameter. The additional term has the function needed to prefer a certain set of parameters over all the possible solutions penalizing all the parameters θ_j different from 0. The final set of θ_j *shrank* around 0, lowering the variance of the parameters but introducing a bias error. Indicating with the superscript l the parameters from the linear regression, the ridge regression parameters are related by the following formula:

$$\theta_j=\frac{\theta_j^l}{1+\lambda}$$

This clearly shows that the larger the λ value, the more the ridge parameters are shrunk around 0.

Lasso regression

Lasso regression is an algorithm similar to ridge regression, the only difference being that the regularization term is the sum of the absolute values of the parameters:

$$J = \frac{1}{2}\sum_{i=0}^{N-1}\left(y_i - h_\theta\left(x^{(i)}\right)\right)^2 + \lambda\sum_{j=0}^{M-1}\left|\theta_j\right| \rightarrow \frac{\partial J}{\partial \theta_j} = \left(y_i - h_\theta\left(x^{(i)}\right)\right)x_j^{(i)} + \lambda sign\left(\theta_j\right)$$

$$\forall j \in 0,..,M-1$$

Logistic regression

Despite the name, this algorithm is used for (binary) classification problems, so we define the labels $y_i \in 0,1$. The model is given the so-called logistic function expressed by:

$$h_\theta\left(x^{(i)}\right) = \frac{1}{1+e^{-\sum_{j=0}^{M-1}\theta_j x_j^{(i)}}}$$

In this case, the cost function is defined as follows:

$$J = \frac{1}{2}\sum_{i=0}^{N-1} y_i \log\left(h_\theta\left(x^{(i)}\right)\right) + \left(1-y_i\right)\log\left(1-h_\theta\left(x^{(i)}\right)\right)$$

From this, the update rule is formally the same as linear regression (but the model definition, h_θ, is different):

$$\frac{\partial J}{\partial \theta_j} = \left(y_i - h_\theta\left(x^{(i)}\right)\right)x_j^{(i)} \; \forall j \in 0,..,M-1$$

Note that the prediction for a point p, $h_\theta\left(x^{(p)}\right)$, is a continuous value between 0 and 1. So usually, to estimate the class label, we have a threshold at $h_\theta\left(x^{(p)}\right) = 0.5$ such that:

$$h_\theta\left(x^{(p)}\right) = \begin{cases} \geq & 0.5 \quad 1 \\ < & 0.5 \quad 0 \end{cases}$$

The logistic regression algorithm is applicable to multiple label problems using the techniques one versus all or one versus one. Using the first method, a problem with K classes is solved by training K logistic regression models, each one assuming the labels of the considered class j as $+1$ and all the rest as 0. The second approach consists of training a model for each pair of labels ($\dfrac{K(K-1)}{2}$ trained models).

Probabilistic interpretation of generalized linear models

Now that we have seen the generalized linear model, let's find the parameters θ_j that satisfy the relationship:

$$y_i = \sum_{j=0}^{M-1} \theta_j x_j^{(i)} + \epsilon_i = h_\theta\left(x^{(i)}\right) + \epsilon_i \ \forall i \in 0, \ldots, N-1$$

In the case of linear regression, we can assume ϵ_i as normally distributed with mean 0 and variance σ^2 such that the probability is $p(\epsilon_i) = \dfrac{1}{\sqrt{2\pi}\sigma} e^{-\frac{\epsilon_i^2}{2\sigma^2}}$ equivalent to:

$$p\left(y_i x^{(i)}; \theta\right) = \frac{1}{\sqrt{2\pi}\sigma} e^{-\frac{\left(y_i - h_\theta\left(x^{(i)}\right)\right)^2}{2\sigma^{\wedge 2}}}$$

Therefore, the total likelihood of the system can be expressed as follows:

$$L(\theta) = \prod_{i=0}^{N-1} p\left(y_i \middle| x^{(i)}; \theta\right) = \prod_{i=0}^{N-1} \frac{1}{\sqrt{2\pi}\sigma} e^{-\frac{\left(y_i - h_\theta\left(x^{(i)}\right)\right)^2}{2\sigma^2}}$$

In the case of the logistic regression algorithm, we are assuming that the logistic function itself is the probability:

$$P\left(y_i = 1 \middle| x^{(i)}; \theta\right) = h_\theta\left(x^{(i)}\right)$$

$$P\left(y_i = 0 \middle| x^{(i)}; \theta\right) = 1 - h_\theta\left(x^{(i)}\right)$$

Then the likelihood can be expressed by:

$$L(\theta) = \prod_{i=0}^{N-1} p\left(y_i \middle| x^{(i)}; \theta\right) = \prod_{i=0}^{N-1} \left(h_\theta\left(x^{(i)}\right)\right)^{y_i} \left(1 - h_\theta\left(x^{(i)}\right)\right)^{(1-y_i)}$$

In both cases, it can be shown that maximizing the likelihood is equivalent to minimizing the cost function, so the gradient descent will be the same.

k-nearest neighbours (KNN)

This is a very simple classification (or regression) method in which given a set of feature vectors $x^{(i)} i \in 0, \ldots, N-1$ with corresponding labels y_i, a test point $x^{(t)}$ is assigned to the label value with the majority of the label occurrences in the K nearest neighbors $x^{(k)} k \in 1, \ldots, K$ found, using a distance measure such as the following:

- **Euclidean:** $\sqrt{\sum_{j=0}^{M-1} \left(x_j^{(k)} - x_j^{(t)} \right)^2}$

- **Manhattan:** $\left| \sum_{j=0}^{M-1} x_j^{(k)} - x_j^{(t)} \right|$

- **Minkowski:** $\left(\sum_{j=0}^{M-1} \left(\left| x_j^{(k)} - x_j^{(t)} \right| \right)^q \right)^{1/q}$ (if q=2, this reduces to the Euclidean
  distance)

In the case of regression, the value y_t is calculated by replacing the majority of occurrences by the average of the labels y_k $k \in 1, \ldots, K$. The simplest average (or the majority of occurrences) has uniform weights, so each point has the same importance regardless of their actual distance from $x^{(t)}$. However, a weighted average with weights equal to the inverse distance from $x^{(t)}$ may be used.

Naive Bayes

Naive Bayes is a classification algorithm based on Bayes' probability theorem and conditional independence hypothesis on the features. Given a set of m features, $x_i i \in 0, \ldots, M-1$, and a set of labels (classes) $y \in 0, \ldots, K-1$, the probability of having label c (also given the feature set x_i) is expressed by Bayes' theorem:

$$P\left(y = c \middle| x_{0,\cdot}, x_{M-1} \right) = \frac{P\left(x_{0,\cdot}, x_{M-1} \middle| y = c \right) P\left(y = c \right)}{P\left(x_{0,\cdot}, x_{M-1} \right)}$$

Here:

- $P\left(x_{0,\cdot\cdot},x_{M-1}\middle|y=c\right)$ is called the likelihood distribution
- $P\left(c\middle|x_{0,\cdot\cdot},x_{M-1}\right)$ is the posteriori distribution
- $P\left(y=c\right)$ is the prior distribution
- $P\left(x_{0,\cdot\cdot},x_{M-1}\right)$ is called the evidence

The predicted class associated with the set of features $x_i, i \in 0,\ldots,M-1$ will be the value p such that the probability is maximized:

$$p = arg \max_{y \in 0,\ldots,K-1} P\left(y\middle|x_{0,\cdot\cdot},x_{M-1}\right)$$

However, the equation cannot be computed. So, an assumption is needed.

Using the rule on conditional probability $P\left(A/B\right) = \dfrac{P\left(A,B\right)}{P\left(B\right)}$, we can write the numerator of the previous formula as follows:

$$P\left(x_{0,\cdots},x_{M-1}\middle|y=c\right)P\left(y=c\right) = P\left(y=c\right)P\left(x_0\middle|y=c\right)p\left(x_{1,\cdot\cdot},x_{M-1}\middle|y=c,x_0\right) =$$

$$P\left(y=c\right)P\left(x_0\middle|y=c\right)P\left(x_1\middle|y=c,x_0\right)p\left(x_{2,\cdot\cdot},x_{M-1}\middle|y=c,x_0,x_1\right) =$$

$$P\left(y=c\right)P\left(x_0\middle|y=c\right)P\left(x_1\middle|y=c,x_0\right)p\left(x_{M-1}\middle|y=c,x_0,x_{1,\cdot\cdot},x_{M-2}\right)$$

We now use the assumption that each feature x_i is conditionally independent given c (for example, to calculate the probability of x_1 given c, the knowledge of the label c makes the knowledge of the other feature x_0 redundant, $P\left(x_1\middle|y=c\right) = p\left(x_1\middle|y=c,x_0\right)$):

$$P\left(y=c\right)\prod_{j=0}^{M-1}P\left(x_j\middle|y=c\right)$$

Under this assumption, the probability of having label c is then equal to:

$$P\left(y=c\middle|x_{0,\cdot\cdot},x_{M-1}\right)=\frac{\prod\limits_{j=0}^{M-1}P\left(x_j\middle|y=c\right)P\left(y=c\right)+1}{\sum\limits_{i=0}^{K-1}\prod\limits_{j=0}^{M-1}P\left(x_j\middle|y=i\right)P\left(y=i\right)+M}$$

————(1)

Here, the *+1* in the numerator and the M in the denominator are constants, useful for avoiding the *0/0* situation (**Laplace smoothing**).

Due to the fact that the denominator of **(1)** does not depend on the labels (it is summed over all possible labels), the final predicted label p is obtained by finding the maximum of the numerator of **(1)**:

$$p=arg\max_{c\in 0,\ldots,K-1}\prod\limits_{j=0}^{M-1}P\left(x_j\middle|y=c\right)P\left(y=c\right)$$

————(2)

Given the usual training set $x^{(i)}i\in 0,..,N-1$, where $x^{(i)}i\in R^M$ (M features) corresponding to the labels set $y_i i\in 0,..,N-1$, the probability $P(y=c)$ is simply calculated in frequency terms as the number of training examples associated with the class c over the total number of examples, $P\left(y=c\right)=\frac{N_{y=c}}{N}$. The conditional probabilities $P\left(x_j\middle|y=i\right)$ instead are evaluated by following a distribution. We are going to discuss two models, **Multinomial Naive Bayes** and **Gaussian Naive Bayes**.

Multinomial Naive Bayes

Let's assume we want to determine whether an e-mail s given by a set of word occurrences $x^{(s)}=\left(x_{0,\cdot\cdot}^{(s)},x_{M-1}^{(s)}\right)$ is spam *(1)* or not *(0)* so that $y\in 0,1$. M is the size of the vocabulary (number of features). There are $w_t t\in 0,..,M-1$ words and N training examples (e-mails).

Each email $x^{(i)}$ with label y_i such that $x_j^{(i)}, j \in 0,.., M-1$ is the number of times the word j in the vocabulary occurs in the training example l. For example, $x_1^{(3)}$ represents the number of times the word 1, or w_1, occurs in the third e-mail. In this case, multinomial distribution on the likelihood is applied:

$$p\left(x^{(s)}|y\right) = \frac{\left(\sum_{j=0}^{M-1} x_j^{(s)}\right)!}{\prod_{j=0}^{M-1} x_j^{(s)}!} \prod_{j=0}^{M-1} P\left(w_j|y\right)^{x_j^{(s)}} \alpha \prod_{j=0}^{M-1} P\left(w_j|y\right)^{x_j^{(s)}}$$

Here, the normalization constants in the front can be discarded because they do not depend on the label y, and so the *arg max* operator will not be affected. The important part is the evaluation of the single word w_j: probability over the training set:

$$p\left(w_j|y\right) = \frac{\sum_{i=0}^{N-1} x_j^{(i)} \delta_{y_i,y}}{\sum_{t=0}^{M-1}\sum_{i=0}^{N-1} x_t^{(i)} \delta_{y_i,y}} = \frac{N_{jy}}{N_y}$$

Here N_{iy} is the number of times the word j occurs, that is associated with label y, and N_y is the portion of the training set with label y.

This is the analogue of $P\left(x_j|y=i\right), p\left(x_j|y=c\right)$ on equation **(1)** and the multinomial distribution likelihood. Due to the exponent on the probability, usually the logarithm is applied to compute the final algorithm *(2)*:

$$p = \arg \max_{y} \log P(y) - \sum_{j=0}^{M-1} x_j^{(s)} \log P\left(w_j|y\right)$$

Gaussian Naive Bayes

If the features vectors $x^{(i)}$ have continuous values, this method can be applied. For example, we want to classify images in K classes, each feature j is a pixel, and $x_j^{(i)}$ is the *j-th* pixel of the *i-th* image in the training set with N images and labels $y_i i \in 0,..,N-1$. Given an unlabeled image represented by the pixels $x_{0,.},.,x_{M-1}$, in this case, $P(x_j|y=i)$ in equation (1) becomes:

$$P(x_j|y=i) = \frac{1}{\sigma_{ji}\sqrt{2\pi}} e^{-\frac{(x_j-\mu_{ij})^2}{2\sigma_{ji}^2}}$$

Here:

$$\mu_{ij} = \frac{\sum_{t=0}^{N-1} x_j^{(t)} \delta_{y_t,i}}{\sum_{t=0}^{N-1} \delta_{y_t,i}}$$

And:

$$\sigma_{ij}^2 = \frac{\sum_{t=0}^{N-1} \left(x_j^{(t)} - \mu_{ij}\right)^2 \delta_{y_t,i}}{\sum_{t=0}^{N-1} \delta_{y_t,i} - 1}$$

Decision trees

This class of algorithms aims to predict the unknown labels splitting the dataset, by generating a set of simple rules that are learnt from the features values. For example, consider a case of deciding whether to take an umbrella today or not based on the values of humidity, wind, temperature, and pressure. This is a classification problem, and an example of the decision tree can be like what is shown in the following figure based on data of 100 days. Here is a sample table:

Humidity (%)	Pressure (mbar)	Wind (Km/h)	Temperature (C)	Umbrella
56	1,021	5	21	Yes
65	1,018	3	18	No
80	1,020	10	17	No
81	1,015	11	20	Yes

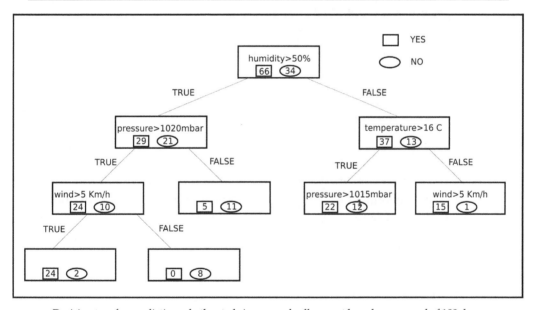

Decision tree for predicting whether to bring an umbrella or not based on a record of 100 days.

In the preceding figure the numbers in squares represent the days on which an umbrella has been brought, while the circled numbers indicate days in which an umbrella was not necessary.

The decision tree presents two types of nodes: decision nodes, which have two (or more) branches when a decision split is applied; and leaf nodes, when data is classified. The stopping criterion is usually a maximum number of decision nodes (depth of the tree) or a minimum of data points to continue to split (typically around 2 to 5). The problem of decision trees learning is to build the *best* tree out of all the possible node combinations, that is, estimate the hierarchy of the rules to be applied (in other words, whether the first decision node should be on humidity or on temperature, and so on). More formally, given a training set of $x^{(i)}, i \in 1,..,N$ with $x^{(i)}$ in R^m and corresponding labels y_i, we need to find the best rule to partition the data S at node k. If the chosen feature, j, is continuous, each split rule is given by a feature j and a threshold t^j_k that splits S in $S_{left}\left(t^j_k, j\right)$ for $x^{(i)}_j < t^j_k$ and $S_{right}\left(t^j_k, j\right)$ for $x^{(i)}_j \geq t^j_k$, $i \in 1,...,N$. The best split rule $\left(t^q_k, q\right)$ for the node k is associated with the minimum of the impurity I function that measures how much the rule is able to separate the data into partitions with different labels (that is, each branch will contain the minimum amount of label mixing):

$$I\left(t^j_k, j\right) = \frac{n_{left}}{N_k} H\left(S_{left}\right) + \frac{n_{right}}{N_k} H\left(S_{right}\right)$$

$$\left(t^q_k, q\right) = a \, rg \min_{\left(t^j_k, j\right)} I\left(t^j_k, j\right)$$

Here, n_{left}, n_{right} are the numbers of data points on the left and right branches, respectively. N_k is the number of data points on node k, and H is a measure that can assume different expressions using the probability of each target value l at branch b (b can be left or right), $p_{bl} = \frac{n_l}{N_b}$:

- Entropy of the branch: $H\left(S_b\right) = \sum_l p_{bl} \log_2 p_{bl}$

- Gini impurity of the branch: $H\left(S_b\right) = \sum_l p_{bl}\left(1 - p_{bl}\right)$

- Misclassification: $H(S_b) = 1 - \max_{l}(p_{bl})$

  ◦ Mean squared error (variance): $H(S_b) = \dfrac{1}{N_b} \sum_{i \in N_b} (y_i - \mu_b)^2$

  (where $\mu_b = \dfrac{\sum_{i \in N_b} y_i}{N_b}$)

Note that the latter is typically used in regression problems while the others are employed in classification. Note also that usually in literature, the *information gain* definition is introduced as the difference between H at node k and $I\left(t_k^j, j\right)$

$$IG = H(S_k) - I\left(t_k^j, j\right) \text{ where } H(S_k) = \sum_{l} p_{kl} \log_2 p_{kl},\, p_{kl} = \frac{n_l}{N_k}$$

If the feature j is discrete with d number of possible values, there is no binary threshold t_k^j to calculate and the data is split into d partitions. The measure H is calculated over d subsets.

For example, we can determine the rule for the first node ($k=0$) for the preceding example using the entropy as the impurity measure H.

All the features are continuous, so the values of t_0^j are needed. Assuming that $j=0$ is the humidity and sorting in increasing order, the possible humidity values in the dataset we have are as follows:

h	0		1		....		98		99	
umbrella	yes		no		....		no		no	
humidity	**58**		62		....		88		89	
	<	>=	<	>=	<	>=	<	>=	<	>=
yes	0	11	14	32	7	20	29	12	78	0
no	0	89	21	33	13	60	10	49	22	0
$I\left(x_0^{(h)}, 0\right)$	**0.5**		0.99		0.85		0.76		0.76	

So, the threshold value for the humidity feature is $t_0^0 = \arg \min\limits_{h \in 1,\dots,N} \left(I\left(x_j^{(h)}, j \right) \right) = 58;$

and in the same way, we can calculate the threshold values for temperature t_0^1, wind t_0^2, and pressure t_0^3. Now we can record to determine the best rule for the first node, computing the impurity for each of the four features:

yes		umbrella		yes		umbrella	
		no				no	
Humidity j=0	$x_0^{(i)} < t_0^0$	0	0	Temperature j=1	$x_0^{(i)} < t_0^1$	21	32
	$x_0^{(i)} \geq t_0^1$	11	89		$x_0^{(i)} \geq t_0^1$	11	36
Impurity: $I\left(t_0^0, 0 \right) = 0.5$				Impurity: $I\left(t_0^1, 1 \right) = 0.88$			
yes		umbrella		yes		umbrella	
		no				no	
Wind j=2	$x_0^{(i)} < t_0^2$	48	5	Pressure j=3	$x_0^{(i)} < t_0^3$	39	3
	$x_0^{(i)} \geq t_0^2$	1	46		$x_0^{(i)} \geq t_0^3$	45	13
Impurity: $I\left(t_0^2, 2 \right) = 0.31$				Impurity: $I\left(t_0^3, 3 \right) = 0.60$			

Therefore, for node 0, the best rule is given by:

$$\left(t_0^q, q \right) = \arg \min\limits_{j=0,1,2,3} \left(I\left(t_0^0, 0 \right), I\left(t_0^1, 1 \right), I\left(t_0^2, 2 \right), I\left(t_0^3, 3 \right) \right) = \left(t_0^2, 2 \right)$$

That is, the wind feature with threshold t_0^2. We can repeat the same procedure to find the best rule for the following decision nodes until the end of the tree.

Decision trees learning is able to handle large datasets, though it tends not to generalize well, especially with a large set of features ($N \approx M$). In such cases, it is advisable to set a small depth of the tree or use some dimensionality reduction techniques. Setting the minimum number of data points to split or the minimum number of data points in a leaf node will also help prevent overfitting. This algorithm may lead to over-complex trees; they can be *pruned* to reduce the branches that do not affect the quality of the prediction. Various pruning techniques are available, but they are beyond the scope of this book. Note also that a series of decision trees can be trained at the same time, composing of a so-called **random forest**. A random forest trains each tree with a random sample of the original data points, and a random subset of features is available for each decision node learning. The result is an average of the predictions in a regression problem or the majority in a classification problem.

Support vector machine

This algorithm, **Support Vector Machine (SVM)**, tries to geometrically separate the dataset $x^{(i)}, i \in 1,..,N$ into two subsets labeled with $y_i = +1$ and $y_i = -1$. The next figure shows the data perfectly separated into two classes (empty circles and black circles), that is, the case the data in which the decision boundary (or hyperplane) given by the black line fully separates the two classes (in other words, there are no misclassified data points):

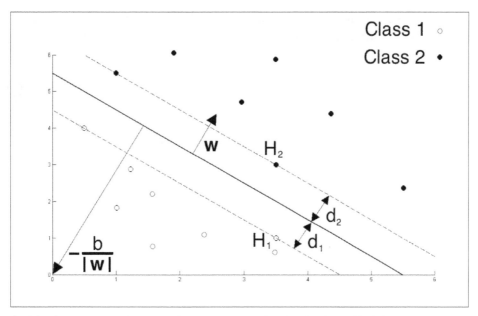

Sketch of the dataset separated into two classes (empty and filled circles) by the black line (decision boundary)

The hyperplane is mathematically described by the equation $w \cdot x + b = 0$, where $|x| = \dfrac{-b}{|w|}$ is the distance of the hyperplane from the origin and w is the normal to the hyperplane. The goal of the algorithm is to maximize the distance of the decision boundary from the data points. In practice, we consider the closest points i to the hyperplane, called support vectors, that lie in two planes H_1, H_2 at distances d_1, d_2 from the decision boundary such that:

$w \cdot x^{(i)} + b = +1$ for H_1 such that $y_i = +1$ --------(1)

$w \cdot x^{(i)} + b = -1$ for H_2 such that $y_i = -1$--------(2)

Assuming $d_1 = d_2$, the common distance is called margin so that the support vector machine method finds the values of w and b that maximize the margin.

Since the distance between H_1 and H_2 is given by $\dfrac{2}{|w|}$, the margin is equal to $\dfrac{1}{|w|}$ and the support vector machine algorithm is equivalent to:

$$min \frac{1}{2}|w|^2 \text{ such that } y_i\left(w.x^{(i)} + b\right) - 1 \geq 0 \ \forall i \in 1,..,N,$$

Here, the square operation and the factor $\dfrac{1}{2}$ have been added to allow the use of a quadratic programming method to solve the mathematical problem. Now, the problem can be rewritten in a Lagrangian form using the Lagrange multipliers $a_i > 0$:

$$L = \frac{1}{2}|w|^2 - \sum_{i=0}^{N-1}\alpha_i\left[y_i\left(x^{(i)} \cdot w + b\right) - 1\right] = \frac{1}{2}|w|^2 - \sum_{i=0}^{N-1}\alpha_i y_i\left(x^{(i)} \cdot w + b\right) + \sum_{i=0}^{N-1}\alpha_i$$

Setting the derivatives with respect to $|w|$ and b to 0, we obtain:

$$w = \sum_{i=0}^{N-1}\alpha_i y_i x^{(i)} \underline{\hspace{1cm}} (3)$$

$$\sum_{i=0}^{N-1}\alpha_i y_i = 0 \underline{\hspace{1cm}} (4)$$

So the optimized Lagrangian becomes:

$$L_d = \sum_{i=0}^{N-1} \alpha_i - \frac{1}{2} \sum_{i,j} \alpha_i H_{ij} \alpha_j \alpha_i \geq 0 \forall i \in 0,.., N-1, \sum_{i=0}^{N-1} y_i \alpha_i = 0$$

Here, $H_{ij} = y_i y_j x^{(i)} \cdot x^{(j)}$.

This is known as a dual form of the original problem, which depends only on the maximization of α_i:

$$\max_{\alpha_i} \left[\sum_{i=0}^{N-1} \alpha_i - \frac{1}{2} \sum_{i,j} \alpha_i H_{ij} \alpha_j \right] \alpha_i \geq 0 \forall i \in 0,.., N-1, \sum_{i=0}^{N-1} y_i \alpha_i = 0$$

The solutions $\alpha_s > 0$ $s \in S$ (the cases $a_i = 0$ return null vectors) are found using a technique called quadratic programming and represent the support vectors w through formula **(3)**:

$$w = \sum_{s \in S} \alpha_s y_s x^{(s)} \qquad \text{---(5).}$$

α_s satisfy the equation (combination of equation **(1)** and **(2)**):

$$y_s = \left(w \cdot x^{(s)} + b \right) = 1$$

Substituting equation **(3)** and multiplying both sides by y_s (which is +1 or -1), we obtain:

$$b = y_s - \sum_{m \in S} \alpha_m y_m x^{(m)} \cdot x^{(s)}$$

Averaging over all the support vectors N_s we can have a better estimate of the parameter b:

$$b = \frac{1}{N} \sum_{s \in S} y_s - \sum_{m \in S} \alpha_m y_m x^{(m)} \cdot x^{(s)} \qquad \text{---(6)}$$

The equations **(5)** and **(6)** return the values of the parameters that define the support vector machines algorithm, from which it is possible to predict the class of all test points *t*:

$$x^{(t)} \cdot w + b \geq 1 \rightarrow y_t = 1$$

$$x^{(t)} \cdot w + b \leq -1 \rightarrow y_t = -1$$

If a line is not able to completely separate the data points into two classes, we need to allow the data points to be misclassified by an error $\xi_i > 0$ such that:

$$x^{(t)} \cdot w + b \geq 1 - \xi_i \rightarrow y_t = 1$$

$$x^{(t)} \cdot w + b \leq -1 + \xi_i \rightarrow y_t = -1$$

And we need to maximize the margin, trying to minimize the misclassification errors. This condition is translated into this equation:

$$min \frac{1}{2}|w|^2 + C \sum_{i=0}^{N-1} \xi_i \text{ such that } y_i \left(w \cdot x^{(i)} + b \right) - 1 + \xi_i \geq 0 \ \forall i \in 1,.., N$$

Here, the parameter *C* is set to balance the size of the margin with the misclassification errors (*C=0* trivially no misclassification and maximum margin, *C>>1* many misclassified points and a narrow margin). Applying the same method as before, the dual problem is subjected to Lagrange multipliers' conditions with an upper bound *C*:

$$\max_{\alpha_i} \left[\sum_{i=0}^{N-1} \alpha_i - \frac{1}{2} \sum_{i,j} \alpha_i H_{ij} \alpha_j \right], C \geq \alpha_i \geq 0 \forall i \in 0,.., N-1, \sum_{i=0}^{N-1} y_i \alpha_i = 0$$

Until now, we have treated problems in which only two classes are considered. Real problems may have multiple classes, and two procedures are commonly used to employ this method (as seen for logistic regression): one versus all or one versus one. Given a problem with M classes, the first method trains M SVM models, each one assuming the labels of the considered class j +1 and all the rest -1. The second method instead trains a model for each pair of classes i, j, leading to $\dfrac{M(M-1)}{2}$ trained models. Clearly, the second method is computationally more expensive but the results are generally more precise.

In a similar way, SVM can be used in regression problems, that is, whenever y_i is continuous between -1 and 1. In this case, the goal is to find the parameters w and b such that:

$$y_i = w \cdot x^{(i)} + b$$

We assume that the true values t_i can differ from the predicted value y_i of a maximum $\in$ and the predictions can further be misclassified of about ξ_i^+, ξ_i^- depending on whether y_i is larger or smaller than t_i. The following figure shows for an example point i the various predictions y_i lying around the true value t_i, and the associated errors:

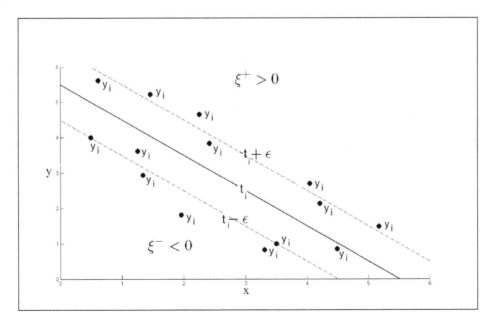

The predictions y_i lie around the true value t_i

The minimization problem becomes:

$$min \frac{1}{2}|w|^2 + C\sum_{i=0}^{N-1}\left(\xi_i^+ + \xi_i^-\right)$$

Such that:

$$t_i - y_i \le \in +\xi_i^+, t_i - y_i \ge -\in -\xi_i^-, \xi_i^+ > 0, \xi_i^- > 0 \forall i \in 0,.., N-1$$

It is possible to show that the associated dual problem is now equal to:

$$\max_{\alpha_i^+,\alpha_i^-}\left[\sum_{i=0}^{N-1}\left(\alpha_i^+ - \alpha_i^-\right)t_i - \in \sum_{i=0}^{N-1}\left(\alpha_i^+ - \alpha_i^-\right) - \frac{1}{2}\sum_{i,j}\left(\alpha_i^+ - \alpha_i^-\right)\left(\alpha_j^+ - \alpha_j^+\right)x^i \cdot x^i\right] \text{ subject}$$

to $C \ge \alpha_i^+, \alpha_i^- \ge 0 \forall i \in 0,.., N-1, \sum_{i=0}^{N-1}\left(\alpha_i^+ - \alpha_i^-\right) = 0$.

Here, α_i^+, α_i^- are the Lagrangian multipliers.

The new prediction, y_p, can be found by applying the formula

$y_p = \sum_{i=0}^{N-1}\left(\alpha_i^+ - \alpha_i^-\right)x^i \cdot x^p + b$, where the parameter b can be obtained as before —

averaging on the subset S given by the support vectors associated with the subset

$C > \alpha_s^+, \alpha_s^- > 0$ and $\xi_s^+, \xi_s^- = 0$:

$$b = \frac{1}{N_s}\sum_{s\in S}t_s - \in -\sum_{m\in S}\left(\alpha_m^+ - \alpha_m^-\right)y_m x^{(m)} \cdot x^{(s)}$$

Kernel trick

There are datasets that are not linearly separable in a certain space, but if it is transformed in the right space, then a hyperplane can separate the data into the desired two or more classes. Consider the example shown in the following figure:

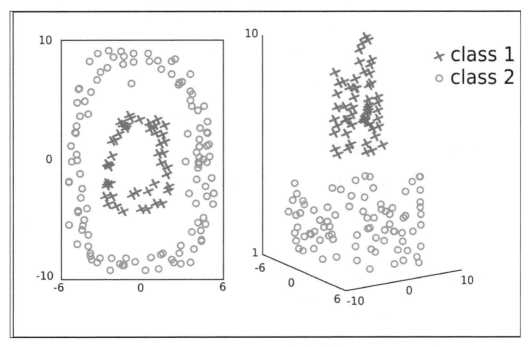

In a two-dimensional space, the dataset shown on the left is not separable. Mapping the dataset in a three-dimensional space, the two classes are separable.

We can clearly see that the two classes are not linearly separable in two-dimensional space (the left figure). Suppose we then apply a kernel function K on the data such that:

$$K\left(x^{(i)}, x^{(j)}\right) = e^{\dfrac{-\left|x^{(i)}, x^{(j)}\right|^2}{2\sigma^2}}$$

The data is now separable by a two-dimensional plane (the right figure). The kernel function on the SVM algorithm is applied to the matrix H_{ij}, replacing the dot product on the variable i, j:

$$H_{ij} = y_i y_j x^{(i)} \cdot x^{(j)} \to H_{ij} = y_i y_j K\left(x^{(i)}, x^{(j)}\right)$$

Popular kernel functions used on the SVM algorithm are:

- Linear kernel: $K\left(x^{(i)}, x^{(j)}\right) = x^{(i)} \cdot x^{(j)}$

- Radial basis kernel (RBF): $K\left(x^{(i)}, x^{(j)}\right) = e^{\frac{-\left|x^{(i)} - x^{(j)}\right|^2}{2\sigma^2}}$

- Polynomial kernel: $K\left(x^{(i)}, x^{(j)}\right) = \left(x^{(i)} \cdot x^{(j)} + a\right)^b$

- Sigmoid kernel: $K\left(x^{(i)}, x^{(j)}\right) = \tanh\left(ax^{(i)} \cdot x^{(j)} - b\right)$

A comparison of methods

We can now test the methods discussed in this chapter to solve a regression problem and a classification problem. To avoid overfitting, the dataset is typically split into two sets: the training set, in which the model parameters are fitted, and a test set, where the accuracy of the model is evaluated. However, it may be necessary to use a third set, the validation set, in which the hyperparameters (for example, C and $\in$ for SVM, or α in ridge regression) can be optimized. The original dataset may be too small to allow splitting into three sets, and also the results may be affected by the particular choice of data points on the training, validation, and test sets. A common way to solve this issue is by evaluating the model following the so-called cross-validation procedure – the dataset is split into k subsets (called folds) and the model is trained as follows:

- A model is trained using *k-1* of the folds as the training data.

- The resulting model is tested on the remaining part of the data.

- This procedure is repeated as many times as the number of folds decided at the beginning, each time with different *k-1* folds to train (and consequently different test fold). The final accuracy is obtained by the average of the accuracies obtained on the different k iterations.

Regression problem

We are using the housing dataset of Boston's suburbs stored at `http://archive.ics.uci.edu/ml/datasets/Housing` and in the author's repository (`https://github.com/ai2010/machine_learning_for_the_web/tree/master/chapter_3/`), in which the code used in this paragraph is also available. The dataset has 13 features:

- **CRIM**: Per capita crime rate by town
- **ZN**: Proportion of residential land zoned for lots over 25,000 sqft
- **INDUS**: Proportion of non-retail business acres per town
- **CHAS**: Charles River dummy variable (= *1* if tract bounds river; *0* otherwise)
- **NOX**: Nitric oxides concentration (parts per 10 million)
- **RM**: Average number of rooms per dwelling
- **AGE**: Proportion of owner-occupied units built prior to 1940
- **DIS**: Weighted distances from five Boston employment centers
- **RAD**: Index of accessibility to radial highways
- **TAX**: Full-value property tax rate per $10,000
- **PTRATIO**: Pupil-teacher ratio by town
- **B**: *1000(Bk - 0.63)^2*, where *Bk* is the proportion of blacks by town
- **LSTAT**: The percentage of lower status of the population and the labels that we want to predict are MEDV, which represent the house value values (in $1000)

To evaluate the quality of the models, the mean squared error defined in the introduction and the coefficient of determination, R^2, are calculated. R^2 is given by:

$$R^2 = 1 - \frac{\sum_{i=0}^{N-1}\left(y_i - y_i^{pred}\right)^2}{\sum_{i=0}^{N-1}\left(y_i - y\right)^2}, y = \frac{\sum_{i=0}^{N-1}y_i}{N}$$

Here, y_i^{pred} indicates the predicted label from the model.

The best result is $R^2=1$, which means the model perfectly fits the data, while $R^2=0$ is associated with a model with a constant line (negative values indicate an increasingly worse fit). The code to compute to train the linear regression, ridge regression, lasso regression, and SVM regression using the `sklearn` library is as follows (IPython notebook at `https://github.com/ai2010/machine_learning_for_the_web/tree/master/chapter_3/`):

```
In [4]:  import pandas as pd
         import numpy as np
         from sklearn import cross_validation
         from sklearn import svm
         from sklearn.tree import DecisionTreeRegressor
         from sklearn.ensemble import RandomForestRegressor
         from sklearn.linear_model import LinearRegression
         from sklearn.linear_model import Ridge
         from sklearn.linear_model import Lasso
         from sklearn.neighbors import KNeighborsRegressor
         from sklearn.metrics import mean_squared_error
```

```
In [7]:  df = pd.read_csv('housing.csv',sep=',',header=None)
         #shuffle the data
         df = df.iloc[np.random.permutation(len(df))]
         X= df[df.columns[:-1]].values
         Y = df[df.columns[-1]].values

         cv = 10
         print 'linear regression'
         lin = LinearRegression()
         scores = cross_validation.cross_val_score(lin, X, Y, cv=cv)
         print("mean R2: %0.2f (+/- %0.2f)" % (scores.mean(), scores.std() * 2))
         predicted = cross_validation.cross_val_predict(lin, X,Y, cv=cv)
         print 'MSE:',mean_squared_error(Y,predicted)

         print 'ridge regression'
         ridge = Ridge(alpha=1.0)
         scores = cross_validation.cross_val_score(ridge, X, Y, cv=cv)
         print("mean R2: %0.2f (+/- %0.2f)" % (scores.mean(), scores.std() * 2))
         predicted = cross_validation.cross_val_predict(ridge, X,Y, cv=cv)
         print 'MSE:',mean_squared_error(Y,predicted)

         print 'lasso regression'
         lasso = Lasso(alpha=0.1)
         scores = cross_validation.cross_val_score(lasso, X, Y, cv=cv)
         print("mean R2: %0.2f (+/- %0.2f)" % (scores.mean(), scores.std() * 2))
         predicted = cross_validation.cross_val_predict(lasso, X,Y, cv=cv)
         print 'MSE:',mean_squared_error(Y,predicted)

         print 'decision tree regression'
         tree = DecisionTreeRegressor(random_state=0)
         scores = cross_validation.cross_val_score(tree, X, Y, cv=cv)
         print("mean R2: %0.2f (+/- %0.2f)" % (scores.mean(), scores.std() * 2))
         predicted = cross_validation.cross_val_predict(tree, X,Y, cv=cv)
         print 'MSE:',mean_squared_error(Y,predicted)

         print 'random forest regression'
         forest = RandomForestRegressor(n_estimators=50, max_depth=None,min_samples_split=1,
                                        random_state=0)
         scores = cross_validation.cross_val_score(forest, X, Y, cv=cv)
         print("mean R2: %0.2f (+/- %0.2f)" % (scores.mean(), scores.std() * 2))
         predicted = cross_validation.cross_val_predict(forest, X,Y, cv=cv)
         print 'MSE:',mean_squared_error(Y,predicted)
         #svm
         print 'linear support vector machine'
         svm_lin = svm.SVR(epsilon=0.2,kernel='linear',C=1)
         scores = cross_validation.cross_val_score(svm_lin, X, Y, cv=cv)
         print("mean R2: %0.2f (+/- %0.2f)" % (scores.mean(), scores.std() * 2))
         predicted = cross_validation.cross_val_predict(svm_lin, X,Y, cv=cv)
         print 'MSE:',mean_squared_error(Y,predicted)

         print 'support vector machine rbf'
         clf = svm.SVR(epsilon=0.2,kernel='rbf',C=1.)
         scores = cross_validation.cross_val_score(clf, X, Y, cv=cv)
         print("mean R2: %0.2f (+/- %0.2f)" % (scores.mean(), scores.std() * 2))
         predicted = cross_validation.cross_val_predict(clf, X,Y, cv=cv)
         print 'MSE:',mean_squared_error(Y,predicted)

         print 'knn'
         knn = KNeighborsRegressor()
         scores = cross_validation.cross_val_score(knn, X, Y, cv=cv)
         print("mean R2: %0.2f (+/- %0.2f)" % (scores.mean(), scores.std() * 2))
         predicted = cross_validation.cross_val_predict(knn, X,Y, cv=cv)
         print 'MSE:',mean_squared_error(Y,predicted)
```

The housing data is loaded using the pandas library and reshuffled to randomize the cross-validation folds subset data (10 folds have been used) by applying the function `df.iloc[np.random.permutation(len(df))]`. The output of this script is as follows:

```
    linear regression
    mean R2: 0.72 (+/- 0.15)
    MSE: 23.5515499366
    ridge regression
    mean R2: 0.72 (+/- 0.16)
    MSE: 23.7397585761
    lasso regression
    mean R2: 0.71 (+/- 0.17)
    MSE: 24.734860679
    decision tree regression
    mean R2: 0.75 (+/- 0.24)
    MSE: 19.8023913043
    random forest regression
    mean R2: 0.87 (+/- 0.12)
    MSE: 10.9910313913
    linear support vector machine
    mean R2: 0.70 (+/- 0.25)
    MSE: 25.833801836
    support vector machine rbf
    mean R2: -0.01 (+/- 0.11)
    MSE: 83.8283880541
    knn
    mean R2: 0.54 (+/- 0.23)
    MSE: 37.8792632411
```

The best model fit is obtained using a random forest (with 50 trees); it returns an average coefficient of determination of *0.86* and *MSE=11.5*. As expected, the decision tree regressor has a lower R^2 and higher MSE than the random forest (*0.67* and *25* respectively). The support vector machine with the **rbf kernel** (*C=1*, $\in= 0.2$) is the worst model, with a huge MSE error *83.9* and *0.0* at R^2, while SVM with the linear kernel (*C=1*, $\in= 0.2$) returns a decent model (*0.69* R^2 and *25.8* MSE). The lasso and ridge regressors have comparable results, around *0.7* R^2 and *24* MSE. An important procedure to improve the model results is feature selection. It often happens that only a subset of the total features is relevant to perform the model training while the other features may not contribute at all to the model R^2. Feature selection may improve R^2 because misleading data is disregarded and training time is reduced (fewer features to consider).

There are many techniques for extracting the best features for a certain model, but in this context, we explore the so-called recursive feature elimination method (RSE), which essentially considers the attributes associated with the largest absolute weights until the desired number of features are selected. In the case of the SVM algorithm, the weights are just the values of w, while for regression, they are the model parameters θ. Using the `sklearn` built-in function `RFE` specifying only the best four attributes (`best_features`):

```
In [9]:  from sklearn.feature_selection import RFE
         best_features=4
         print 'feature selection on linear regression'
         rfe_lin = RFE(lin,best_features).fit(X,Y)
         mask = np.array(rfe_lin.support_)
         scores = cross_validation.cross_val_score(lin, X[:,mask], Y, cv=cv)
         print("R2: %0.2f (+/- %0.2f)" % (scores.mean(), scores.std() * 2))
         predicted = cross_validation.cross_val_predict(lin, X[:,mask],Y, cv=cv)
         print 'MSE:',mean_squared_error(Y,predicted)

         print 'feature selection ridge regression'
         rfe_ridge = RFE(ridge,best_features).fit(X,Y)
         mask = np.array(rfe_ridge.support_)
         scores = cross_validation.cross_val_score(ridge, X[:,mask], Y, cv=cv)
         print("R2: %0.2f (+/- %0.2f)" % (scores.mean(), scores.std() * 2))
         predicted = cross_validation.cross_val_predict(ridge, X[:,mask],Y, cv=cv)
         print 'MSE:',mean_squared_error(Y,predicted)

         print 'feature selection on lasso regression'
         rfe_lasso = RFE(lasso,best_features).fit(X,Y)
         mask = np.array(rfe_lasso.support_)
         scores = cross_validation.cross_val_score(lasso, X[:,mask], Y, cv=cv)
         print("R2: %0.2f (+/- %0.2f)" % (scores.mean(), scores.std() * 2))
         predicted = cross_validation.cross_val_predict(lasso, X[:,mask],Y, cv=cv)
         print 'MSE:',mean_squared_error(Y,predicted)

         print 'feature selection on decision tree'
         rfe_tree = RFE(tree,best_features).fit(X,Y)
         mask = np.array(rfe_tree.support_)
         scores = cross_validation.cross_val_score(tree, X[:,mask], Y, cv=cv)
         print("R2: %0.2f (+/- %0.2f)" % (scores.mean(), scores.std() * 2))
         predicted = cross_validation.cross_val_predict(tree, X[:,mask],Y, cv=cv)
         print 'MSE:',mean_squared_error(Y,predicted)

         print 'feature selection on random forest'
         rfe_forest = RFE(forest,best_features).fit(X,Y)
         mask = np.array(rfe_forest.support_)
         scores = cross_validation.cross_val_score(forest, X[:,mask], Y, cv=cv)
         print("R2: %0.2f (+/- %0.2f)" % (scores.mean(), scores.std() * 2))
         predicted = cross_validation.cross_val_predict(forest, X[:,mask],Y, cv=cv)
         print 'MSE:',mean_squared_error(Y,predicted)

         print 'feature selection on linear support vector machine'
         rfe_svm = RFE(svm_lin,best_features).fit(X,Y)
         mask = np.array(rfe_svm.support_)
         scores = cross_validation.cross_val_score(svm_lin, X[:,mask], Y, cv=cv)
         print("R2: %0.2f (+/- %0.2f)" % (scores.mean(), scores.std() * 2))
         predicted = cross_validation.cross_val_predict(svm_lin, X,Y, cv=cv)
         print 'MSE:',mean_squared_error(Y,predicted)
```

The output is:

```
        feature selection on linear regression
        R2: 0.61 (+/- 0.31)
        MSE: 33.182126206
        feature selection ridge regression
        R2: 0.61 (+/- 0.32)
        MSE: 33.2543979822
        feature selection on lasso regression
        R2: 0.68 (+/- 0.20)
        MSE: 27.4174043724
        feature selection on decision tree
        R2: 0.70 (+/- 0.35)
        MSE: 24.1185968379
        feature selection on random forest
        R2: 0.84 (+/- 0.14)
        MSE: 13.6755712332
        feature selection on linear support vector machine
        R2: 0.60 (+/- 0.33)
```

The RFE function returns a list of Booleans (the support_ attribute) to indicate which features are selected (true values) and which are not (false values). The selected features are then used to evaluate the model as we have done before.

Even by using only four features, the best model remains the random forest with 50 trees, and the R^2 is just marginally lower than that for the model trained with the full set of features (*0.82* against *0.86*). The other models—lasso, ridge, decision tree, and linear SVM regressors—have a more significant R^2 drop, but the results are still comparable with their corresponding full-trained models. Note that the KNN algorithm does not provide weights on the features, so the RFE method cannot be applied.

Classification problem

To test the classifiers learned in this chapter, the dataset about car evaluation quality (inaccurate, accurate, good, and very good) based on six features that describe the main characteristics of a car (buying price, maintenance cost, number of doors, number of persons to carry, size of luggage boot, and safety). The dataset can be found at http://archive.ics.uci.edu/ml/datasets/Car+Evaluation or on my GitHub account, together with the code discussed here (https://github.com/ai2010/machine_learning_for_the_web/tree/master/chapter_3/). To evaluate the accuracy of the classification, we will use the precision, recall, and f-measure. Given a dataset with only two classes (positive and negative), we define the number of true positive points (*tp*) the points correctly labeled as positive, the number of false positive (*fp*) the points wrongly labeled as positive (negative points) and the number of false negative (*fn*) the number of points erroneously assigned to the negative class. Using these definitions, the precision, recall and f-measure can be calculated as:

$$Precision = \frac{tp}{tp+fn}$$

$$Recall = \frac{tp}{tp+fn}$$

$$f-measure = 2\frac{(precision \cdot recall)}{(precision + recall)}$$

In a classification problem, a perfect precision (*1.0*) for a given class *C* means that each point assigned to class *C* belongs to class *C* (there is no information about the number of points from class *C* erroneously labeled), whereas a recall equal to *1.0* means that each point from class *C* was labeled as belonging to class *C* (but there is no information about the other points wrongly assigned to class *C*).

Note that in the case of multiple classes, these metrics are usually calculated as many times the number of labels, each time considering a class as the positive and all others as the negative. Different averages over the multiple classes' metrics are then used to estimate the total precision, recall, and f-measure.

The code to classify the cars dataset is as follows. First, we load all the libraries and the data into a pandas data frame.

```
In [1]: import pandas as pd
        import numpy as np
        from sklearn import cross_validation
        from sklearn import svm
        from sklearn.tree import DecisionTreeClassifier
        from sklearn.ensemble import RandomForestClassifier
        from sklearn.naive_bayes import MultinomialNB
        from sklearn.linear_model import LogisticRegression
        from sklearn.neighbors import KNeighborsClassifier
        from sklearn.metrics import f1_score
        from sklearn.metrics import precision_score
        from sklearn.metrics import recall_score
```

```
In [10]: #read data in
         df = pd.read_csv('data_cars.csv',header=None)
         for i in range(len(df.columns)):
             df[i] = df[i].astype('category')
         df.head()
```

Out[10]:

	0	1	2	3	4	5	6
0	vhigh	vhigh	2	2	small	low	unacc
1	vhigh	vhigh	2	2	small	med	unacc
2	vhigh	vhigh	2	2	small	high	unacc
3	vhigh	vhigh	2	2	med	low	unacc
4	vhigh	vhigh	2	2	med	med	unacc

The following are the feature values that are categorical:

```
buying 0        v-high, high, med, low
maintenance 1   v-high, high, med, low
doors 2         2, 3, 4, 5-more
persons 3       2, 4, more
lug_boot 4      small, med, big
safety 5        low, med, high
car evaluation 6 unacc,acc,good,vgood
```

These are mapped into numbers to be used in the classification algorithms:

```python
In [14]:  #map catgories to values
          map0 = dict( zip( df[0].cat.categories, range( len(df[0].cat.categories ))))
          #print map0
          map1 = dict( zip( df[1].cat.categories, range( len(df[1].cat.categories ))))
          map2 = dict( zip( df[2].cat.categories, range( len(df[2].cat.categories ))))
          map3 = dict( zip( df[3].cat.categories, range( len(df[3].cat.categories ))))
          map4 = dict( zip( df[4].cat.categories, range( len(df[4].cat.categories ))))
          map5 = dict( zip( df[5].cat.categories, range( len(df[5].cat.categories ))))
          map6 = dict( zip( df[6].cat.categories, range( len(df[6].cat.categories ))))

          cat_cols = df.select_dtypes(['category']).columns
          df[cat_cols] = df[cat_cols].apply(lambda x: x.cat.codes)

          df = df.iloc[np.random.permutation(len(df))]
          print df.head()

                0  1  2  3  4  5  6
          570   0  0  1  0  1  1  2
          951   2  3  3  0  0  1  2
          1633  1  1  0  1  1  2  0
          412   3  1  3  0  0  2  2
          156   3  0  1  2  1  1  2
```

Since we need to calculate and save the measures for all the methods, we write a standard function, `CalcMeasures`, and divide the labels' vector `Y` from the features `X`:

```python
In [40]:  df_f1 = pd.DataFrame(columns=['method']+sorted(map6, key=map6.get))
          df_precision = pd.DataFrame(columns=['method']+sorted(map6, key=map6.get))
          df_recall = pd.DataFrame(columns=['method']+sorted(map6, key=map6.get))
          def CalcMeasures(method,y_pred,y_true,df_f1=df_f1
                      ,df_precision=df_precision,df_recall=df_recall):

              df_f1.loc[len(df_f1)] = [method]+list(f1_score(y_pred,y_true,average=None))
              df_precision.loc[len(df_precision)] = [method]+list(precision_score(y_pred,y_true,average=None))
              df_recall.loc[len(df_recall)] = [method]+list(recall_score(y_pred,y_true,average=None))

          X= df[df.columns[:-1]].values
          Y = df[df.columns[-1]].values
```

A `10` crossing validation folds has been used and the code is:

```
In [41]:  cv = 10
          method = 'linear support vector machine'
          clf = svm.SVC(kernel='linear',C=50)
          y_pred = cross_validation.cross_val_predict(clf, X,Y, cv=cv)
          CalcMeasures(method,y_pred,Y)

          method = 'rbf support vector machine'
          clf = svm.SVC(kernel='rbf',C=50)
          y_pred = cross_validation.cross_val_predict(clf, X,Y, cv=cv)
          CalcMeasures(method,y_pred,Y)

          method = 'poly support vector machine'
          clf = svm.SVC(kernel='poly',C=50)
          y_pred = cross_validation.cross_val_predict(clf, X,Y, cv=cv)
          CalcMeasures(method,y_pred,Y)

          method = 'decision tree'
          clf = DecisionTreeClassifier(random_state=0)
          y_pred = cross_validation.cross_val_predict(clf, X,Y, cv=cv)
          CalcMeasures(method,y_pred,Y)

          method = 'random forest'
          clf = RandomForestClassifier(n_estimators=50,random_state=0,max_features=None)
          y_pred = cross_validation.cross_val_predict(clf, X,Y, cv=cv)
          CalcMeasures(method,y_pred,Y)

          method = 'naive bayes'
          clf = MultinomialNB()
          y_pred = cross_validation.cross_val_predict(clf, X,Y, cv=cv)
          CalcMeasures(method,y_pred,Y)

          method = 'logistic regression'
          clf = LogisticRegression()
          y_pred = cross_validation.cross_val_predict(clf, X,Y, cv=cv)
          CalcMeasures(method,y_pred,Y)

          method = 'k nearest neighbours'
          clf = KNeighborsClassifier(weights='distance',n_neighbors=5)
          y_pred = cross_validation.cross_val_predict(clf, X,Y, cv=cv)
          CalcMeasures(method,y_pred,Y)
```

The measures' values are stored in the data frames:

```
In [45]: df_f1
```

Out[45]:

	method	acc	good	unacc	vgood
0	linear support vector machine	0.271318	0.000000	0.846757	0.000000
1	rbf support vector machine	0.990921	1.000000	0.997933	0.984375
2	poly support vector machine	0.788918	0.841270	0.938010	0.800000
3	decision tree	0.957309	0.882353	0.989238	0.946565
4	random forest	0.963918	0.915493	0.991275	0.961832
5	naive bayes	0.040404	0.000000	0.825701	0.000000
6	logistic regression	0.265781	0.000000	0.820967	0.078947
7	k nearest neighbours	0.801609	0.534653	0.952988	0.666667

```
In [46]: df_precision
```

Out[46]:

	method	acc	good	unacc	vgood
0	linear support vector machine	0.182292	0.000000	0.981818	0.000000
1	rbf support vector machine	0.994792	1.000000	0.997521	0.969231
2	poly support vector machine	0.778646	0.768116	0.950413	0.738462
3	decision tree	0.963542	0.869565	0.987603	0.953846
4	random forest	0.973958	0.942029	0.985950	0.969231
5	naive bayes	0.020833	0.000000	0.998347	0.000000
6	logistic regression	0.208333	0.000000	0.919008	0.046154
7	k nearest neighbours	0.778646	0.391304	0.988430	0.507692

```
In [47]: df_recall
```

Out[47]:

	method	acc	good	unacc	vgood
0	linear support vector machine	0.530303	0.000000	0.744361	0.000000
1	rbf support vector machine	0.987080	1.000000	0.998346	1.000000
2	poly support vector machine	0.799465	0.929825	0.925926	0.872727
3	decision tree	0.951157	0.895522	0.990879	0.939394
4	random forest	0.954082	0.890411	0.996658	0.954545
5	naive bayes	0.666667	0.000000	0.703963	0.000000
6	logistic regression	0.366972	0.000000	0.741828	0.272727
7	k nearest neighbours	0.825967	0.843750	0.920000	0.970588

Each measure has been evaluated four times—the number of car evaluation classes that fill the arrays according to the index mapping:

```
'acc': 0, 'unacc': 2, 'good': 1, 'vgood': 3
```

The best model is SVM with rbf kernel (*C=50*), but random forest (50 trees) and decision trees also return excellent results (measures over *0.9* for all the four classes). Naive Bayes, logistic regression, and SVM with linear kernel (*C=50*) return poor models, especially for the accurate, good, and very good classes, because there are few points with those labels:

```
In [42]:  labels_counts=df[6].value_counts()
          pd.Series(map6).map(labels_counts)

Out[42]:  acc        384
          good        69
          unacc     1210
          vgood       65
          dtype: int64
```

In percentage, the very good (v-good) and good are 3.993% and 3.762% respectively, compared to 70.0223% of inaccurate and 22.222% of accurate. So, we can conclude that these algorithms are not suitable for predicting classes that are scarcely represented in a dataset.

Hidden Markov model

Although this method cannot be strictly considered a supervised learning algorithm, it can be also used to perform something that is really similar to classification, so we decided to include it here. To introduce the subject, we are going to present an example. Consider the simplistic case of predicting whether a salesman in front of you is lying or not (two states s_i $i \in 0,1$) by observing his glance: eye contact, looking down, or looking aside (each observation O_i has the values *0, 1*, and *2* respectively). Imagine a sequence of observations of the salesman's glances O=O_0, O_1, O_2, O_3, O_4,... are *0, 1, 0, 2,...* We want to infer the transition matrix *A* between states S_i at consecutive times *t, t+1* (or, in this example, two consecutive sentences):

$$A = \begin{bmatrix} 0.7 & 0.3 \\ 0.6 & 0.4 \end{bmatrix} a_i = \sum_j a_{ij} = 1, , a_{ij} = P\left(s_i \, at\, t+1 \middle| s_j \, at\, t\right)$$

Any entry of A, a_{ij} represents the probability to stay at state S_i at time $t+1$ given the state S_j at time t. Therefore, 0.3 (a_{01}) is the probability that the salesman is not lying on the sentence at time $t+1$ given that he is lying on the sentence at time t, 0.6 (a_{10}) is vice versa, 0.7 (a_{00}) represents the probability that the salesman is lying on the sentence at time t and at time $t+1$ 0.4 (a_{11}) is the probability that he is not lying on the sentence at time $t+1$ after he was sincere at time t. In a similar way, it is possible to define the matrix B that correlates the salesman's intention with his three possible behaviors:

$$B = \begin{bmatrix} 0.7 & 0.1 & 0.2 \\ 0.1 & 0.6 & 0.3 \end{bmatrix} b(k) = \sum_j b_j(k) = 1, \; b_j(k) = P\left(k \, at \, t \, \middle| \, s_j \, at \, t\right)$$

Any entry $b_{j(k)}$ is the probability to have observation k at time t given the state S_j at time t. For example, 0.7 (b_{00}), 0.1 (b_{01}), and 0.2 (b_{02}) are the probabilities that the salesman is lying given the behavioral observations — eye contact, looking down, and looking aside — respectively. These relationships are described in the following figure:

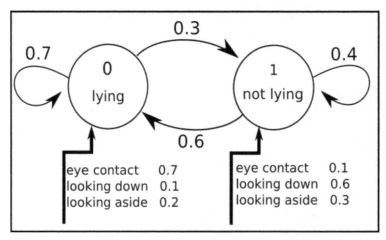

Salesman behavior – two states hidden Markov model

The initial state distribution of the salesman can be also defined: $\pi = [0.6, 0.4]$ (he is slightly more inclined to lie than to tell the truth in the first sentence at time *0*). Note that all of these matrices π, A, B are row stochastic; that is, the rows sum to *1* and there is no direct dependency on time. A **hidden Markov model** (HMM) is given by the composition of the three matrices ($\lambda = (\pi, A, B)$) that describe the relationship between the known sequence of observations $O=O_0, O_1, \dots O_{T-1}$ and the corresponding hidden states sequence $S=S_0, S_1, \dots S_{T-1}$. In general, the standard notation symbols employed by this algorithm are summarized as follows:

- T is the length of the observation sequence $O=O_0, O_1, \dots O_{T-1}$ and the hidden states sequence $S=S_0, S_1, \dots S_{T-1}$
- N is the number of possible (hidden) states in the model
- M is the number of the possible observation values: $O_k k \in 0,1..,M-1$
- A is the state transition matrix
- B is the observation probability matrix
- π is the initial state distribution

In the preceding example, *M=3*, *N=2*, and we imagine to predict the sequence of the salesman's intentions over the course of his speech (which are the hidden states) $S=S_0, S_1, \dots S_{T-1}$, observing the values of his behavior $O=O_0, O_1, \dots O_{T-1}$. This is achieved by calculating the probability of each state sequence *S* as:

$$P(S) = \pi_{s_0} b_{s_0}(O_0) a_{s_0 s_1} b_{s1}(O_1) \dots a_{s_{T-2} s_{T-1}} b_{s_{T-1}}(O_{T-1})$$

For instance, fixing *T=4*, *S=0101*, and *O=1012*:

$$p(0101) = 0.6(0.1)(0.3)(0.1)(0.6)(0.1)(0.3)(0.3) = 9.722 \cdot 10^{-6}$$

In the same way, we can calculate the probability of all other combinations of hidden states and find the most probable sequence S. An efficient algorithm for finding the most probable sequence S is the **Viterbi algorithm**, which consists of computing the maximum probability of the set of partial sequences from 0 to t until $T-1$. In practice, we calculate the following quantities:

- $\delta_0 = \pi_i b_i(O_0) i \in 0,..,N-1$
- For $t=1,...,T-1$ and $i=0,...,N-1$, the maximum probability of being at state i at time t among the possible paths coming from different states j is

  $\delta_t(i) = \max\limits_{j\in 1,...,N-1}\left[\delta_{T-1}a_{ji}b_i(O_t)\right]$. The partial sequence associated with the maximum of $\delta_t(i)$ is the most probable partial sequence until time t.
- The final most probable sequence is associated with the maximum of the probability at time $T-1$: $\delta_{T-1}(i)$.

For example, given the preceding model, the most likely sequence of length $T=2$ can be calculated as:

- *P(10)=0.0024*
- *P(00)=0.0294*
  - So $\delta_1(0)$=*P(00)*=0.0294
- *P(01)=0.076*
- *P(11)=0.01*
  - So $\delta_1(1)$=*P(01)*=0.076

And the final most probable sequence is *00* (two consecutive false sentences).

Another way to think about the most likely sequence is by maximizing the number of correct states; that is, consider for each time t the state i with the maximum probability $\max\limits_{j}(Y_t(i))$. Using an algorithm called backward algorithm, it is possible to show that the probability of a given state i, $Y_t(i)$, is:

$$Y_t(i) = \frac{\alpha_t(i)\beta_t(i)}{P(O|\lambda)}$$

Here:

- $$P(O|\lambda) = \sum_{i=0}^{N-1} \alpha_{T-1}(i)$$

- $\alpha_0(i) = \pi_i b_i(O_0)$ $i \in 0,..,N-1$ and $\alpha_t(i) = \left[\sum_{j=0}^{N-1} \alpha_{t-1}(j) a_{ji}\right] b_i(O_t)$

  Probabilities of the partial observation sequence until time t, where the HMM is on state i: $\alpha_t(i) = P(O_{0,.},O_t,s_t = i|\lambda)$

- $\beta_t(i) = \sum_{j=0}^{N-1} a_{ij} b_j(O_{t+1}) \beta_{t+1}(j) t < T-1$ and $\beta_{T-1}(i) = 1$ $i \in 1,...,N-1$

  Probability of the partial sequence after time t until $T-1$ given the state at time t equal to i: $\beta_t(i) = P(O_{t+1},..,O_{t-1},S_t = i|\lambda)$

- The combination of the probabilities to stay on state i before and after time t result in the value of $Y_t(i) = \dfrac{\alpha_t(i)\beta_t(i)}{P(O|\lambda)}$.

Note that the two methods of calculating the most likely sequence do not necessarily return the same result.

The reverse problem—find the optimal HMM $\lambda = (\pi, A, B)$ given a sequence $O = O_0, O_1, ... O_{T-1}$ and the values of the parameters N, M—is also solvable iteratively using the **Baum-Welch algorithm**. Defining the probability of occurring at state i at time t and to go at state j at time $t+1$ as:

$$Y_t(i,j) = P(s_t = i, s_{t+1} = j|O,\lambda) = \frac{\alpha_t(i) a_{ij} b_j(O_{t+1}) \beta_{t+1}(j)}{P(O|\lambda)} \text{ where}$$

$$Y_t(i) = \sum_{j=0}^{N-1} Y_t(i,j) \text{ for } T \in 0,...,T-2 \text{ and } Y_{T-1}(i) = \frac{\alpha_{T-1}}{P(O|\lambda)}.$$

Then the Baum-Welch algorithm is as follows:

- Initialize $\lambda = (\pi, A, B)$
- Calculate $\alpha_t(i), \beta_t(i), Y_t(i, j)$ and $Y_t(i)$ $i \in 0, .., N-1$
- Recompute the model matrices as:

$$\pi(i) = Y_0(i), a_{ij} = \frac{\sum_{t=0}^{T-2} Y_t(i, j)}{\sum_{t=0}^{T-2} Y_t(i, j)}, b_j(O_k) = \frac{\sum_{t=0}^{T-1} \delta o_t o_k Y_t(j)}{\sum_{t=0}^{T-1} Y_t(j)} \quad \text{where}$$

$i, j \in 0, .., N-1; k \in 0, .., M-1$ and δ_{ij} is Kronacker symbol, which is equal to *1* if $i = j$ and *0* otherwise

- Iterate until the convergence of: $P(O|\lambda) = \sum_{t=0}^{N-1} \alpha_{T-1}(i)$

In the next section, we are going to show a piece of Python code that implements these equations to test the HMM algorithm.

A Python example

As usual, the `hmm_example.py` file discussed hereafter is available at `https://github.com/ai2010/machine_learning_for_the_web/tree/master/chapter_3/`.

We start defining a class in which we pass the model matrices:

```
class HMM:
    def __init__(self):
        self.pi = pi
        self.A = A
        self.B = B
```

The Viterbi algorithm and the maximization of the number of correct states are implemented in the following two functions:

```
    def ViterbiSequence(self,observations):
        deltas = [{}]
        seq = {}
        N = self.A.shape[0]
        states = [i for i in range(N)]
```

```
        T = len(observations)
        #initialization
        for s in states:
            deltas[0][s] = self.pi[s]*self.B[s,observations[0]]
            seq[s] = [s]
        #compute Viterbi
        for t in range(1,T):
            deltas.append({})
            newseq = {}
            for s in states:
                (delta,state) = max((deltas[t-1][s0]*self.A[s0,s]*self.B[
s,observations[t]],s0) for s0 in states)
                deltas[t][s] = delta
                newseq[s] = seq[state] + [s]
            seq = newseq

        (delta,state) = max((deltas[T-1][s],s) for s in states)
        return  delta,' sequence: ', seq[state]


    def maxProbSequence(self,observations):
        N = self.A.shape[0]
        states = [i for i in range(N)]
        T = len(observations)
        M = self.B.shape[1]
        # alpha_t(i) = P(O_1 O_2 ... O_t, q_t = S_i | hmm)
        # Initialize alpha
        alpha = np.zeros((N,T))
        c = np.zeros(T) #scale factors
        alpha[:,0] = pi.T * self.B[:,observations[0]]
        c[0] = 1.0/np.sum(alpha[:,0])
        alpha[:,0] = c[0] * alpha[:,0]
        # Update alpha for each observation step
        for t in range(1,T):
            alpha[:,t] = np.dot(alpha[:,t-1].T, self.A).T *
self.B[:,observations[t]]
            c[t] = 1.0/np.sum(alpha[:,t])
```

```
        alpha[:,t] = c[t] * alpha[:,t]


    # beta_t(i) = P(O_t+1 O_t+2 ... O_T | q_t = S_i , hmm)
    # Initialize beta
    beta = np.zeros((N,T))
    beta[:,T-1] = 1
    beta[:,T-1] = c[T-1] * beta[:,T-1]
    # Update beta backwards froT end of sequence
    for t in range(len(observations)-1,0,-1):
        beta[:,t-1] = np.dot(self.A, (self.B[:,observations[t]] *
beta[:,t]))
        beta[:,t-1] = c[t-1] * beta[:,t-1]


    norm = np.sum(alpha[:,T-1])
    seq = ''
    for t in range(T):
        g,state = max(((beta[i,t]*alpha[i,t])/norm,i) for i in
states)
        seq +=str(state)


    return seq
```

Since the multiplication of probabilities will result in an underflow problem, all the $\alpha_t(i)$ and $\beta_t(i)$ have been multiplied by a constant such that for $i \in 0,..,N-1$:

- $$c_0 = \frac{1}{\sum_{j=0}^{N-1} \alpha_0(j)}$$

- $$c_t = \frac{1}{\sum_{j=0}^{N-1} \alpha'_{t-1}(j) a_{ji} b_i(O_t)}, \alpha'_t(i) = \sum_{j=0}^{N-1} c_{t-1}\alpha'_{t-1} a_{ji} b_i(O_t) \text{ where}$$

  $$\alpha'_0(i) = \alpha_0(i)$$

Now we can initialize the HMM model with the matrices in the salesman's intentions example and use the two preceding functions:

```
pi = np.array([0.6, 0.4])
A = np.array([[0.7, 0.3],
                    [0.6, 0.4]])
B = np.array([[0.7, 0.1, 0.2],
                    [0.1, 0.6, 0.3]])
hmmguess = HMM(pi,A,B)
print 'Viterbi sequence:',hmmguess.ViterbiSequence(np.array([0,1,0,2]))
print 'max prob sequence:',hmmguess.maxProbSequence(np.array([0,1,0,2]))
```

The result is:

```
Viterbi: (0.0044, 'sequence: ', [0, 1, 0, 0])
Max prob sequence: 0100
```

In this particular case, the two methods return the same sequence, and you can easily verify that by changing the initial matrices, the algorithms may lead to different results. We obtain that the sequence of behaviors; eye contact, looking down, eye contact, looking aside is likely associated with the salesman states' sequence; lie, not lie, lie, lie with a probability of *0.0044*.

It is also possible to implement the Baum-Welch algorithm to find the optimal HMM given the sequence of observations and the parameters N and M. Here is the code:

```
    def train(self,observations,criterion):

        N = self.A.shape[0]
        T = len(observations)
        M = self.B.shape[1]

        A = self.A
        B = self.B
        pi = copy(self.pi)

        convergence = False
        while not convergence:

            # alpha_t(i) = P(O_1 O_2 ... O_t, q_t = S_i | hmm)
            # Initialize alpha
```

```
alpha = np.zeros((N,T))
c = np.zeros(T) #scale factors
alpha[:,0] = pi.T * self.B[:,observations[0]]
c[0] = 1.0/np.sum(alpha[:,0])
alpha[:,0] = c[0] * alpha[:,0]
# Update alpha for each observation step
for t in range(1,T):
    alpha[:,t] = np.dot(alpha[:,t-1].T, self.A).T *
self.B[:,observations[t]]
    c[t] = 1.0/np.sum(alpha[:,t])
    alpha[:,t] = c[t] * alpha[:,t]


#P(O=O_0,O_1,...,O_T-1 | hmm)
P_O = np.sum(alpha[:,T-1])
# beta_t(i) = P(O_t+1 O_t+2 ... O_T | q_t = S_i , hmm)
# Initialize beta
beta = np.zeros((N,T))
beta[:,T-1] = 1
beta[:,T-1] = c[T-1] * beta[:,T-1]
# Update beta backwards froT end of sequence
for t in range(len(observations)-1,0,-1):
    beta[:,t-1] = np.dot(self.A, (self.B[:,observations[t]] *
beta[:,t]))
    beta[:,t-1] = c[t-1] * beta[:,t-1]


gi = np.zeros((N,N,T-1));


for t in range(T-1):
    for i in range(N):

        gamma_num = alpha[i,t] * self.A[i,:] *
self.B[:,observations[t+1]].T * \
                    beta[:,t+1].T
        gi[i,:,t] = gamma_num / P_O


# gamma_t(i) = P(q_t = S_i | O, hmm)
```

```
        gamma = np.squeeze(np.sum(gi,axis=1))
        # Need final gamma element for new B
        prod =   (alpha[:,T-1] * beta[:,T-1]).reshape((-1,1))
        gamma_T = prod/P_O
        gamma = np.hstack((gamma,   gamma_T)) #append one Tore to
gamma!!!


        newpi = gamma[:,0]
        newA = np.sum(gi,2) / np.sum(gamma[:,:-1],axis=1).
reshape((-1,1))
        newB = copy(B)


        sumgamma = np.sum(gamma,axis=1)
        for ob_k in range(M):
            list_k = observations == ob_k
            newB[:,ob_k] = np.sum(gamma[:,list_k],axis=1) / sumgamma


        if np.max(abs(pi - newpi)) < criterion and \
                np.max(abs(A - newA)) < criterion and \
                np.max(abs(B - newB)) < criterion:
            convergence = True;


        A[:],B[:],pi[:] = newA,newB,newpi


    self.A[:] = newA
    self.B[:] = newB
    self.pi[:] = newpi
    self.gamma = gamma
```

Note that the code uses the shallow copy from the module `copy`, which creates a new container populated with references to the contents of the original object (in this case, pi, B). That is, `newpi` is a different object from `pi` but `newpi[0]` is a reference of `pi[0]`. The NumPy squeeze function instead is needed to drop the redundant dimension from a matrix.

Using the same behaviors sequence *O=0, 1, 0, 2*, we obtain that the optimal model is given by:

$$\pi = \begin{bmatrix} 1.0 & 0.0 \end{bmatrix}, A = \begin{bmatrix} 0.0 & 1.0 \\ 1.0 & 0.0 \end{bmatrix}, B = \begin{bmatrix} 1.0 & 0.0 & 0.0 \\ 0.0 & 0.38 & 0.62 \end{bmatrix}$$

This means that the state sequence must start from a true salesman's sentence and continuously oscillate between the two states *lie* and *not lie*. A true salesman's sentence (not lie) is certainly related to the eye contact value, while a lie is related to the looking down and looking aside behaviors.

In this simple introduction on HMM, we have assumed that each observation is a scalar value, but in real applications, each O_i is usually a vector of features. And usually, this method is used as a classification training as many HMM l_j as classes to predict and then a test time chooses the class with the highest $P(O|\lambda_i)$. Continuing with this example, we can imagine building a *true machine* to test each salesman we talk to. Imagine that for each sentence (observation) O_i of our speaker, we can extract three features glances with three possible values e_i (eye contact, looking down, and looking aside), voice sound v_i with three possible values (too loud, too low, and flat), and hand movement h_i with two possible values (shaking and calm) $O_i=(e_i, v_i, h_{ij}$. At training time, we ask our friend to tell lies and we use these observations to train an HMM λ_0 using Baum-Welch. We repeat the training process but with true sentences and train λ_1. At test time, we record the sentence of the salesman O and calculate both: $P(O|\lambda_0), P(O|\lambda_1)$. The class prediction will be the one with the highest probability.

Note that HMM has been applied in various fields, but the applications in which it performs quite well are speech recognition tasks, handwritten character recognition, and action recognition.

Summary

In this chapter, the major classification and regression algorithms, together with the techniques to implement them, were discussed. You should now be able to understand in which situation each method can be used and how to implement it using Python and its libraries (sklearn and pandas).

In the next chapter, we will cover the most relevant techniques used to learn from web data (web data mining).

4
Web Mining Techniques

Web data mining techniques are used to explore the data available online and then extract the relevant information from the Internet. Searching on the web is a complex process that requires different algorithms, and they will be the main focus of this chapter. Given a search query, the relevant pages are obtained using the data available on each web page, which is usually divided in the page content and the page hyperlinks to other pages. Usually, a search engine has multiple components:

- A web crawler or spider for collecting web pages
- A parser that extracts content and preprocesses web pages
- An indexer to organize the web pages in data structures
- A retrieval information system to score the most important documents related to a query
- A ranking algorithm to order the web pages in a meaningful manner

These parts can be divided into web structure mining techniques and web content mining techniques.

The web crawler, indexer, and ranking procedures refer to the web structure (the network of hyperlinks). The other parts (parser and retrieval system) of a search engine are web content analysis methods because the text information on web pages is used to perform such operations.

Furthermore, the content of a collection of web pages can be further analyzed using some natural language processing techniques, such as **latent Dirichlet allocation** opinion mining or sentiment analysis tools. These techniques are especially important for extracting subjective information about web users, and so they are widely found in many commercial applications, from marketing to consultancy. These sentiment analysis techniques will be discussed at the end of the chapter. Now we will start discussing the web structure mining category.

Web structure mining

This field of web mining focuses on the discovery of the relationships among web pages and how to use this link structure to find the relevance of web pages. For the first task, usually a spider is employed, and the links and the collected web pages are stored in a indexer. For the the last task, the web page ranking evaluates the importance of the web pages.

Web crawlers (or spiders)

A spider starts from a set of URLs (seed pages) and then extracts the URL inside them to fetch more pages. New links are then extracted from the new pages and the process continues until some criteria are matched. The unvisited URLs are stored in a list called **frontier**, and depending on how the list is used, we can have different crawler algorithms, such as breadth-first and preferential spiders. In the **breadth-first** algorithm, the next URL to crawl comes from the head of the frontier while the new URLs are appended to the frontier tail. Preferential spider instead employs a certain importance estimate on the list of unvisited URLs to determine which page to crawl first. Note that the extraction of links from a page is performed using a parser, and this operation is discussed in more detail in the related paragraph of the web content mining section.

A web crawler is essentially a graph search algorithm in which the structure of the neighborhood of the starting pages is retrieved, following certain criteria such as the maximum number of links to follow (depth of the graph), maximum number of pages to crawl, or time limit. A spider can then extract a portion of the Web that has interesting structures, such as hubs and authorities. A hub is a web page that contains a large number of links, while an authority is defined as, a page, with a large number of times that its URL occurs on other web pages (it is a measure of the page's popularity). A popular Python implementation of the crawler is given by the Scrapy library, which also employs concurrency methods (asynchronous programming using Twisted) to speed up operations. A tutorial on this module is given in *Chapter 7, Movie Recommendation System Web Application* when the crawler will be used to extract information about movie reviews.

Indexer

An indexer is a way to store web pages found by the crawler in a structured database to allow subsequent fast retrieval on a given search query. The simplest indexing approach is to directly store all the pages and, at query time, just scan for all the documents that contain the keywords in the query. However, this method is not feasible if the number of pages is large (which in practice, it is) due to high computational costs. The most common method to speed up the retrieval is called **inverted index scheme**, which is used by the most popular search engines.

Given a set of web pages $p_1, ..., p_k$ and a vocabulary V containing all the words $w_i \in V$ in the pages, the inverted index database is obtained by storing lists such as

$$w_1 : id_{p_1}, id_{p_3}, ..., w_i : id_{p_2}, id_{p_7},$$

Here, id_{p_j} is the ID of the web page j. Extra information can be stored for each word, for example, the frequency count of the word or its position on each page. The implementation of the indexer is beyond the scope of this book, but the general concepts have been described in this paragraph for completeness.

Therefore, a search query with a list of words will retrieve all the inverted lists related to each word and then merge the lists. The order of the final lists will be chosen using the ranking algorithm together with an information retrieval system to measure the relevance of the documents to the query.

Ranking – PageRank algorithm

A ranking algorithm is important because the usual number of web pages that a single information retrieval query can return may be huge, so there is a problem of how to choose the most relevant pages. Furthermore, the information retrieval model can easily be spammed by just inserting many keywords into the page to make the page relevant to a large number of queries. So, the problem to evaluate the importance (that is, ranking score) of a web page on the Internet has been addressed considering the fact that the web has a graph in which the hyperlinks – links from a page to another – are the primary source of information to estimate the relevance of web pages. The hyperlinks can be divided as:

- in-links of page i: hyperlinks that point to page i
- out-links of page i: hyperlinks that point to other pages from page i

Intuitively, the more in-links a web page has, the more important the page should be. The study of this hyperlink structure is part of social network analysis, and many algorithms have been used and proposed. But for historical reasons, we will explain the most well known algorithm, called **PageRank**, which was presented by Sergey Brin and Larry Page (the founders of Google) in 1998. The whole idea is to calculate the prestige of a page as the sum of the prestiges of the pages that point to it. If the prestige of a page j is $P(j)$ it is equally distributed to all the pages N_j that it points to so that each out-link receives a portion of prestige equal to $P(j) | N_j$. Formally, the prestige or page rank score of a page i can be defined as:

$$P(i) = \sum_j A_{ji} P(j)$$

Here, $A_{ji} = \dfrac{1}{N_j}$ if page j points to page i; otherwise it is equal to 0. A_{ij} is called adjacency matrix and it represents the portion of prestige that propagates from node j to node i. Considering N total nodes in the graph, the preceding equation can be rewritten in matrix form:

$$P = A^T P, P = \left(P(1), ..., P(N)\right)^T$$

Note that this equation is equivalent to an eigensystem with eigenvalue $\lambda = 1$ if the adjacency matrix satisfies certain conditions. Another way to interpret the preceding equation is to use the Markov chain terminology — the entry A_{ij} becomes the transition probability from node j to node i and the prestige of node i, $p(i)$, is the probability to visit node i. In this scenario, it may happen that two nodes (or more) point to each other but do not point to other pages. Once one of these two nodes has been visited, a loop will occur and the user will be trapped in it. This situation is called **rank sink**, (the matrix A is called **periodic**) and the solution is to add a transition matrix term that allows jumping from each page to another page at random without following the Markov chain described by A:

$$P = \left(\frac{(1-d)E}{N} + d\, A^T\right) P$$

Here, $E=ee^T$ is a matrix of one entry of dimensions $N'N$ (e is a unit vector), and d (also called the **damping factor**) is the probability to follow the transition given by the transition matrix A. *(1-d)* is the probability to visit a page randomly. In this final form, all the nodes are linked to each other so that even if the adjacency matrix has a row with many *0* entries for a particular node s, A_{sj}, there is always a small probability equal to $\dfrac{1}{N}$ that s is visited from all the N nodes in the graph. Note that A has to be stochastic, which means each row has to sum to *1*; $\sum_{j} A_{ij} = 1 \forall i1,\ldots,N$ (at least one entry per row different from *0* or at least one out-link per page). The equation can be simplified by normalizing the P vector as $e^T P=N$:

$$P=(1-d)e+d\,A^T P \rightarrow P(i)=(1-d)+d\sum_{j=1}^{N} A_{ji}P(j) \ \ \forall i1,..,N$$

This can be solved using the power iteration method. This algorithm will be used in *Chapter 8, Sentiment Analyser Application on Movie Reviews* to implement an example of a movie review sentiment analysis system. The main advantages of this algorithm is that it does not depend on the query (so the PageRank scores can be computed offline and retrieved at query time), and it is very robust to spamming since it is not feasible for a spammer to insert in-links to their page on influential pages.

Web content mining

This type of mining focuses on extracting information from the content of web pages. Each page is usually gathered and organized (using a parsing technique), processed to remove the unimportant parts from the text (natural language processing), and then analyzed using an information retrieval system to match the relevant documents to a given query. These three components are discussed in the following paragraphs.

Parsing

A web page is written in HTML format, so the first operation is to extract the relevant pieces of information. An HTML parser builds a tree of tags from which the content can be extracted. Nowadays, there are many parsers available, but as an example, we use the Scrapy library see *Chapter 7, Movie Recommendation System Web Application* which provides a command-line parser. Let's say we want to parse the main page of Wikipedia, https://en.wikipedia.org/wiki/Main_Page. We simply type this in a terminal:

```
scrapy shell 'https://en.wikipedia.org/wiki/Main_Page'
```

A prompt will be ready to parse the page using the response object and the xpath language. For example we want to obtain the title's page:

```
In [1]: response.xpath('//title/text()').extract()
Out[1]: [u'Wikipedia, the free encyclopedia']
```

Or we want to extract all the embedded links in page (this operation is needed for the crawler to work), which are usually put on <a>, and the URL value is on an href attribute:

```
In [2]: response.xpath("//a/@href").extract()
Out[2]:
[u'#mw-head',
 u'#p-search',
 u'/wiki/Wikipedia',
 u'/wiki/Free_content',
 u'/wiki/Encyclopedia',
 u'/wiki/Wikipedia:Introduction',
 ...
 u'//wikimediafoundation.org/',
 u'//www.mediawiki.org/']
```

Note that a more robust way to parse content can be used since the web pages are usually written by non-programmers, so the HTML may contain syntax errors that browsers typically repair. Note also that web pages may contain a large amount of data due to advertisements, making the parsing of relevant information complicated. Different algorithms have been proposed (for instance, tree matching) to identify the main content of a page but no Python libraries are available at the moment, so we have decided not to discuss this topic further. However, note that a nice parsing implementation for extracting the body of a web article can be found in the newspaper library and it will also be used in *Chapter 7, Movie Recommendation System Web Application*.

Natural language processing

Once the text content of a web page has been extracted, the text data is usually preprocessed to remove parts that do not bring any relevant information. A text is tokenized, that is, transformed into a list of words (tokens), and all the punctuation marks are removed. Another usual operation is to remove all the *stopwords*, that is, all the words used to construct the syntax of a sentence but not containing text information (such as conjunctions, articles, and prepositions) such as *a*, *about*, *an*, *are*, *as*, *at*, *be*, *by*, *for*, *from*, *how*, *in*, *is*, *of*, *on*, *or*, *that*, *the*, *these*, *this*, *to*, *was*, *what*, *when*, *where*, *who*, *will*, *with*, and many others.

Many words in English (or any language) share the same root but have different suffixes or prefixes. For example, the words *think*, *thinking*, and *thinker* all share the same root — *think* indicating that the meaning is the same — but the role in a sentence is different (verb, noun, and so on). The procedure to reduce all the words in a set to its roots it is called **stemming**, and many algorithms have been invented to do so (Porter, Snowball, and Lancaster). All of these techniques are parts of a broader range of algorithms called **natural language processing**, and they are implemented in Python on the `nltk` library (installed as usual through `sudo pip install nltk`). As an example, the following code preprocesses a sample text using the techniques described previously (using the Python interface terminal):

```
>>> import nltk
>>> from nltk.tokenize import WordPunctTokenizer
>>> nltk.download('stopwords')
[nltk_data] Downloading package 'stopwords' to
[nltk_data]     /Users/andrea/nltk_data...
[nltk_data]   Package stopwords is already up-to-date!
True
>>> from nltk.corpus import stopwords
>>> stopwords = stopwords.words('english')
>>> tknzr = WordPunctTokenizer()
>>> from nltk.stem.porter import PorterStemmer
>>> stemmer = PorterStemmer()
>>> text = 'The European languages are members of the same family. Many words in a language trans
late into familiar words in another. For science, music, sport, etc, Europe uses the same vocabul
ary.  Everyone realizes why a new common language would be desirable: one could refuse to pay tra
nslators.'
>>> words = tknzr.tokenize(text)
>>> words
['The', 'European', 'languages', 'are', 'members', 'of', 'the', 'same', 'family', '.', 'Many', 'w
ords', 'in', 'a', 'language', 'translate', 'into', 'familiar', 'words', 'in', 'another', '.', 'Fo
r', 'science', ',', 'music', ',', 'sport', ',', 'etc', ',', 'Europe', 'uses', 'the', 'same', 'voc
abulary', '.', 'Everyone', 'realizes', 'why', 'a', 'new', 'common', 'language', 'would', 'be', 'd
esirable', ':', 'one', 'could', 'refuse', 'to', 'pay', 'translators', '.']
>>> words_clean = [w.lower() for w in words if w not in stopwords]
>>> words_clean
['the', 'european', 'languages', 'members', 'family', '.', 'many', 'words', 'language', 'translat
e', 'familiar', 'words', 'another', '.', 'for', 'science', ',', 'music', ',', 'sport', ',', 'etc'
, ',', 'europe', 'uses', 'vocabulary', '.', 'everyone', 'realizes', 'new', 'common', 'language',
'would', 'desirable', ':', 'one', 'could', 'refuse', 'pay', 'translators', '.']
>>> words_clean_stem = [stemmer.stem(w) for w in words_clean]
>>> words_clean_stem
['the', 'european', 'languag', 'member', 'famili', '.', 'mani', 'word', 'languag', 'translat', 'f
amiliar', 'word', 'anoth', '.', 'for', 'scienc', ',', 'music', ',', 'sport', ',', 'etc', ',', 'eu
rop', 'use', 'vocabulari', '.', 'everyon', 'realiz', 'new', 'common', 'languag', 'would', 'desir'
, ':', 'one', 'could', 'refus', 'pay', 'translat', '.']
```

Note that the `stopwords` list has been downloaded using the `nltk dowloader` `nltk.download('stopwords')`.

Information retrieval models

The information retrieval methods are needed to find the most relevant documents to a given query. The words contained in the web pages can be modeled using different approaches such as Boolean models, vector space models, and probabilistic models, and in this book, we have decided to discuss the vector space models and how to implement them. Formally, given a vocabulary of V words, each web page d_i (or document) in a collection of N pages, can be thought of as a vector of words, $d_i = w_{1i}, ..., w_{|V|i}$, where each word j belonging to the document i is represented by w_{ij}, which can be either a number (weight) or a vector depending on the chosen algorithm:

- Term frequency-inverse document frequency (TF-IDF), w_{ij}, is a real number

- **Latent Semantic Analysis (LSA)**, w_{ij}, is a real number (representation independent of the document i)

- Doc2Vec (or word2vec), w_{ij}, is a vector of real numbers (representation independent of the document i)

Since the query can also be represented by a vector of words, $q = w_{1q}, ... w_{|V|q}$, the web pages most similar to the vector q are found by calculating a similarity measure between the query vector and each document. The most used similarity measure is called cosine similarity, for any document i given by:

$$\frac{d_i \cdot q}{|d_i||q|} = \frac{\sum_{j=1}^{|V|} w_{ij} w_{jq}}{\sqrt{\sum_{j=1}^{|V|} w_{ij}^2} \sqrt{\sum_{j=1}^{|V|} w_{qj}^2}}$$

Note that there are other measures used in literature (okapi and pivoted normalization weighting), but for the purpose of this book, they are not necessary.

The following sections will give some details about the three methods before being applied in a text case in the final paragraph of the section.

TF-IDF

This method calculates w_{ij}, taking into account the fact that a word that appears many times and in a large number of pages is likely to be less important than a word that occurs many times but only in a subset of documents. It is given by the multiplication of two factors:

$w_{ij} = tf_{ij} x\, idf_i$ where:

- $tf_{ij} = \dfrac{f_{ij}}{max\, f_{1i}, ..., f_{|V|i}}$ is the normalized frequency of the word j in the document I

- $idf_i = \log \dfrac{N}{df_j}$ is the inverse document frequency and df_j is the number of web pages that contain the word j

Latent Semantic Analysis (LSA)

The name of this algorithm comes from the idea that there is a latent space in which each word (and each document) can be efficiently described, assuming that words with similar meanings also occur in similar text positions. Projection on this subspace is performed using the (truncated) SVD method already discussed in *Chapter 2, Machine Learning Techniques – Unsupervised Learning*. We contextualize the method for LSA as follows: the web pages are collected together in matrix X ($V \times N$), in which each column is a document:

$$X = U_t \sum_t V_t^T$$

Here, U_t ($V \times d$) is the matrix of the words projected in the new latent space with d dimensions, $\sum_t V_t^T$ ($d \times N$) is the transpose matrix of the documents transformed into the subspace, and $\sum_t$ ($d \times d$) is the diagonal matrix with singular values. The query vector itself is projected into the latent space by:

$$q_t = q U_t \sum_t^{-1}$$

Now, each document represented by each row of V_t can be compared with q_t using the cosine similarity. Note that the true mathematical representation of the documents on the latent space is given by $\Sigma_t V_t$ (not V_t) because the singular values are the scaling factors of the space axis components and they must be taken into account. Therefore, this matrix should be compared with $\Sigma_t q_t$. Nevertheless, it usually computes the similarity between V_t and q_t, and in practice, it is still unknown which method returns the best results.

Doc2Vec (word2vec)

This method represents each word j, w_j, as a vector V_{w_j} but independent of the document d_i it occurs in. Doc2Vec is an extension of the word2vec algorithm originally proposed by Mikolov and others, and it employs neuron networks and backpropagation to generate the word (and document) vectors. Due to the increasing importance of neuron networks (especially deep learning) in many machine learning applications, we decided to include the main concepts and formulas of this quite advanced method here to give you an introduction to a subject that will become extremely important in the future of machine learning in various fields. The following description is based on the paper Rong (2014) and Le and Mikolov (2014), and the notation also reflects the name currently used in literature.

Word2vec – continuous bag of words and skip-gram architectures

Each word j in the vocabulary V is represented by a vector of length $|V|$, with binary entries $x_j = (x_{1j}, \dots, x_{Vj})$, where only $x_{jj}=1$; otherwise, 0. The word2vec method trains a single (hidden) layer of N neurons (weights), choosing between two different network architectures (shown in the following figure). Note that both architectures have only one layer of N neurons or weights, h. This means that the method has to be considered *shallow* learning and not deep, which typically refers to networks with many hidden layers. The **Continuous Bag Of Words (CBOW)** method (displayed to the right in the following figure) trains the model using a set of C words as an input called *context* trying to predict the word (target) that occurs adjacent to the input text. The reverse approach is called **Skip-gram**, in which the input is the target word and the network is trained to predict the context set (displayed to the left in the following figure). Note that C is called the window parameter and it sets how far from the target word the context words are selected:

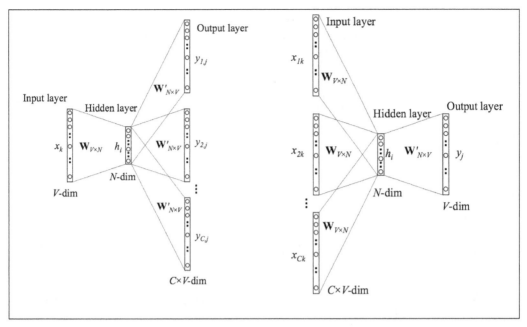

Skip-gram (left) and CBOW (right) architectures of the word2vec algorithm; figures taken from word2vec Parameter Learning Explained by X Rong (2015)

In both cases, the matrix W transforms the input vectors into the hidden layer and W' transforms from the hidden layer to the output layer y, where the target (or context) is evaluated. In the training phase, the error from the true target (or context) is computed and used to calculate a stochastic gradient descent to update both the matrices W and W'. We will give a more mathematical description of the CBOW method in the following section. Note that the Skip-gram equations are similar and we will refer to the Rong (2015) paper for further details.

Mathematical description of the CBOW model

Starting from the input layer, the hidden layer h can be obtained by computing,

$h = \frac{1}{C} W \cdot \left(x_1 + .. + x_C \right) = \frac{1}{C} \left(v_{w_1} + .. + v_{w_c} \right) = v_C$, where v_{w_i} is a vector of length N that represents the word w_i on the hidden layer and w_C is the average of the C context vectors v_{w_i}. Choosing a target word w_j, the score at the output layer u_j is obtained by multiplying the vector v'_{w_j} (the j-th column of W') by h:

$$u_j = v'_{w_j} \cdot h$$

This is not the final value on the output layer y_j because we want to evaluate the posterior conditional probability to have the target word w_j given the context C expressed by the **softmax** formula:

$$y_j = p\left(w_j \mid w_{1,.,}w_C\right) = \frac{e^{u_j}}{\sum\limits_{i=1}^{|V|} e^{u_i}} = \frac{e^{v_j'^T v_C}}{\sum\limits_{i=1}^{|V|} e^{v_i'^T v_C}}$$

Now the training objective is to maximize this probability for all the words in the vocabulary, which is equivalent to

$$max \; p\left(w_j \mid w_{1,.,}w_C\right) \rightarrow E = -\underset{j}{max} \log p\left(w_j \mid w_{1,.,}w_C\right) = -v_{w_{jM}}'^T \cdot h + \log \sum\limits_{i=1}^{|V|} e^{v_{wi}' \cdot h} \quad,$$

where $\underset{j}{max}\left(v_{w_j}'^T \cdot h\right) = v_{w_{jM}}'^T \cdot h$ and the index j^M represents the vector of W' in which the product is maximum, that is, the most probable target word.

The stochastic gradient descent equations are then obtained by calculating the derivatives of E with respect to the entries of W (w_{ij}) and W' (w'_{ij}). The final equations for each output target word w_j are:

$$v_{w_j}'^{new} = v_{w_j}'^{old} - \alpha \frac{\partial E}{\partial u_j} h \;\; \forall j \in 1,...|V|$$

$v_{w_j}'^{new} = v_{w_j}'^{old} - \alpha \frac{1}{C}\frac{\partial E}{\partial h} \;\; \forall j \in 1,...,C$ where $\frac{\partial E}{\partial h} = \left(\frac{\partial E}{\partial h_1},...,\frac{\partial E}{\partial h_N}\right)$ and a is the learning rate of the gradient descent. The derivative $\frac{\partial E}{\partial u_j} = y_j - \delta_{j,j^M}$ represents the error of the network with respect to the true target word so that the error is back propagated on the system, which can learn iteratively. Note that the vectors $v_{w_j} \; \forall j1,..,|V|$ are the usual word representations used to perform the semantic operations.

Further details can be found in the Rong (2015) paper.

Doc2Vec extension

As explained in Le and Mikolov (2014), Doc2Vec is a natural extension of the word2vec method in which a document is considered as an additional word vector. So in the case of the CBOW architecture, the hidden layer vector h is just the average of the context vectors and the document vector d_i:

$$h = \frac{1}{C} W \cdot \left(x_1 + .. + x_C + d_i \right) = \frac{1}{C} \left(v_{w_1} + .. + v_{w_c} + v_{d_i} \right) = v_C$$

This architecture is shown in the following figure, and it is called the **distributed memory model** (**DM**) because the document d_i vector just remembers the information of the document not represented by the context words. The vector v_{d_i} is shared with all the context words sampled from the document d_i but the matrix W (and W') is the same for all the documents:

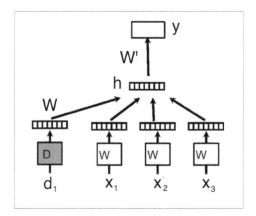

A distributed memory model example with a context of three words (window=3); figure taken from Distributed Representations of Sentences and Documents by Le and Mikolov (2014)

The other proposed architecture is called **distributed bag of words** (**DBOW**), which considers only a document vector in the input layer and a set of context words sampled from the document in the output layer. It has been shown that the DM architecture performs better than DBOW, and it is therefore the default model in the `gensim` library implementation. The reader is advised to read the paper of Le and Mikolov (2014) for further details.

Movie review query example

To show in action the three information retrieval methods discussed previously, we use the IMBD movie reviews in the *polarity dataset v2.0* and *Pool of 27886 unprocessed html files* at `http://www.cs.cornell.edu/people/pabo/movie-review-data/`, provided by Bo Pang and Lillian Lee (the dataset and the code are also stored in the GitHub account of the author at `https://github.com/ai2010/machine_learning_for_the_web/tree/master/chapter_4/`. Download and unzip the `movie.zip` file from the website (called `polarity_html.zip`), which creates the `movie` folder with all the web page movie reviews (about 2000 files). First of all, we need to prepare the data from the files:

```
In [1]:  #import files
         import os
         import numpy as np
         #get titles
         from BeautifulSoup import BeautifulSoup
         moviehtmldir = './movie/'
         moviedict = {}
         for filename in [f for f in os.listdir(moviehtmldir) if f[0]!='.']:
             id = filename.split('.')[0]
             f = open(moviehtmldir+'/'+filename)
             parsed_html = BeautifulSoup(f.read())
             try:
                 title = parsed_html.body.h1.text

             except:
                 title = 'none'
             moviedict[id] = title
```

This time we use **BeautifulSoup** to parse the title of the movie from each HTML web page and create a dictionary, `moviedict`. The `polarity dataset v2.0.tar.gz` contains a folder, `review_polarity`, which is inside the `txt_sentoken/` folder that split the positive and negative reviews into two separate subfolders (pros and cons). These files are preprocessed using the following code:

```
In [99]:  import nltk
          from nltk.corpus import stopwords
          from nltk.tokenize import WordPunctTokenizer
          tknzr = WordPunctTokenizer()
          nltk.download('stopwords')
          stoplist = stopwords.words('english')
          from nltk.stem.porter import PorterStemmer
          stemmer = PorterStemmer()
          def ListDocs(dirname):
              docs = []
              titles = []
              for filename in [f for f in os.listdir(dirname) if str(f)[0]!='.']:
                  f = open(dirname+'/'+filename,'r')
                  id = filename.split('.')[0].split('_')[1]
                  titles.append(moviedict[id])
                  docs.append(f.read())
              return docs,titles

          dir = './review_polarity/txt_sentoken/'
          pos_textreviews,pos_titles = ListDocs(dir+'pos/')
          neg_textreviews,neg_titles = ListDocs(dir+'neg/')
          tot_textreviews = pos_textreviews+neg_textreviews
          tot_titles = pos_titles+neg_titles
```

Now all the 2,000 reviews are stored in the `tot_textreviews` list and the corresponding titles in `tot_titles`. The TF-IDF model can be trained using `sklearn`:

```
In [4]: #test tf-idf
        from sklearn.feature_extraction.text import TfidfVectorizer

        def PreprocessTfidf(texts,stoplist=[],stem=False):
            newtexts = []
            for text in texts:
                if stem:
                    tmp = [w for w in tknzr.tokenize(text) if w not in stoplist]
                else:
                    tmp = [stemmer.stem(w) for w in [w for w in tknzr.tokenize(text) if w not in stoplist]]
                newtexts.append(' '.join(tmp))
            return newtexts
        vectorizer = TfidfVectorizer(min_df=1)
        processed_reviews = PreprocessTfidf(tot_textreviews,stoplist,True)
        mod_tfidf = vectorizer.fit(processed_reviews)
        vec_tfidf = mod_tfidf.transform(processed_reviews)
        tfidf = dict(zip(vectorizer.get_feature_names(),vectorizer.idf_))
```

After the `PreprocessTfidf` function, apply all the preprocessing techniques (removing stop words, tokenizing, and stemming) to each document. In the same way, we can train the LSA model using the `gensim` library, specifying 10 latent dimensions:

```
In [5]: #test LSA
        import gensim
        from gensim import models
        class GenSimCorpus(object):
            def __init__(self, texts, stoplist=[],stem=False):
                self.texts = texts
                self.stoplist = stoplist
                self.stem = stem
                self.dictionary = gensim.corpora.Dictionary(self.iter_docs(texts, stoplist))


            def __len__(self):
                return len(self.texts)
            def __iter__(self):
                for tokens in self.iter_docs(self.texts, self.stoplist):
                    yield self.dictionary.doc2bow(tokens)
            def iter_docs(self,texts, stoplist):
                for text in texts:
                    if self.stem:
                        yield (stemmer.stem(w) for w in [x for x in tknzr.tokenize(text) if x not in stoplist])
                    else:
                        yield (x for x in tknzr.tokenize(text) if x not in stoplist)

        corpus = GenSimCorpus(tot_textreviews,stoplist,True)
        dict_corpus = corpus.dictionary
        ntopics = 10
        lsi = models.LsiModel(corpus, num_topics=ntopics, id2word=dict_corpus)
```

Note that the `GenSimCorpus` function just preprocesses the documents with the usual techniques and transforms them into a format that the gensim LSA implementation can read. From the `lsi` object, it is possible to obtain the matrices *U*, *V*, and *S* that are needed to transform the query into the latent space:

```
In [6]:  U = lsi.projection.u
         Sigma = np.eye(ntopics)*lsi.projection.s
         #calculate V
         V = gensim.matutils.corpus2dense(lsi[corpus], len(lsi.projection.s)).T / lsi.projection.s
         dict_words = {}
         for i in range(len(dict_corpus)):
             dict_words[dict_corpus[i]] = i
```

Also the indexed dictionary of words, `dict_words`, has been calculated to transform a query word into the corresponding index word in `dict_corpus`.

The last model to train is Doc2Vec. First, we prepare the data in a format that the gensim Doc2Vec implementation can handle:

```
In [7]:  from collections import namedtuple

         def PreprocessDoc2Vec(text,stop=[],stem=False):
             words = tknzr.tokenize(text)
             if stem:
                 words_clean = [stemmer.stem(w) for w in [i.lower() for i in words if i not in stop]]
             else:
                 words_clean = [i.lower() for i in words if i not in stop]
             return words_clean

         Review = namedtuple('Review','words tags')
         dir = './review_polarity/txt_sentoken/'
         do2vecstem = False
         reviews_pos = []
         cnt = 0
         for filename in [f for f in os.listdir(dir+'pos/') if str(f)[0]!='.']:
             f = open(dir+'pos/'+filename,'r')
             reviews_pos.append(Review(PreprocessDoc2Vec(f.read(),stoplist,do2vecstem),['pos_'+str(cnt)]))
             cnt+=1

         reviews_neg = []
         cnt= 0
         for filename in [f for f in os.listdir(dir+'neg/') if str(f)[0]!='.']:
             f = open(dir+'neg/'+filename,'r')
             reviews_neg.append(Review(PreprocessDoc2Vec(f.read(),stoplist,do2vecstem),['neg_'+str(cnt)]))
             cnt+=1

         tot_reviews = reviews_pos + reviews_neg
```

Each review has been placed in a `namedtuple` object, which contains the words preprocessed by the `PreprocessDoc2Vec` function (stopwords removed and tokenization performed) and the tag that is the name of the file. Note that we chose not to apply a stemmer because the results are generally better without it (the reader can test the results by applying the stemmer, setting the Boolean flag `doc2vecstem` to `True`). The Doc2Vec training is finally performed by the following code:

```
In [8]:  #define doc2vec
         from gensim.models import Doc2Vec
         import multiprocessing

         cores = multiprocessing.cpu_count()
         vec_size = 500
         model_d2v = Doc2Vec(dm=1, dm_concat=0, size=vec_size, window=10, negative=0, hs=0, min_count=1, workers=cores)

         #build vocab
         model_d2v.build_vocab(tot_reviews)
         #train
         numepochs= 20
         for epoch in range(numepochs):
             try:
                 print 'epoch %d' % (epoch)
                 model_d2v.train(tot_reviews)
                 model_d2v.alpha *= 0.99
                 model_d2v.min_alpha = model_d2v.alpha
             except (KeyboardInterrupt, SystemExit):
                 break
```

We set the DM architecture (`dm=1`), the hidden layer with 500 dimensions (`size`), a window size of 10 words, and all the words that occur at least once have been taken into account by the model (`min_count=1`).The other parameters are related to the efficiency optimization method (`negative` for negative sampling and `hs` for hierarchical softmax). The training lasted for `20` epochs, with a learning rate equal to `0.99`.

We can now verify which results each method returns, defining a query to retrieve all the web documents related to sci-fi movies, that is, movies usually described by this list of words:

```
In [9]:  #query
         query = ['science','future','action']
```

The TF-IDF method returns the five most similar web pages using the following script:

```
In [10]:  #similar tfidf
          #sparse matrix so the metrics transform into regular vectors before computing cosine
          from sklearn.metrics.pairwise import cosine_similarity
          query_vec = mod_tfidf.transform(PreprocessTfidf([' '.join(query)],stoplist,True))
          sims= cosine_similarity(query_vec,vec_tfidf)[0]
          indxs_sims = sims.argsort()[::-1]
          for d in list(indxs_sims)[:5]:
              print 'sim:',sims[d],' title:',tot_titles[d]
```

Note that the model uses a sparse matrix format to store data, so the `cosine_similarity` function converts the vectors into regular vectors. Then it computes the similarity. In a similar way, the query is converted in a q_k in LSA terminology and the five most similar web pages are printed out:

```
In [11]:  #LSA query
          def TransformWordsListtoQueryVec(wordslist,dict_words,stem=False):
              q = np.zeros(len(dict_words.keys()))
              for w in wordslist:
                  if stem:
                      q[dict_words[stemmer.stem(w)]]=1.
                  else:
                      q[dict_words[w]] = 1.
              return q

          q = TransformWordsListtoQueryVec(query,dict_words,True)

          qk =   np.dot(np.dot(q,U),Sigma)

          sims = np.zeros(len(tot_textreviews))
          for d in range(len(V)):
              sims[d]=np.dot(qk,V[d])
          indxs_sims = np.argsort(sims)[::-1]
          for d in list(indxs_sims)[:5]:
              print 'sim:',sims[d],' doc:',tot_titles[d]
```

Finally, the `doc2vec` model transforms the query list into a vector using the `infer_vector` function, and the most similar reviews are returned by the `most_similar` function:

```
In [12]:  #doc2vec query
          #force inference to get the same result
          model_d2v.random = np.random.RandomState(1)
          query_docvec = model_d2v.infer_vector(PreprocessDoc2Vec(' '.join(query),stoplist,do2vecstem))

          reviews_related = model_d2v.docvecs.most_similar([query_docvec], topn=5)
          for review in reviews_related:
              print 'relevance:',review[1],' title:',tot_titles[review[0]]
```

Note that the `random` parameter of the model needs to be set up to a fixed value to return deterministic results whenever an optimization approach is used (negative sampling or hierarchical softmax). The results are as follows:

- **TF-IDF**:

```
sim: 0.177948650457  title: No Telling (1991)
sim: 0.177821146567  title: Total Recall (1990)
sim: 0.173783798661  title: Time Machine, The (1960)
sim: 0.163031796224  title: Bicentennial Man (1999)
sim: 0.160582512878  title: Andromeda Strain, The (1971)
```

- **LSA**:

```
sim: 4.0370254245   doc: Star Wars: Episode I - The Phantom Menace (1999)
sim: 3.41798397445  doc: Alien&#179; (1992)
sim: 3.41131742531  doc: Rocky Horror Picture Show, The (1975)
sim: 2.99980957062  doc: Starship Troopers (1997)
sim: 2.86164366049  doc: Wild Things (1998)
```

- Doc2vec:

```
relevance: 0.129549503326   title: Lost World: Jurassic Park, The (1997)
relevance: 0.124721623957   title: In the Heat of the Night (1967)
relevance: 0.122562259436   title: Charlie's Angels (2000)
relevance: 0.119273915887   title: Batman & Robin (1997)
relevance: 0.118506141007   title: Pok&#233;mon: The Movie 2000 (2000)
```

All three methods show movies related to the query. Interestingly, TF-IDF performs better than the more advanced LSA and Doc2Vec algorithms because *In the Heat of the Night*, *Pokemon*, *Rocky Horror Picture Show*, and *Wild Things* are not related to the query compared with the TF-IDF results which show only one movie (*No Telling*) as unrelated. The movies *Charlie's Angels* and *Batman & Robin* are action movies, so they are mostly related to the single query word *action*. Doc2Vec returns the worst results mostly because the training dataset is too small to learn good vector representations (as an example, Google released a word2vec trained dataset based on billions of documents, or more). The website `http://www.cs.cornell.edu/people/pabo/movie-review-data/` provides a larger dataset, so the reader can try to train Doc2Vec with more data as an exercise.

Postprocessing information

Once the web pages are collected from the Web, there are natural language processing algorithms that are able to extract relevant information for different commercial purposes apart from building a web search engine. We will discuss here algorithms that are able to extract the main topics on the collection of documents (latent Dirichlet analysis) and to extract the sentiment or opinion of each web page (opinion mining techniques).

Latent Dirichlet allocation

Latent Dirichlet allocation (LDA) is a natural language processing algorithm that belongs to the generative model category. The technique is based on the observations of some variables that can be explained by other underlined unobserved variables, which are the reasons the observed data is similar or different.

For example, consider text documents in which words are the observations. Each document can be the result of a mixture of topics (unobserved variables) and each word refers to a specific topic.

For instance, consider the two following documents describing two companies:

- **doc1**: Changing how people search for fashion items and, share and buy fashion via visual recognition, TRUELIFE is going to become the best approach to search the ultimate trends …

- **doc2**: Cinema4you enabling any venue to be a cinema is a new digital filmed media distribution company currently in the testing phase. It applies technologies used in Video on Demand and broadcasting to …

LDA is a way of automatically discovering latent topics that these documents contain. For example, given these documents and asked for two topics, LDA might return the following words associated with each topic:

- **topic 1**: people Video fashion media…
- **topic 2**: Cinema technologies recognition broadcasting…

Therefore, the second topic can be labeled as *technology* while the first as *business*.

Documents are then represented as mixtures of topics that spit out words with certain probabilities:

- **doc1**: topic 1 42%,topic 2 64%
- **doc2**: topic 1 21%, topic 2 79%

This representation of the documents can be useful in various applications such as clustering of pages in different groups, or to extract the main common subjects of a collection of pages. The mathematical model behind this algorithm is explained in the next paragraph.

Model

Documents are represented as random mixtures over latent topics, where each topic is characterized by a distribution over words. LDA assumes the following process for a corpus consisting of M documents, $d=(d_1, ..., d_M)$, with each i containing N_i words. If V is the length of the vocabulary, a word of document i is represented by a vector w_i of length V, where only an element $w_i^v=1$ and the others are 0:

$$w_i = \left(0,,, w_i^v = 1,. ...\right)$$

The number of latent dimensions (topics) is K, and for each document, $z = \left(z_{1,}..z_{N_1}\right)$ is the vector of topics associated with each word w_i, where z_i is a vector of 0's of length K except for the element j, $z_i^j=1$, that represents the topic w_i has been drawn from.

b indicates the $K\,'V$ matrix, where b_{ij} represents the probability that each word j in the vocabulary is drawn from topic i: $\beta_{ij} = p\left(w^j = 1\,|\,z^i = 1\right)$.

So, each row i of b is the word's distribution of topic i, while each column j is the topic's distribution of word j. Using these definitions, the process is described as follows:

1. From a chosen distribution (usually Poisson), draw the length of each document N_i.

2. For each document d_i, draw the topic distribution q_i, as a Dirichlet distribution $Dir(a)$, where $i \in 1,..., M$ and a is a parameter vector of length K

   such that $p\left(\theta_i\,|\,\alpha\right) = \dfrac{\Gamma\left(\sum\limits_{d=0}^{K}\alpha_d\right)}{\prod\limits_{d=0}^{K}\Gamma\left(\alpha_d\right)}\prod\limits_{d=0}^{K}\left(\theta_i\right)_d^{\alpha_i-1}$.

3. For each document d_i, for each word n, draw a topic from the multinomial $z_n \sim Multinomial\left(\theta_i\right)$.

4. For each document d_i, for each word n, and for each topic z_n, draw a word w_n from a multinomial given by the row z_n of b, $w_n \sim \beta_{z_n}$.

The objective of the algorithm is to maximize the posterior probability for each document:

$$p(\theta_i, z \mid d_i, \alpha, \beta) = \frac{p(\theta_i, z, d_i \mid \alpha, \beta)}{p(d_i \mid \alpha, \beta)}$$

Applying the conditional probability definition, the numerator becomes the following:

$$p(\theta_i, z, d_i \mid \alpha, \beta) = p(d_i \mid z, \beta) \, p(z \mid \theta_i) \, p(\theta_i \mid \alpha)$$

So, the probability that the document *i* is given by topic vector *z* and word probability matrix b can be expressed as a multiplication of the single word probabilities:

$$p(d_i \mid z, \beta) = \prod_{n=1}^{N_i} \beta_{z_n, w_n}$$

Considering that z_n is a vector with only one component *j* different from 0, $z^j_n = 1$, then $p(z \mid \theta_i) = (\theta_i)_j$. Substituting these expressions on (2):

$$p(\theta_i, z, d_i \mid \alpha, \beta) = \left(\frac{\Gamma\left(\sum_{d=0}^{K} \alpha_d \right)}{\prod_{d=0}^{K} \Gamma(\alpha_d)} \prod_{d=0}^{K} (\theta_i)_d^{\alpha_i - 1} \prod_{n=1}^{N_i} \beta_{z_n, w_n} (\theta_i)_{z_n} \right)$$

The denominator of (1) is obtained simply by integration over q_i and summation over z. The final values of the topic distribution q_i and the words per topic distribution (rows of b) are obtained by calculating this probability by approximated inference techniques; those are beyond the scope of this book.

The parameter a is called the concentration parameter, and it indicates how much the distribution is spread over the possible values. A concentration parameter of 1 (or k, the dimension of the Dirichlet distribution, by the definition used in topic modeling literature) results in all sets of probabilities being equally probable. Meanwhile, in the limit as the concentration parameter tends towards zero, only distributions with nearly the entire mass concentrated on one of their components are likely (the words are less shared among different topics and they concentrate on a few topics).

As an example, a 100,000-dimension categorical distribution has a vocabulary of 100,000 words even though a topic may be represented by a couple of hundred words. As a consequence, typical values for the concentration parameter are between 0.01 and 0.001, or lower if the vocabulary's size is millions of words or higher.

According to L. Li and Y. Zhang's paper *An empirical study of text classification using Latent Dirichlet Allocation*, LDA can be used as an effective dimension reduction method for text modeling. However, even though the method has performed well in various applications, there are certain issues to consider. The initialization of the model is random, which means it can lead to different results in each run. Also, the choice of concentration parameters is important, but there is no standard method to choose them.

Example

Consider again the movie reviews' web pages, `textreviews`, already preprocessed in the *Movie review query example* section, and LDA is applied to test whether it is possible to gather reviews on different topics. As usual, the following code is available in `postprocessing.ipynb` at `https://github.com/ai2010/machine_learning_for_the_web/tree/master/chapter_4/`:

```
In [6]:  #LDA
         import gensim.models
         from gensim import models

         from nltk.tokenize import RegexpTokenizer
         tknzr = RegexpTokenizer(r'((?<=[^\w\s])\w(?=[^\w\s])|(\W))+', gaps=True)

         from nltk.stem.porter import PorterStemmer
         stemmer = PorterStemmer()
         class GenSimCorpus(object):
                 def __init__(self, texts, stoplist=[],bestwords=[],stem=False):
                     self.texts = texts
                     self.stoplist = stoplist
                     self.stem = stem
                     self.bestwords = bestwords
                     self.dictionary = gensim.corpora.Dictionary(self.iter_docs(texts, stoplist))

                 def __len__(self):
                     return len(self.texts)
                 def __iter__(self):
                     for tokens in self.iter_docs(self.texts, self.stoplist):
                         yield self.dictionary.doc2bow(tokens)
                 def iter_docs(self,texts, stoplist):
                     for text in texts:
                         if self.stem:
                             yield (stemmer.stem(w) for w in [x for x in tknzr.tokenize(text) if x not in stoplist])
                         else:
                             if len(self.bestwords)>0:
                                 yield (x for x in tknzr.tokenize(text) if x in self.bestwords)
                             else:
                                 yield (x for x in tknzr.tokenize(text) if x not in stoplist)

         num_topics = 10
         corpus = GenSimCorpus(tot_textreviews, stoplist,[],False)
         dict_lda = corpus.dictionary
```

As usual we have transformed each document in tokens (a different tokenizer has been used) and the stop words have been removed. To achieve better results, we filter out the most frequent words (such as `movie` and `film`) that do not add any information to the pages. We ignore all the words with more than 1,000 occurrences or observed less than three times:

```
In [7]:  import copy
         #filter out very common words like mobie and film or very unfrequent terms
         out_ids = [tokenid for tokenid, docfreq in dict_lda.dfs.iteritems() if docfreq > 1000 or docfreq < 3 ]
         dict_lfq = copy.deepcopy(dict_lda)
         dict_lfq.filter_tokens(out_ids)
         dict_lfq.compactify()
         corpus = [dict_lfq.doc2bow(tknzr.tokenize(text)) for text in tot_textreviews]
```

Now we can train the LDA model with 10 topics (`passes` is the number of training passes through the corpus):

```
In [8]:  lda_lfq = models.LdaModel(corpus, num_topics=num_topics, id2word=dict_lfq,passes=10, iterations=50,alpha=0.01,eta=0.01)
         for t in range(num_topics):
             print 'topic ',t,' words: ',lda_lfq.print_topic(t,topn=10)
             print
```

The code returns the following 10 most probable words associated with each topic:

```
topic  0    words:  0.009*best + 0.008*life + 0.008*although + 0.008*great + 0.007*director + 0.006*own + 0.006*see +
0.006*town + 0.006*doesn + 0.005*still

topic  1    words:  0.014*see + 0.010*know + 0.008*bad + 0.008*off + 0.008*think + 0.007*plot + 0.007*could +
0.007*re + 0.007*life + 0.007*m

topic  2    words:  0.011*disney + 0.009*off + 0.009*action + 0.009*plot + 0.008*love + 0.008*life + 0.007*wild +
0.007*could + 0.006*mulan + 0.006*new

topic  3    words:  0.009*scene + 0.008*life + 0.007*new + 0.007*know + 0.007*doesn + 0.007*off + 0.007*could +
0.006*bad + 0.006*director + 0.006*see

topic  4    words:  0.014*truman + 0.009*life + 0.009*best + 0.008*doesn + 0.007*scene + 0.007*own + 0.007*world +
0.007*sandler + 0.007*see + 0.006*new

topic  5    words:  0.009*bad + 0.008*big + 0.008*off + 0.007*plot + 0.007*doesn + 0.007*director + 0.007*scene +
0.007*go + 0.006*see + 0.006*better

topic  6    words:  0.013*plot + 0.012*action + 0.012*alien + 0.011*bad + 0.009*new + 0.008*off + 0.008*planet +
0.008*see + 0.007*could + 0.006*scene

topic  7    words:  0.013*action + 0.009*plot + 0.007*war + 0.007*off + 0.007*see + 0.007*re + 0.007*van +
0.006*director + 0.006*great + 0.006*made

topic  8    words:  0.012*love + 0.009*best + 0.008*see + 0.007*could + 0.007*life + 0.006*new + 0.006*scene +
0.006*off + 0.006*go + 0.006*re

topic  9    words:  0.016*life + 0.010*world + 0.007*scene + 0.007*could + 0.006*mother + 0.006*own + 0.006*love +
0.006*role + 0.006*off + 0.006*father
```

Although not all the topics have an easy interpretation, we can definitely see that topic 2 is associated with the words `disney`, `mulan` (a Disney movie), `love`, and `life` is a topic about animation movies, topic 6 is associated with the words `action`, `alien`, `bad`, and `planet` is related to fantasy sci-fi movies. In fact, we can query all the movies with most probable topic equal to 6 like this:

```
In [9]:  #topics for each doc
         def GenerateDistrArrays(corpus):
                 for i,dist in enumerate(corpus[:10]):
                     dist_array = np.zeros(num_topics)
                     for d in dist:
                         dist_array[d[0]] =d[1]
                     if dist_array.argmax() == 6 :
                         print tot_titles[i]
         corpus_lda = lda_lfq[corpus]
         GenerateDistrArrays(corpus_lda)
```

This will return:

```
Rock Star (2001)
Star Wars: Episode I - The Phantom Menace (1999)
Zoolander (2001)
Star Wars: Episode I - The Phantom Menace (1999)
Matrix, The (1999)
Volcano (1997)
Return of the Jedi (1983)
Daylight (1996)
Blues Brothers 2000 (1998)
Alien&#179; (1992)
Fallen (1998)
Planet of the Apes (2001)
```

Most of these titles are clearly sci-fi and fantasy movies, so the LDA algorithm clusters them correctly.

Note that with the documents' representations in the topic space (`lda_lfq[corpus]`), it would be possible to apply a cluster algorithm (see *Chapter 2, Machine Learning Techniques – Unsupervised Learning*) but this is left to the reader as an exercise. Note also that each time the LDA algorithm is run, it may lead to different results due to the random initialization of the model (that is, it's normal if your results are different from what it is shown in this paragraph).

Opinion mining (sentiment analysis)

Opinion mining or sentiment analysis is the field of study of text to extract the opinion of the writer, which can usually be positive or negative (or neutral). This analysis is particularly useful especially in marketing to find the public opinion on products or services. The standard approach is to consider the sentiment (or polarity), negative or positive, as the target of a classification problem. A dataset of documents will have as many features as the number of different words contained in the vocabulary, and classification algorithms such as SVM and Naive Bayes are typically used. As an example, we consider the 2,000 movie reviews already used for testing LDA and information retrieval models that are already labeled (positive or negative). All of the code discussed in this paragraph is available on the `postprocessing.ipynb` IPython notebook at `https://github.com/ai2010/machine_learning_for_the_web/tree/master/chapter_4/`. As before, we import the data and preprocess:

```
In [10]:  import nltk
          from nltk.corpus import stopwords
          from nltk.tokenize import WordPunctTokenizer
          tknzr = WordPunctTokenizer()

          from nltk.tokenize import RegexpTokenizer
          tknzr = RegexpTokenizer(r'((?<=[^\w\s])\w(?=[^\w\s])|(\W))+', gaps=True)

          nltk.download('stopwords')
          stoplist = stopwords.words('english')
          from nltk.stem.porter import PorterStemmer
          stemmer = PorterStemmer()


          from collections import namedtuple

          def PreprocessReviews(text,stop=[],stem=False):
              #print profile
              words = tknzr.tokenize(text)
              if stem:
                  words_clean = [stemmer.stem(w) for w in [i.lower() for i in words if i not in stop]]
              else:
                  words_clean = [i.lower() for i in words if i not in stop]
              return words_clean

          Review = namedtuple('Review','words title tags')
          dir = './review_polarity/txt_sentoken/'
          do2vecstem = True
          reviews_pos = []
          cnt = 0
          for filename in [f for f in os.listdir(dir+'pos/') if str(f)[0]!='.']:
              f = open(dir+'pos/'+filename,'r')
              id = filename.split('.')[0].split('_')[1]
              reviews_pos.append(Review(PreprocessReviews(f.read(),stoplist,do2vecstem),moviedict[id],['pos_'+str(cnt)]))
              cnt+=1

          reviews_neg = []
          cnt= 0
          for filename in [f for f in os.listdir(dir+'neg/') if str(f)[0]!='.']:
              f = open(dir+'neg/'+filename,'r')
              id = filename.split('.')[0].split('_')[1]
              reviews_neg.append(Review(PreprocessReviews(f.read(),stoplist,do2vecstem),moviedict[id],['neg_'+str(cnt)]))
              cnt+=1

          tot_reviews = reviews_pos + reviews_neg
```

The data is then split into a training set (80%) and a test set (20%) in a way the `nltk` library can process (a list of tuples each or those with a dictionary containing the document words and the label):

```
In [11]:  #split in test training sets
          def word_features(words):
              return dict([(word, True) for word in words])
          negfeatures = [(word_features(r.words), 'neg') for r in reviews_neg]
          posfeatures = [(word_features(r.words), 'pos') for r in reviews_pos]
          portionpos = int(len(posfeatures)*0.8)
          portionneg = int(len(negfeatures)*0.8)
          print portionpos,'-',portionneg
          trainfeatures = negfeatures[:portionneg] + posfeatures[:portionpos]
          print len(trainfeatures)
          testfeatures = negfeatures[portionneg:] + posfeatures[portionpos:]
          #shuffle(testfeatures)
```

Now we can train and test a `NaiveBayesClassifier` (multinomial) using the `nltk` library and check the error:

```
In [12]:  from nltk.classify import NaiveBayesClassifier
          #training naive bayes
          classifier = NaiveBayesClassifier.train(trainfeatures)
          ##testing
          err = 0
          print 'test on: ',len(testfeatures)
          for r in testfeatures:
              sent = classifier.classify(r[0])
              if sent != r[1]:
                  err +=1.
          print 'error rate: ',err/float(len(testfeatures))
```

The code returns an error of 28.25%, but it is possible to improve the result by computing the best bigrams in each document. A bigram is defined as a pair of consecutive words, and the X^2 test is used to find bigrams that do not occur by chance but with a larger frequency. These particular bigrams contain relevant information for the text and are called collocations in natural language processing terminology. For example, given a bigram of two words, **w1** and **w2**, in our corpus with a total number of N possible bigrams, under the null hypothesis that **w1** and **w2** occur independently to each other, we can fill a two-dimensional matrix O by collecting the occurrences of the bigram (**w1**, **w2**) and the rest of the possible bigrams, such as these:

	w1	Not w1
w2	10	901
Not w2	345	1,111,111

The X^2 measure is then given by $X^2 = \dfrac{\sum\limits_{i=0,j=0}^{1,1} \left(O_{ij} - E_{ij}\right)^2}{E_{ij}}$, where O_{ij} is the

number of occurrences of the bigram given by the words (i, j) (so that $O_{00}{=}10$ and so on) and E_{ij} is the expected frequency of the bigram (i, j) (for example,

$E_{00} = \left(\dfrac{(O_{00} + O_{01})}{N} + \dfrac{(O_{00} + O_{10})}{N}\right) N$). Intuitively, X^2 is higher the more the

observed frequency O_{ij} differs from the expected mean E_{ij}, so the null hypothesis is likely to be rejected. The bigram is a good collocation and it contains *more information* than a bigram that follows the expected means. It can be shown that the X^2 can be calculated as the f test (also called **mean square contingency coefficient**) multiplied by the total number of bigram occurrences N, as follows:

$$X^2 = N\phi, \quad \phi = \dfrac{O_{00}O_{11} - O_{01}O_{10}}{\sqrt{(O_{10} + O_{11})(O_{01} + O_{00})(O_{01} + O_{11})(O_{00} + O_{10})}}$$

More information about the collocations and the X^2 methods can be found in *Foundations of Statistical Natural Language Processing* by C. D. Manning and H. Schuetze (1999). Note also that the X^2, as the information gain measure (not discussed here), can be thought of as a feature selection method as defined in *Chapter 3, Supervised Machine Learning*. Using the `nltk` library, we can use the X^2 measure to select the 500 best bigrams per document and then train a Naive Bayes classifier again, as follows:

```
In [16]:  import itertools
          from nltk.collocations import BigramCollocationFinder
          from nltk.metrics import BigramAssocMeasures
          from random import shuffle

          #train bigram:
          def bigrams_words_features(words, nbigrams=200,measure=BigramAssocMeasures.chi_sq):
              bigram_finder = BigramCollocationFinder.from_words(words)
              bigrams = bigram_finder.nbest(measure, nbigrams)
              return dict([(ngram, True) for ngram in itertools.chain(words, bigrams)])


          negfeatures = [(bigrams_words_features(r.words,500), 'neg') for r in reviews_neg]
          posfeatures = [(bigrams_words_features(r.words,500), 'pos') for r in reviews_pos]
          portionpos = int(len(posfeatures)*0.8)
          portionneg = int(len(negfeatures)*0.8)
          print portionpos,'-',portionneg
          trainfeatures = negfeatures[:portionpos] + posfeatures[:portionneg]
          print len(trainfeatures)
          classifier = NaiveBayesClassifier.train(trainfeatures)
          ##test bigram
          testfeatures = negfeatures[portionneg:] + posfeatures[portionpos:]
          shuffle(testfeatures)
          err = 0
          print 'test on: ',len(testfeatures)
          for r in testfeatures:
              sent = classifier.classify(r[0])
              #print r[1],'-pred: ',sent
              if sent != r[1]:
                  err +=1.
          print 'error rate: ',err/float(len(testfeatures))
```

This time the error rate is 20%, which is lower than in the normal method. The X^2 test can also be used to extract the most informative words from the whole corpus. We can measure how much the single word frequency differs from the frequency of the positive (or negative) documents to score its importance (for example, if the word great has a high X^2 value on positive reviews but low on negative reviews, it means that the word gives information that the review is positive). The 10,000 most significant words of the corpus can be extracted by calculating for each of them, the the overall frequency on the entire corpus and the frequencies over the positive and negative subsets:

```
In [21]:  import nltk.classify.util, nltk.metrics
          tot_poswords = [val for l in [r.words for r in reviews_pos] for val in l]
          tot_negwords = [val for l in [r.words for r in reviews_neg] for val in l]
          from nltk.probability import FreqDist, ConditionalFreqDist
          word_fd = FreqDist()
          label_word_fd = ConditionalFreqDist()

          for word in tot_poswords:
              word_fd[word.lower()] +=1
              label_word_fd['pos'][word.lower()] +=1

          for word in tot_negwords:
              word_fd[word.lower()] +=1
              label_word_fd['neg'][word.lower()] +=1
          pos_words = len(tot_poswords)
          neg_words = len(tot_negwords)

          tot_words = pos_words + neg_words
          #select the best words in terms of information contained in the two classes pos and neg
          word_scores = {}

          for word, freq in word_fd.iteritems():
              pos_score = BigramAssocMeasures.chi_sq(label_word_fd['pos'][word],
                      (freq, pos_words), tot_words)
              neg_score = BigramAssocMeasures.chi_sq(label_word_fd['neg'][word],
                      (freq, neg_words), tot_words)
              word_scores[word] = pos_score + neg_score
          print 'total: ',len(word_scores)
          best = sorted(word_scores.iteritems(), key=lambda (w,s): s, reverse=True)[:10000]
          bestwords = set([w for w, s in best])
```

Now we can simply train a Naive Bayes classifier again using only the words in the
bestwords set for each document:

```
In [22]:  #training naive bayes with chi square feature selection of best words
          def best_words_features(words):
              return dict([(word, True) for word in words if word in bestwords])

          negfeatures = [(best_words_features(r.words), 'neg') for r in reviews_neg]
          posfeatures = [(best_words_features(r.words), 'pos') for r in reviews_pos]
          portionpos = int(len(posfeatures)*0.8)
          portionneg = int(len(negfeatures)*0.8)
          print portionpos,'-',portionneg
          trainfeatures = negfeatures[:portionpos] + posfeatures[:portionneg]
          print len(trainfeatures)
          classifier = NaiveBayesClassifier.train(trainfeatures)
          ##test with feature chi square selection
          testfeatures = negfeatures[portionneg:] + posfeatures[portionpos:]
          shuffle(testfeatures)
          err = 0
          print 'test on: ',len(testfeatures)
          for r in testfeatures:
              sent = classifier.classify(r[0])
              #print r[1],'-pred: ',sent
              if sent != r[1]:
                  err +=1.
          print 'error rate: ',err/float(len(testfeatures))
```

The error rate is 12.75%, which is remarkably low considering the relatively small dataset. Note that to have a more reliable result, a cross-validation method (see *Chapter 3, Supervised Machine Learning*) should be applied, but this is given to the reader as an exercise. Also note that the Doc2Vec vectors (compute in the *Movie review query example* section) can be used to train a classifier. Assuming that the Doc2Vec vectors have already been trained and stored in the `model_d2v.doc2vec` object, as usual we split the data into a training dataset (80%) and a test set (20%):

```
In [23]:  #split train,test sets
          trainingsize = 2*int(len(reviews_pos)*0.8)

          train_d2v = np.zeros((trainingsize, vec_size))
          train_labels = np.zeros(trainingsize)
          test_size = len(tot_reviews)-trainingsize
          test_d2v = np.zeros((test_size, vec_size))
          test_labels = np.zeros(test_size)

          cnt_train = 0
          cnt_test = 0
          for r in reviews_pos:
              name_pos = r.tags[0]
              if int(name_pos.split('_')[1])>= int(trainingsize/2.):
                  test_d2v[cnt_test] = model_d2v.docvecs[name_pos]
                  test_labels[cnt_test] = 1
                  cnt_test +=1
              else:
                  train_d2v[cnt_train] = model_d2v.docvecs[name_pos]
                  train_labels[cnt_train] = 1
                  cnt_train +=1

          for r in reviews_neg:
              name_neg = r.tags[0]
              if int(name_neg.split('_')[1])>= int(trainingsize/2.):
                  test_d2v[cnt_test] = model_d2v.docvecs[name_neg]
                  test_labels[cnt_test] = 0
                  cnt_test +=1
              else:
                  train_d2v[cnt_train] = model_d2v.docvecs[name_neg]
                  train_labels[cnt_train] = 0
                  cnt_train +=1
```

Then we can train an SVM classifier (**radial basis function kernel (RBF)** kernel) or a logistic regression model:

```
In [27]:  #train log regre
          from sklearn.linear_model import LogisticRegression
          classifier = LogisticRegression()
          classifier.fit(train_d2v, train_labels)
          print 'accuracy:',classifier.score(test_d2v,test_labels)

          from sklearn.svm import SVC
          clf = SVC()
          clf.fit(train_d2v, train_labels)
          print 'accuracy:',clf.score(test_d2v,test_labels)
```

Logistic regression and SVM give very low accuracies, of 0.5172 and 0.5225 respectively. This is mostly due to the small size of the training dataset, which does not allow us to train algorithms that have a large number of parameters to train, such as neuron networks.

Summary

In this chapter both the most common and advanced algorithms used to manage web data were discussed and implemented using a series of Python libraries. Now you should have a clear understanding of the challenges faced in the web mining area and should be able to handle some of these issues with Python. In the next chapter, we will discuss the most important recommendation systems algorithms used to date in the commercial environment.

5
Recommendation Systems

Recommendation systems find their natural application whenever a user is exposed to a wide choice of products or services that they cannot evaluate in a reasonable timeframe. These engines are an important part of an e-commerce business because they assist the clients on the web to facilitate the task of deciding the appropriate items to buy or choose over a large number of candidates not relevant to the end user. Typical examples are Amazon, Netflix, eBay, and Google Play stores that suggest each user the items they may like to buy using the historical data they have collected. Different techniques have been developed in the past 20 years and we will focus on the most important (and employed) methods used in the industry to date, specifying the advantages and disadvantages that characterize each of these methods. The recommendation systems are classified in **Content-based Filtering (CBF)** and **Collaborative Filtering (CF)** techniques and other different approaches (association rules, the log-likelihood method, and hybrid methods) will be discussed together with different ways to evaluate their accuracy. The methods will be tested on the MovieLens database (from `http://grouplens.org/datasets/movielens/`) consisting of 100,000 movie ratings (1 to 5 values) from 943 users on 1,682 movies. Each user has at least 20 ratings and each movie has a list of genres that it belongs to. All the codes shown in this chapter are available, as usual, at `https://github.com/ai2010/machine_learning_for_the_web/tree/master/chapter_5` in the `rec_sys_methods.ipynb` file.

We will start by introducing the main matrix used to arrange the dataset employed by the recommendation system and the metric measures typically used before starting to discuss the algorithms in the following sections.

Utility matrix

The data used in a recommendation system is divided in two categories: the users and the items. Each user likes certain items, and the rating value r_{ij} (from 1 to 5) is the data associated with each user i and item j and represents how much the user appreciates the item. These rating values are collected in matrix, called utility matrix R, in which each row i represents the list of rated items for user i while each column j lists all the users who have rated item j. In our case, the data folder ml-100k contains a file called u.data (and also u.item with the list of movie titles) that has been converted into a Pandas DataFrame (and saved into a csv, utilitymatrix.csv) by the following script:

```
In [34]:  import numpy as np
          import pandas as pd
          import copy
          import collections
          from scipy import linalg
          import math
          from collections import defaultdict
```

```
In [35]:  #data
          df = pd.read_csv('./data/ml-100k/u.data',sep='\t',header=None)
          #movie list
          df_info = pd.read_csv('./data/ml-100k/u.item',sep='|',header=None)
          movielist = [df_info[1].tolist()[indx]+';'+str(indx+1) for indx in xrange(len(df_info[1].tolist()))]
          nmovies = len(movielist)
          nusers = len(df[0].drop_duplicates().tolist())

          min_ratings = 50
          movies_rated  = list(df[1])
          counts = collections.Counter(movies_rated)
          dfout = pd.DataFrame(columns=['user']+movielist)

          toremovelist = []
          for i in range(1,nusers):
              tmpmovielist = [0 for j in range(nmovies)]
              dftmp =df[df[0]==i]
              for k in dftmp.index:
                  if counts[dftmp.ix[k][1]]>= min_ratings:
                      tmpmovielist[dftmp.ix[k][1]-1] = dftmp.ix[k][2]

                  else:
                      toremovelist.append(dftmp.ix[k][1])

              dfout.loc[i] = [i]+tmpmovielist

          toremovelist = list(set(toremovelist))
          dfout.drop(dfout.columns[toremovelist], axis=1, inplace=True)
          dfout.to_csv('data/utilitymatrix.csv',index=None)
```

The output of the first two lines is as follows:

```
In [38]:  df = pd.read_csv('data/utilitymatrix.csv')
          df.head(2)
```

Out[38]:

	user	Toy Story (1995);1	GoldenEye (1995);2	Four Rooms (1995);3	Get Shorty (1995);4	Copycat (1995);5	Twelve Monkeys (1995);7	Babe (1995);8	Dead Man Walking (1995);9	Richard III (1995);10	...	Cool Runnings (1993);1035	Hamlet (1996);1039
0	1	5	3	4	3	3	4	1	5	3	...	0	0
1	2	4	0	0	0	0	0	0	0	2	...	0	0

2 rows × 604 columns

Each column name, apart from the first (which is the user id), defines the name of the movie and the ID of the movie in the MovieLens database (separated by a semicolon). The 0 values represent the missing values and we expect to have a large number of them because the users evaluated far fewer than 1,600 movies. Note that the movies with less than 50 ratings have been removed from the utility matrix, so the number of columns is 604 (603 movies rated more than 50 times). The goal of the recommendation system is to predict these values, but for some techniques to work properly it will be necessary for us to initially set these values (imputation). Usually, two imputation approaches are used: ratings average per user or ratings average per item, and both of them are implemented in the following function:

```
In [4]:  def imputation(inp,Ri):
             Ri = Ri.astype(float)
             def userav():
                 for i in xrange(len(Ri)):
                     Ri[i][Ri[i]==0] = sum(Ri[i])/float(len(Ri[i][Ri[i]>0]))
                 return Ri
             def itemav():
                 for i in xrange(len(Ri[0])):
                     Ri[:,i][Ri[:,i]==0] = sum(Ri[:,i])/float(len(Ri[:,i][Ri[:,i]>0]))
                 return Ri
             switch = {'useraverage':userav(),'itemaverage':itemav()}
             return switch[inp]
```

This function will be called by many of the algorithms implemented in this chapter, so we decided to discuss it here as a reference for future use. Furthermore, in this chapter the utility matrix R will have dimensions $N{\times}M$ with N number of users and M number of items. Due to the recurrent use of the similarity measures by different algorithms, we will define the most commonly used definitions hereafter.

Similarities measures

In order to compute similarity s between two different vectors x and y, which can be users (rows of utility matrix) or items (columns of utility matrix), two measures are typically used:

- Cosine similarity: $s(x, y) = \dfrac{\sqrt{\sum_i x_i y_i}}{\sqrt{\sum_i x_i^2} \sqrt{\sum_i y_i^2}}$

- Pearson correlation: $s(x, y) = \dfrac{\sum_i (x_i - \bar{x})(y_i - \bar{y})}{\sqrt{\sum_i (x_i - \bar{x})^2} \sqrt{\sum_i (y_i - \bar{y})^2}}$, where x and y

    are the averages of the two vectors.

Note that the two measures coincide if the average is 0. We can now start discussing the different algorithms, starting from the CF category. The following `sim()` function will be used to evaluate the similarity between two vectors:

```
In [8]: from scipy.stats import pearsonr
        from scipy.spatial.distance import cosine
        def sim(x,y,metric='cos'):
            if metric == 'cos':
                return 1.-cosine(x,y)
            else:#correlation
                return pearsonr(x,y)[0]
```

The `SciPy` library has been used to compute both similarities (note that the cosine scipy definition is the opposite of what has been defined previously, so the value is subtracted from 1).

Collaborative Filtering methods

This class of methods is based on the idea that any user will like items appreciated by other users similar to them. In simple terms, the fundamental hypothesis is that a user A, who is similar to user B, will likely rate an item as B did rather than in another way. In practice, this concept is implemented by either comparing the taste of different user's and inferring the future rating for a given user using the most similar users taste (memory-based) or by extracting some rating patterns from what the users like (model-based) and trying to predict the future rating following these patterns. All these methods require a large amount of data to work because the recommendations to a given user rely on how many similar users can be found in the data. This problem is called **cold start** and it is very well studied in literature, which usually suggests using some hybrid method between CF and CBF to overcome the issue. In our MovieLens database example we assume we have enough data to avoid the cold start problem. Other common problems of CF algorithms are the scalability, because the computation grows with the number of users and products (it may be necessary some parallelization technique), and the sparsity of the utility matrix due to small number of items that any user usually rates (imputation is usually an attempt to handle the problem).

Memory-based Collaborative Filtering

This subclass employs the utility matrix to calculate either the similarity between users or items. The methods suffer from scalability and cold start issues, but when they are applied to a large or too small utility matrix, they are currently used in many commercial systems today. We are going to discuss user-based Collaborative Filtering and iteFiased Collaborative Filtering hereafter.

User-based Collaborative Filtering

The approach uses a k-NN method (see *Chapter 3, Supervised Machine Learning*) to find the users whose past ratings are similar to the ratings of the chosen user so that their ratings can be combined in a weighted average to return the current user's missing ratings.

The algorithm is as follows:

For any given user i and item not yet rated j:

1. Find the K that is most similar users that have rate j using a similarity metric s.

2. Calculate the predicted rating for each item *j* not yet rated by *i* as a weighted average over the ratings of the users *K*:

$$p_{ij} = r_i + \frac{\sum_{k=0}^{K} s(i,k)(r_{kj} - \overline{r_k})}{\left| \sum_{k=0}^{K} s(i,k) \right|}$$

Here $\overline{r_i}, \overline{r_k}$ are the average ratings for users *i* and *k* to compensate for subjective judgment (some users are generous and some are picky) and *s(i, k)* is the similarity metric, as seen in the previous paragraph. Note that we can even normalize by the spread of the ratings per user to compare more homogeneous ratings:

$$p_{ij} = \overline{r_i} + \frac{\sigma_i \sum_{k=0}^{K} s(i,k)(r_{kj} - \overline{r_k}) / \sigma_k}{\left| \sum_{k=0}^{K} s(i,k) \right|}$$

Here, σ_i and σ_k are the standard deviations of ratings of users *i* and *k*.

This algorithm has as an input parameter, the number of neighbors, *K* but usually a value between 20 and 50 is sufficient in most applications. The Pearson correlation has been found to return better results than cosine similarity, probably because the subtraction of the user ratings means that the correlation formula makes the users more comparable. The following code is used to predict the missing ratings of each user.

The u_vec represents the user ratings values from which the most similar other users *K* are found by the function FindKNeighbours. CalcRating just computes the predicted rating using the formula discussed earlier (without the spreading correction). Note that in case the utility matrix is so sparse that no neighbors are found, the mean rating of the user is predicted. It may happen that the predicted rating is beyond 5 or below 1, so in such situations the predicted rating is set to 5 or 1 respectively.

```
In [51]:  def CF_userbased(u_vec,K,data,indxs=False):
              def FindKNeighbours(r,data,K):
                  neighs = []
                  cnt=0
                  for u in xrange(len(data)):
                      if data[u,r]>0 and cnt<K:
                          neighs.append(data[u])
                          cnt +=1
                      elif cnt==K:
                          break
                  return np.array(neighs)

              def CalcRating(u_vec,r,neighs):
                  rating = 0.
                  den = 0.
                  for j in xrange(len(neighs)):
                      rating += neighs[j][-1]*float(neighs[j][r]-neighs[j][neighs[j]>0][:-1].mean())
                      den += abs(neighs[j][-1])
                  if den>0:
                      rating = np.round(u_vec[u_vec>0].mean()+(rating/den),0)
                  else:
                      rating = np.round(u_vec[u_vec>0].mean(),0)
                  if rating>5:
                      return 5.
                  elif rating<1:
                      return 1.
                  return rating
              #add similarity col
              data = data.astype(float)
              nrows = len(data)
              ncols = len(data[0])
              data_sim = np.zeros((nrows,ncols+1))
              data_sim[:,:-1] = data
              #calc similarities:
              for u in xrange(nrows):
                  if np.array_equal(data_sim[u,:-1],u_vec)==False: #list(data_sim[u,:-1]) != list(u_vec):
                      data_sim[u,ncols] = sim(data_sim[u,:-1],u_vec,'pearson')
                  else:
                      data_sim[u,ncols] = 0.
              #order by similarity:
              data_sim =data_sim[data_sim[:,ncols].argsort()][::-1]
              #find the K users for each item not rated:
              u_rec = np.zeros(len(u_vec))
              for r in xrange(ncols):
                  if u_vec[r]==0:
                      neighs = FindKNeighbours(r,data_sim,K)
                      #calc the predicted rating
                      u_rec[r] = CalcRating(u_vec,r,neighs)
              if indxs:
                      #take out the rated movies
                      seenindxs = [indx for indx in xrange(len(u_vec)) if u_vec[indx]>0]
                      u_rec[seenindxs] = -1
                      recsvec = np.argsort(u_rec)[::-1][np.argsort(u_rec)>0]

                      return recsvec
              return u_rec
```

Item-based Collaborative Filtering

This approach is conceptually the same as user-based CF except that the similarity is calculated on the items rather than the users. Since most of the time the number of users can become much larger than the number of items, this method offers a more scalable recommendation system because the items' similarities can be precomputed and they will not change much when new users arrive (if the number of users N is significantly large).

The algorithm for each user i and item j is as follows:

1. Find the K most similar items using a similarity metric s that i has already rated.

2. Calculate the predicted rating as a weighted average of the ratings of the K items:

$$p_{ij} = \frac{\sum_{k=0}^{K} s(jk) r_{ik}}{\left| \sum_{k=0}^{K} s(jk) \right|}$$

Note that the similarity metric may have a negative value, so we need to restrict the summation to only positive similarities in order to have meaningful (that is, positive) P_{ij} (the relative ordering of items will be correct anyway if we are only interested in the best item to recommend instead of the ratings). Even in this case, a K value between 20 and 50 is usually fine in most applications.

The algorithm is implemented using a class, as follows:

```
In [32]: class CF_itembased(object):
             def __init__(self,data):
                 #calc item similarities matrix
                 nitems = len(data[0])
                 self.data = data
                 self.simmatrix = np.zeros((nitems,nitems))
                 for i in xrange(nitems):
                     for j in xrange(nitems):
                         if j>=i:#triangular matrix
                             self.simmatrix[i,j] = sim(data[:,i],data[:,j])
                         else:
                             self.simmatrix[i,j] = self.simmatrix[j,i]

             def GetKSimItemsperUser(self,r,K,u_vec):
                 items = np.argsort(self.simmatrix[r])[::-1]
                 items = items[items!=r]
                 cnt=0
                 neighitems = []
                 for i in items:
                     if u_vec[i]>0 and cnt<K:
                         neighitems.append(i)
                         cnt+=1
                     elif cnt==K:
                         break
                 return neighitems

             def CalcRating(self,r,u_vec,neighitems):
                 rating = 0.
                 den = 0.
                 for i in neighitems:
                     rating +=  self.simmatrix[r,i]*u_vec[i]
                     den += abs(self.simmatrix[r,i])
                 if den>0:
                     rating = np.round(rating/den,0)
                 else:
                     rating = np.round(self.data[:,r][self.data[:,r]>0].mean(),0)
                 return rating

             def CalcRatings(self,u_vec,K,indxs=False):
                 #u_rec = copy.copy(u_vec)
                 u_rec = np.zeros(len(u_vec))
                 for r in xrange(len(u_vec)):
                     if u_vec[r]==0:
                         neighitems = self.GetKSimItemsperUser(r,K,u_vec)
                         #calc predicted rating
                         u_rec[r] = self.CalcRating(r,u_vec,neighitems)
                 if indxs:
                     #take out the rated movies
                     seenindxs = [indx for indx in xrange(len(u_vec)) if u_vec[indx]>0]
                     u_rec[seenindxs]=-1
                     recsvec = np.argsort(u_rec)[::-1][np.argsort(u_rec)>0]

                     return recsvec
                 return u_rec
```

The constructor of the class `CF_itembased` calculates the item similarity matrix `simmatrix` to use any time we want to evaluate missing ratings for a user through the function `CalcRatings`. The function `GetKSimItemsperUser` finds K: most similar users to the chosen user (given by `u_vec`) and `CalcRating` just implements the weighted average rating calculations discussed previously. Note that in case no neighbors are found, the rating is set to the average or the item's ratings.

Simplest item-based Collaborative Filtering – slope one

Instead of computing the similarity using the metric discussed previously, a very simple but effective method can be used. We can compute a matrix D in which each entry d_{ij} is the average difference between the ratings of items i and j:

$$d_{ij} = \frac{\sum_{k=1}^{K}\left(r_{ki} - r_{kj}\right)n_{ij}^{k}}{\sum_{k=1}^{N}n_{ij}^{k}}$$

Here, $n_{ij}^{k} = \begin{cases} 1\,if\,r_{ki}, r_{kj} > 0 \\ 0\,else\,(missing\,data) \end{cases}$ is a variable that counts if the user k has rated both i and j items, so $\sum_{k=1}^{N}n_{ij}^{k}$ is the number of users who have rated both i and j items.

Then the algorithm is as explained in the *Item-based Collaborative Filtering* section. For each user i and item j:

1. Find the K items with the smallest differences from j,

    $d_{j}*,\ldots,d_{j}* = d_{j1},\ldots,d_{jK}$ (the * indicates the possible index values, but
    K
    for simplicity we relabel them from 1 to K).

2. Compute the predicted rating as a weighted average:

$$p_{ij} = \frac{\sum_{k=1}^{K}\left(d_{jk} + r_{ik}\right)\sum_{l=1}^{N}n_{jk}^{l}}{\sum_{k=1}^{K}\sum_{l=1}^{N}n_{jk}^{l}}$$

Although this algorithm is much simpler than the other CF algorithms, it often matches their accuracy, is computationally less expensive, and is easy to implement. The implementation is very similar to the class used for item-based CF:

```
In [34]: class SlopeOne(object):
            def __init__(self,Umatrix):
                #calc item similarities matrix
                nitems = len(Umatrix[0])
                self.difmatrix = np.zeros((nitems,nitems))
                self.nratings = np.zeros((nitems,nitems))
                def diffav_n(x,y):
                    xy = np.vstack((x, y)).T
                    xy = xy[(xy[:,0]>0) & (xy[:,1]>0)]
                    nxy = len(xy)
                    if nxy == 0:
                        #print 'no common'
                        return [1000.,0]
                    return [float(sum(xy[:,0])-sum(xy[:,1]))/nxy,nxy]

                for i in xrange(nitems):
                    for j in xrange(nitems):
                        if j>=i:#triangular matrix
                            self.difmatrix[i,j],self.nratings[i,j] = diffav_n(Umatrix[:,i],Umatrix[:,j])
                        else:
                            self.difmatrix[i,j] = -self.difmatrix[j,i]
                            self.nratings[i,j] = self.nratings[j,i]

            def GetKSimItemsperUser(self,r,K,u_vec):
                items = np.argsort(self.difmatrix[r])
                items = items[items!=r]
                cnt=0
                neighitems = []
                for i in items:
                    if u_vec[i]>0 and cnt<K:
                        neighitems.append(i)
                        cnt+=1
                    elif cnt==K:
                        break
                return neighitems

            def CalcRating(self,r,u_vec,neighitems):
                rating = 0.
                den = 0.
                for i in neighitems:
                    if abs(self.difmatrix[r,i])!=1000:
                        rating += (self.difmatrix[r,i]+u_vec[i])*self.nratings[r,i]
                        den += self.nratings[r,i]
                if den==0:
                    #print 'no similar diff'
                    return 0.
                rating = np.round(rating/den,0)
                if rating >5:
                    return 5.
                elif rating <1.:
                    return 1.
                return rating

            def CalcRatings(self,u_vec,K):
                #u_rec = copy.copy(u_vec)
                u_rec = np.zeros(len(u_vec))
                for r in xrange(len(u_vec)):
                    if u_vec[r]==0:
                        neighitems = self.GetKSimItemsperUser(r,K,u_vec)
                        #calc predicted rating
                        u_rec[r] = self.CalcRating(r,u_vec,neighitems)
                return u_rec
```

The only difference is the matrix: now `difmatrix` is used to calculate the differences $d(i, j)$ between items i, j, as explained earlier, and the function `GetKSimItemsperUser` now looks for the smallest `difmatrix` values to determine the K nearest neighbors. Since it is possible (although unlikely) that two items have not been rated by at least one user, `difmatrix` can have undefined values that are set to `1000` by default. Note that it is also possible that the predicted rating is beyond `5` or below `1`, so in such situations the predicted rating must be set to `5` or `1` appropriately.

Model-based Collaborative Filtering

This class of methods uses the utility matrix to generate a model to extract the pattern of how the users rate the items. The pattern model returns the predicted ratings, filling or approximating the original matrix (matrix factorization).Various models have been studied in the literature and we will discuss particular *matrix factorization* algorithms — the **Singular Value Decomposition (SVD**, also with expectation maximization), the **Alternating Least Square (ALS)**, the **Stochastic Gradient Descent (SGD)**, and the general **Non-negative matrix factorization (NMF)** class of algorithms.

Alternative least square (ALS)

This is the simplest method to factorize the matrix R. Each user and each item can be represented in a feature space of dimension K so that:

$$R \simeq PQ^T = \hat{R}$$

Here, $P\ N \times K$ is the new matrix of users in the feature space, and $Q\ M \times K$ is the projection of the items in the same space. So the problem is reduced to minimize a regularized cost function J:

$$J = \min_{p,q} \sum_{ij} e_{ij}^2 = \min_{p,q} \sum_{ij} M_{ij} \left(r_{ij} - \sum_{k=1}^{K} p_{ik} q_{kj} \right)^2 + \frac{\lambda}{2} \left(|p_i|^2 + |q_j^T|^2 \right)$$

Here, λ is the regularization parameter, which is useful to avoid overfitting by penalizing the learned parameters and ensuring that the magnitudes of the vectors p_i and q_j^T are not too large. The matrix entries Mc_{ij} are needed to check that the pair of user i and item j are actually rated, so Mc_{ij} is 1 if $r_{ij}>0$, and it's 0 otherwise. Setting the derivatives of J to 0 for each user vector p_i and item vector q_j, we obtain the following two equations:

$$ p_i = \left(Q^T Mc_i Q + \frac{\lambda}{2} I \right)^{-1} Q^T Mc_i R_i $$

$$ q_j = \left(P^T Mc_j P + \frac{\lambda}{2} I \right)^{-1} P^T Mc_i R_j $$

Here R_i and Mc_i refer to the row i of the matrices R and Mc, and R_j and Mc_j refer to the column j of the matrices Mc and R. Alternating the fixing of the matrix P, Q, the previous equations can be solved directly using a least square algorithm and the following function implements the ALS algorithm in Python:

```
In [12]:  def ALS(Umatrix, K, iterations=50, l=0.001, tol=0.001):

              nrows = len(Umatrix)
              ncols = len(Umatrix[0])
              P = np.random.rand(nrows,K)
              Q = np.random.rand(ncols,K)
              Qt = Q.T
              err = 0.
              Umatrix = Umatrix.astype(float)
              mask = Umatrix>0.
              mask[mask==True]=1
              mask[mask==False]=0
              mask = mask.astype(np.float64, copy=False)
              for it in xrange(iterations):
                  for u, mask_u in enumerate(mask):
                      P[u] = np.linalg.solve(np.dot(Qt, np.dot(np.diag(mask_u), Qt.T)) + l*np.eye(K),
                                  np.dot(Qt, np.dot(np.diag(mask_u), Umatrix[u].T))).T
                  for i, mask_i in enumerate(mask.T):
                      Qt[:,i] = np.linalg.solve(np.dot(P.T, np.dot(np.diag(mask_i), P)) + l*np.eye(K),
                                  np.dot(P.T, np.dot(np.diag(mask_i), Umatrix[:,i])))
                  err=np.sum((mask*(Umatrix - np.dot(P, Qt)))**2)
                  if err < tol:
                      break
              return np.round(np.dot(P,Qt),0)
```

The matrix Mc is called `mask`, the variable `l` represents the regularization parameter lambda and is set to `0.001` by default, and the least square problem has been solved using the `linalg.solve` function of the `Numpy` library. This method usually is less precise than both **Stochastic Gradient Descent (SGD)** and **Singular Value Decomposition (SVD)** (see the following sections) but it is very easy to implement and easy to parallelize (so it can be fast).

Stochastic gradient descent (SGD)

This method also belongs to the matrix factorization subclass because it relies on the approximation of the utility matrix R as:

$$R \simeq PQ^T = \hat{R}$$

Here, the matrices P (N×K) and Q (M×K) represent the users and the items in a latent feature space of K dimensions. Each approximated rating $\hat{r}_{ij}$ can be expressed as follows:

$$\hat{r}_{ij} = \sum_{k=1}^{K} p_{ik} q_{kj}$$

The matrix $\hat{R}$ is found, solving the minimization problem of the regularized squared errors e^2_{ij} as with the ALS method (cost function J as in *Chapter 3, Supervised Machine Learning*):

$$\min_{p,q} \sum_{ij} e^2_{ij} = \min_{p,q} \sum_{ij} \left(r_{ij} - \sum_{k=1}^{K} p_{ik} q_{kj} \right)^2 + \frac{\lambda}{2} \left(\left| p_i \right|^2 + \left| q_j^T \right|^2 \right)$$

This minimization problem is solved using the gradient descent (see *Chapter 3, Supervised Machine Learning*):

$$p_{ik} = p_{ik} + \alpha \frac{\partial e^2_{ij}}{\partial p_{ik}} = p_{ik} + \alpha \left(2 e_{ij} q_{kj} - \lambda p_{ik} \right)$$

$$p_{kj} = q_{kj} + \alpha \frac{\partial e^2_{ij}}{\partial p_{kj}} = q_{kj} + \alpha \left(2 e_{ij} q_{ik} - \lambda q_{kj} \right)$$

Here, α is the learning rate (see *Chapter 3, Supervised Machine Learning*) and
$e_{ij} = \left(r_{ij} - \sum_{k=1}^{K} p_{ik} q_{kj} \right)$. The technique finds R alternating between the two previous
equations (fixing q_{kj} and solving P_{ik}, and vice versa) until convergence. SGD is usually
easier to parallelize (so it can be faster) than SVD (see the following section) but is
less precise at finding good ratings. The implementation in Python of this method is
given by the following script:

```
In [11]:  def SGD(Umatrix, K, iterations=100, alpha=0.00001, l=0.001, tol=0.001):

              nrows = len(Umatrix)
              ncols = len(Umatrix[0])
              P = np.random.rand(nrows,K)
              Q = np.random.rand(ncols,K)
              Qt = Q.T
              cost=-1
              for it in xrange(iterations):
                  for i in xrange(nrows):
                      for j in xrange(ncols):
                          if Umatrix[i][j] > 0:
                              eij = Umatrix[i][j] -np.dot(P[i,:],Qt[:,j])
                              for k in xrange(K):
                                  P[i][k] += alpha*(2*eij*Qt[k][j]-l*P[i][k])
                                  Qt[k][j] += alpha*(2*eij*P[i][k]-l*Qt[k][j])
                  cost = 0
                  for i in xrange(nrows):
                      for j in xrange(ncols):
                          if Umatrix[i][j]>0:
                              cost += pow(Umatrix[i][j]-np.dot(P[i,:],Qt[:,j]),2)
                              for k in xrange(K):
                                  cost += float(1/2.0)*(pow(P[i][k],2)+pow(Qt[k][j],2))
                  if cost < tol:
                      break
              return np.round(np.dot(P,Qt),0)
```

This SGD function has default parameters that are learning rate $a = 0.0001$,
regularization parameter $\lambda = l = 0.001$, maximum number of iterations 1000, and
convergence tolerance tol = 0.001. Note also that the items not rated (0 rating
values) are not considered in the computation, so an initial filling (imputation) is not
necessary when using this method.

Non-negative matrix factorization (NMF)

This is a group of methods that finds the decomposition of the matrix R again as a product of two matrices P ($N \times K$) and Q ($M \times K$) (where K is a dimension of the feature space), but their elements are required to be non-negative. The general minimization problem is as follows:

$$J = \min_{p,q} \sum_{ij} e_{ij}^2 = \min_{p \geq 0, q \geq 0} \frac{1}{2}\sum_{ij}\left(r_{ij} - \sum_{k=1}^{K} p_{ik}q_{kj}\right)^2 + (1-a)\frac{\lambda}{2}\left(|p_i|^2 + |q_j^T|^2\right) + a\lambda\left(|p_i| + |q_j^T|\right)$$

Here, α is a parameter that defines which regularization term to use (0 squared, 1 a lasso regularization, or a mixture of them) and λ is the regularization parameter. Several techniques have been developed to solve this problem, such as projected gradient, coordinate descent, and non-negativity constrained least squares. It is beyond the scope of this book to discuss the details of these techniques, but we are going to use the coordinate descent method implemented in `sklearn` NFM wrapped in the following function:

```
In [13]:  from sklearn.decomposition import NMF
          def NMF_alg(Umatrix,K,inp='none',l=0.001):
              R_tmp = copy.copy(Umatrix)
              R_tmp = R_tmp.astype(float)
              #imputation
              if inp != 'none':
                  R_tmp = imputation(inp,Umatrix)
              nmf = NMF(n_components=K,alpha=l)
              P = nmf.fit_transform(R_tmp)
              R_tmp = np.dot(P,nmf.components_)
              return R_tmp
```

Note that an imputation may be performed before the actual factorization takes place and that the function `fit_transform` returns the P matrix while the Q^T matrix is stored in the `nmf.components_` object. The a value is assumed to be 0 (squared regularization) and $\lambda = l = 0.01$ by default. Since the utility matrix has positive values (ratings), this class of methods is certainly a good fit to predict these values.

Singular value decomposition (SVD)

We have already discussed this algorithm in *Chapter 2, Unsupervised Machine Learning*, as a dimensionality reduction technique to approximate a matrix by decomposition into matrices U, Σ, V (you should read the related section in *Chapter 2, Unsupervised Machine Learning*, for further technical details). In this case, SVD is used as a matrix factorization technique, but an imputation method is required to initially estimate the missing data for each user; typically, the average of each utility matrix row (or column) or a combination of both (instead of leaving the zero values) is used. Apart from directly applying the SVD to the utility matrix, another algorithm that exploits an expectation-maximization (see *Chapter 2, Unsupervised Machine Learning*) can be used as follows, starting from the matrix $\hat{R} = R$:

1. **m-step**: Perform $\hat{R} = SVD\left(\hat{R}\right)$

2. **e-step**: $\hat{r}_{ij} = \begin{cases} r_{ij} \text{ if } r_{ij} \text{ is filled by the user} \\ \quad \hat{r}_{ij} \text{ else (missing data)} \end{cases}$

This procedure is repeated until the sum of squared errors $\sum_{ij}\left(r_{ij} - \hat{r}_{ij}\right)^2$ is less than a chosen tolerance. The code that implements this algorithm and the simple SVD factorization is as follows:

```
In [14]: from sklearn.decomposition import TruncatedSVD
         def SVD(Umatrix,K,inp='none'):
             R_tmp = copy.copy(Umatrix)
             R_tmp = R_tmp.astype(float)
             #imputation
             if inp != 'none':
                 R_tmp = imputation(inp,Umatrix)

             means = np.array([ R_tmp[i][R_tmp[i]>0].mean() for i in xrange(len(R_tmp))]).reshape(-1,1)
             R_tmp = R_tmp-means
             svd = TruncatedSVD(n_components=K, random_state=4)
             R_k = svd.fit_transform(R_tmp)
             R_tmp = svd.inverse_transform(R_k)
             R_tmp = means+R_tmp

             return np.round(R_tmp,0)

In [15]: def SVD_EM(Umatrix,K,inp='none',iterations=50,tol=0.001):
             R_tmp = copy.copy(Umatrix)
             R_tmp = R_tmp.astype(float)
             nrows = len(Umatrix)
             ncols = len(Umatrix[0])
             #imputation
             if inp != 'none':
                 R_tmp = imputation(inp,Umatrix)
             #define svd
             svd = TruncatedSVD(n_components=K, random_state=4)
             err = -1
             for it in xrange(iterations):
                 #m-step
                 R_k = svd.fit_transform(R_tmp)
                 R_tmp = svd.inverse_transform(R_k)
                 #e-step and error evaluation
                 err = 0
                 for i in xrange(nrows):
                     for j in xrange(ncols):
                         if Umatrix[i][j]>0:
                             err += pow(Umatrix[i][j]-R_tmp[i][j],2)
                             R_tmp[i][j] = Umatrix[i][j]

                 if err < tol:
                     print it,'toll reached!'
                     break
             return np.round(R_tmp,0)
```

Note that the SVD is given by the `sklearn` library and both imputation average methods (user ratings' average and item ratings' average) have been implemented, although the function default is *none*, which means that the zero values are left as initial values. For the expect-maximization SVD, the other default parameters are the convergence tolerance (0.0001) and the maximum number of iterations (10,000). This method (especially with expectation-maximization) is slower than the ALS, but the accuracy is generally higher. Also note that the SVD method decomposes the utility matrix subtracted by the user ratings' mean since this approach usually performs better (the user ratings' mean is then added after the SVD matrix has been computed).

We finish remarking that SVD factorization can also be used in memory-based CF to compare users or items in the reduced space (matrix U or V^T) and then the ratings are taken from the original utility matrix (SVD with k-NN approach).

CBF methods

This class of method relies on the data that describes the items, which is then used to extract the features of the users. In our MovieLens example, each movie j has a set of G binary fields to indicate if it belongs to one of the following genres: unknown, action, adventure, animation, children's, comedy, crime, documentary, drama, fantasy, film noir, horror, musical, mystery, romance, sci-fi, thriller, war, or western.

Based on these features (genres), each movie is described by a binary vector m_j with G dimensions (number of movie genres) with entries equal to 1 for all the genres contained in movie j, or 0 otherwise. Given the `dataframe` that stores the utility matrix called `dfout` in the *Utility matrix* section mentioned earlier, these binary vectors m_j are collected from the MoviesLens `database` into a dataframe using the following script:

```
In [ ]:  #matrix movies's content
         movieslist = [int(m.split(';')[-1]) for m in dfout.columns[1:]]
         moviescats = ['unknown','Action','Adventure','Animation','Children\'s','Comedy','Crime','Documentary',
                       'Drama','Fantasy','Film-Noir','Horror','Musical','Mystery',
                       'Romance','Sci-Fi','Thriller','War','Western']
         dfout_movies = pd.DataFrame(columns=['movie_id']+moviescats)
         startcatsindx = 5
         cnt= 0
         for m in movieslist:
             dfout_movies.loc[cnt] = [m]+df_info.iloc[m-1][startcatsindx:].tolist()
             cnt +=1
         print dfout_movies.head()

         dfout_movies.to_csv('data/movies_content.csv',index=None)
```

The movies content matrix has been saved in the `movies_content.csv` file ready to be used by the CBF methods.

The goal of the content-based recommendation system is to generate the user's profile with the same fields to indicate how much the user likes each genre. The problem with this method is that the content description of the item is not always available, so it is not always possible to employ this technique in the e-commerce environment. The advantage is that the recommendations to a specific user are independent of the other users' ratings, so it does not suffer from cold start problems due to an insufficient number of users' ratings for particular items. Two approaches are going to be discussed to find the best recommendation methodologies. The first methodology simply generates the user's profile associated with the average ratings of the movies seen by each user to each genre and the cosine similarity is used to find the movies most similar to the user preferences. The second methodology is a regularized linear regression model to generate the user's profile features from the ratings and the movie features so that the ratings of the movies not yet seen by each user can be predicted using these users' profiles.

Item features average method

The approach is really simple and we are going to explain it using the features that describe the movies in the MovieLens example, as discussed previously. The objective of the method is to generate the movie genres' preferences vector $v_i = (v_{i0}, \ldots, v_{iG-1})$ for each user i (length equal to G). This is done by calculating the average rating $\overline{r_i}$ and each genre entry g; v_{ig} is given by the sum of ratings of the movies seen by user i (Mi) containing the genre g, minus the average $\overline{r_i}$ and divided by the number of movies containing genre g:

$$v_{ig} = \frac{\sum_{k=0}^{M_i} \left(r_{ik} - \overline{r_i} \right) I_{kg}}{\sum_{k=0}^{M_i} I_{kg}}$$

Here, I_{kg} is 1 if the movie k contains genre g; otherwise it is 0.

The vectors v_i are then compared to the binary vectors m_j using the cosine similarity and the movies with the highest similarity values are recommended to the user i. The implementation of the method is given by the following Python class:

```
In [16]: class CBF_averageprofile(object):
             def __init__(self,Movies,Movieslist):
                 #calc user profiles:
                 self.nfeatures = len(Movies[0])
                 self.Movieslist = Movieslist
                 self.Movies = Movies

             def GetRecMovies(self,u_vec,indxs=False):
                 #generate user profile
                 nmovies = len(u_vec)
                 nfeatures = self.nfeatures
                 mean_u = u_vec[u_vec>0].mean()
                 diff_u = u_vec-mean_u
                 features_u = np.zeros(nfeatures).astype(float)
                 cnts = np.zeros(nfeatures)
                 for m in xrange(nmovies):
                     if u_vec[m]>0:#u has rated m
                         features_u += self.Movies[m]*(diff_u[m])
                         cnts += self.Movies[m]
                 #average:
                 for m in xrange(nfeatures):
                     if cnts[m]>0:
                         features_u[m] = features_u[m]/float(cnts[m])

                 #calc sim:
                 sims = np.zeros(nmovies)
                 for m in xrange(nmovies):
                     if u_vec[m]==0:#sim only for movies not yet rated by the user
                         sims[m] = sim(features_u,self.Movies[m])
                 #order movies
                 order_movies_indxs = np.argsort(sims)[::-1]
                 if indxs:
                     return order_movies_indxs
                 return self.Movieslist[order_movies_indxs]
```

The constructor stores the list of the movie titles in Movieslist and the movie features in the Movies vector, and the GetRecMovies function generates the user genres' preferences vector, that is, v_i (applying the preceding formula) called features_u, and returns the most similar items to this vector.

Regularized linear regression method

The method learns the movie preferences of the users as parameters $\theta_i \in 0, \ldots, N-1$ of a linear model, with $\theta_i \in R^{G+1} : \theta_{i0} = 1$, where N is the number of users and G is the number of features (movie genres) of each item. We add an intercept value on the user parameters θ_i ($\theta_{i0} = 1$) and also the movie vector m_j that has the same value $m_{j0}=1$, and so $m_j \in R^{G+1}$. To learn the vectors of parameters q_i, we solve the following regularized minimization problem:

$$\min_{\theta_0, \ldots, \theta_{N-1}} \frac{1}{2} \sum_{i=0}^{N-1} \sum_{j=0}^{M-1} \left(\theta_i^T m_j - r_{ij} \right)^2 I_{ij} + \frac{\lambda}{2} \sum_{i=0}^{N-1} \sum_{k=0}^{G-1} \theta_{ik}^2$$

Here, I_{ij} is 1; that is, user i watched the movie, otherwise j is 0 and λ is the regularization parameter (see *Chapter 3, Supervised Machine Learning*).

The solution is given by applying gradient descent (see *Chapter 3, Supervised Machine Learning*). For each user i:

- $\theta_{i0} = \theta_{i0} - \alpha \sum_{j=0}^{M-1} \left(\theta_i^T m_j - r_{ij} \right) m_{j0} I_{ij}$ (k=0)

- $\theta_{ik} = \theta_{ik} - \alpha \left(\sum_{j=0}^{M-1} \left(\theta_i^T m_j - r_{ij} \right) m_{j0} I_{ij} \right) m_{j0} I_{ij} + \lambda \theta_{ik}$ (k>0)

Since we are adding 1 entry to the movie and user vectors respectively, the distinction between learning the intercept parameter (*k=0*) and the others is necessary (there is no possibility of overfitting on the intercept, so no need to regularize on it). After the parameters θ_i are learned, the recommendation is performed by simply applying for any missing rating r_{ij} in the formula $r_{ij} = \theta_i^T m_j$.

The method is implemented by the following code:

```
In [35]: class CBF_regression(object):
             def __init__(self,Movies,Umatrix,alpha=0.01,l=0.0001,its=50,tol=0.001):
                 #calc parameters:
                 self.nfeatures = len(Movies[0])+1#intercept
                 nusers = len(Umatrix)
                 nmovies = len(Umatrix[0])
                 #add intercept col
                 movies_feats = np.ones((nmovies,self.nfeatures))
                 movies_feats[:,1:] = Movies
                 self.movies_feats = movies_feats.astype(float)

                 #set Umatrix as float
                 self.Umatrix = Umatrix.astype(float)
                 #initialize the matrix:
                 Pmatrix = np.random.rand(nusers,self.nfeatures)
                 Pmatrix[:,0]=1.
                 err = 0.
                 cost = -1
                 for it in xrange(its):
                     print 'it:',it,' -- ',cost
                     for u in xrange(nusers):
                         for f in xrange(self.nfeatures):
                             if f==0:#no regularization
                                 for m in xrange(nmovies):
                                     if self.Umatrix[u,m]>0:
                                         diff = np.dot(Pmatrix[u],self.movies_feats[m])-self.Umatrix[u,m]
                                         Pmatrix[u,f] += -alpha*(diff*self.movies_feats[m][f])
                             else:
                                 for m in xrange(nmovies):
                                     if self.Umatrix[u,m]>0:
                                         diff = np.dot(Pmatrix[u],self.movies_feats[m])-self.Umatrix[u,m]
                                         Pmatrix[u,f] += -alpha*(diff*self.movies_feats[m][f] +l*Pmatrix[u][f])

                     cost = 0
                     for u in xrange(nusers):
                         for m in xrange(nmovies):
                             if self.Umatrix[u][m]>0:
                                 cost += 0.5*pow(Umatrix[u][m]-np.dot(Pmatrix[u],self.movies_feats[m]),2)
                         for f in xrange(1,self.nfeatures):
                             cost += float(1/2.0)*(pow(Pmatrix[u][f],2))
                     if cost < tol:
                         print 'err',cost
                         break
                 self.Pmatrix = Pmatrix

             def CalcRatings(self,u_vec):
                 #find u_vec
                 s = 0.
                 u_feats = np.zeros(len(self.Pmatrix[0]))
                 #in case the user is not present in the utility matrix find the most similar
                 for u in xrange(len(self.Umatrix)):
                     #print self.Umatrix[u]
                     tmps = sim(self.Umatrix[u],u_vec)
                     if tmps > s:
                         s = tmps
                         u_feats = self.Pmatrix[u]
                     if s == 1.:
                         break
                 new_vec = np.zeros(len(u_vec))
                 for r in xrange(len(u_vec)):
                     if u_vec[r]==0:
                         new_vec[r] = np.dot(u_feats,self.movies_feats[r])
                 return new_vec
```

The constructor of the class CBF_regression just performs the gradient descent to find the parameters θ_i (called Pmatrix) while the function CalcRatings finds the most similar rating vector in the stored utility matrix R (in case the user is not present in the utility matrix) and then it uses the corresponding parameters' vector to predict the missing ratings.

Association rules for learning recommendation system

Although this method is not used often in many commercial recommendation systems, association rules learning is certainly a method worth knowing about because of historical data reasons, and it can be employed to solve a wide range of problems in real-world examples. The main concept of this method is to find relationships among items based on some statistical measure of the occurrences of the items in the database of transactions T (for example, a transaction could be the movies seen by a user i or the products bought by i). More formally, a rule could be *{item1,item2} => {item3}*, that is, a set of items *({item1,item2})* implies the presence of another set *({item3})*. Two definitions are used to characterize each $X=>Y$ rule:

- **Support**: Given a set of items X, the support *supp(X)* is the portion of transactions that contains the set X over the total transactions.

- **Confidence**: It is the fraction of transactions that contains the set X that also contains the set Y: *conf(X=>Y)=supp(X U Y)/supp(X)*. Note that the confidence *conf(X=>Y)* can have a very different value than *conf(Y=>X)*.

Support represents the frequency of a certain rule on the transaction database, while the confidence indicates the probability that set Y will occur if set X is present. In other words, the support value is chosen to filter the number of rules we want to mine from the database (the higher the support, the fewer rules will satisfy the condition), while the confidence can be thought of as a *similarity* metric between sets X and Y. In the case of the movie recommendation system, the transaction database can be generated from the utility matrix R considering the movies each user likes, and we look for rules composed by sets X and Y that contain only one item (movie). These rules are collected in a matrix, `ass_matrix`, in which each entry *ass_matrixij* represents the confidence of the rule $i =>j$. The recommendations for the given user are obtained by simply multiplying the `ass_matrix` by his ratings `u_vec`: *recitems = u vec · ass matrix* , and sorting all the values *recitems* by the largest value corresponding to the most recommended movie to the least. Therefore, this method does not predict the ratings, but the list of movie recommendations; however, it is fast and it also works well with a sparse utility matrix. Note that to find all the possible combinations of items to form sets X and Y as fast as possible, two algorithms have been developed in the literature: *apriori* and *fp-growth* (not discussed here since we only require rules with one item per set X and Y).

The class that implements the method is as follows:

```
In [36]: class AssociationRules(object):
             def __init__(self,Umatrix,Movieslist,min_support=0.1,min_confidence=0.1,likethreshold=3):
                 self.min_support = min_support
                 self.min_confidence = min_confidence
                 self.Movieslist = Movieslist
                 #transform utility matrix to sets of liked items
                 nitems = len(Umatrix[0])
                 transactions = []
                 for u in Umatrix:
                     s = [i for i in xrange(len(u)) if u[i]>likethreshold]
                     if len(s)>0:
                         transactions.append(s)
                 #find sets of 2 items
                 flat = [item for sublist in transactions for item in sublist]
                 inititems = map(frozenset,[ [item] for item in frozenset(flat)])
                 set_trans = map(set, transactions)
                 sets_init, self.dict_sets_support = self.filterSet(set_trans, inititems)
                 setlen = 2
                 items_tmp = self.combine_lists(sets_init, setlen)
                 self.freq_sets, sup_tmp = self.filterSet(set_trans, items_tmp)
                 self.dict_sets_support.update(sup_tmp)
                 self.ass_matrix = np.zeros((nitems,nitems))
                 for freqset in self.freq_sets:
                     #print 'freqset',freqset
                     list_setitems = [frozenset([item]) for item in freqset]
                     #print "freqSet", freqset, 'H1', list_setitems
                     self.calc_confidence_matrix(freqset, list_setitems)

             def filterSet(self,set_trans, likeditems):
                 itemscnt = {}
                 for id in set_trans:
                     for item in likeditems:
                         if item.issubset(id):
                             itemscnt.setdefault(item, 0)
                             itemscnt[item] += 1
                 num_items = float(len(set_trans))
                 freq_sets = []
                 dict_sets = {}
                 for key in itemscnt:
                     support = itemscnt[key] / num_items
                     if support >= self.min_support:
                         freq_sets.insert(0, key)
                     dict_sets[key] = support
                 return freq_sets, dict_sets

             def combine_lists(self,freq_sets, setlen):
                 setitems_list = []
                 nsets = len(freq_sets)
                 for i in range(nsets):
                     for j in range(i + 1, nsets):
                         setlist1 = list(freq_sets[i])[:setlen - 2]
                         setlist2 = list(freq_sets[j])[:setlen - 2]
                         if set(setlist1) == set(setlist2):
                             setitems_list.append(freq_sets[i].union(freq_sets[j]))
                 return setitems_list

             def calc_confidence_matrix(self,freqset, list_setitems):
                 for target in list_setitems:
                     confidence = self.dict_sets_support[freqset] / self.dict_sets_support[freqset - target]
                     if confidence >= self.min_confidence:
                         self.ass_matrix[list(freqset - target)[0]][list(target)[0]] = confidence

             def GetRecItems(self,u_vec,indxs=False):
                 vec_recs = np.dot(u_vec,self.ass_matrix)
                 sortedweight = np.argsort(vec_recs)
                 seenindxs = [indx for indx in xrange(len(u_vec)) if u_vec[indx]>0]
                 seenmovies = np.array(self.Movieslist)[seenindxs]
                 #remove seen items
                 recitems = np.array(self.Movieslist)[sortedweight]
                 recitems = [m for m in recitems if m not in seenmovies]
                 if indxs:
                     vec_recs[seenindxs]=-1
                     recsvec = np.argsort(vec_recs)[::-1][np.argsort(vec_recs)>0]
                     return recsvec
                 return recitems[::-1]
```

The class constructor takes as input parameters the utility matrix `Umatrix`, the movie titles list `Movieslist`, the support `min_support`, confidence `min_confidence` thresholds (default `0.1`), and the `likethreshold`, which is the minimum rating value to consider a movie in a transaction (default 3). The function `combine_lists` finds all the possible rules, while `filterSet` just reduces the rules to the subset that satisfies the minimum support threshold. `calc_confidence_matrix` fills the `ass_matrix` with the confidence value that satisfies the minimum threshold (otherwise 0 is set by default) and `GetRecItems` returns the list of recommended movies given the user ratings `u_vec`.

Log-likelihood ratios recommendation system method

The **log-likelihood ratio (LLR)** is a measure of how two events A and B are unlikely to be independent but occur together more than by chance (more than the single event frequency). In other words, the LLR indicates where a significant co-occurrence might exist between two events A and B with a frequency higher than a normal distribution (over the two events variables) would predict.

It has been shown by Ted Dunning (`http://tdunning.blogspot.it/2008/03/surprise-and-coincidence.html`) that the LLR can be expressed based on binomial distributions for events A and B using a matrix k with the following entries:

	A	**Not A**
B	k11	k12
Not B	k21	k22

$$LLR = 2N\left(H\left(\left[k_{11},k_{12},k_{21},k_{22,}\right]\right) - H\left(\left[k_{11},k_{12},k_{21},k_{22,}\right]\right) - \left(\left[k_{11},k_{12},k_{21},k_{22,}\right]\right)\right)$$

Here, $N = k_{11} + k_{12} + k_{21} + k_{22}$ and $H(p) = \sum_{i=0}^{len(p)} p_i / N \log(p_i / N)$ is the **Shannon** entropy that measures the information contained in the vector p.

Note: $H\left(\left[k_{11},k_{12},k_{21},k_{22}\right]\right) - H\left(\left[k_{11}+k_{12}+k_{21}+k_{22}\right]\right) - H\left(\left[k_{11}+k_{21}+k_{12}+k_{22}\right]\right)$ is also called the **Mutual Information (MI)** of the two event variables A and B, measuring how the occurrence of the two events depend on each other.

This test is also called *G2*, and it has been proven effective to detect co-occurrence of rare events (especially in text analysis), so it's useful with sparse databases (or a utility matrix, in our case).

In our case, the events *A* and *B* are the like or dislike of two movies *A* and *B* by a user, where the event of *like a movie* is defined when the rating is greater than 3 (and vice versa for dislike). Therefore, the implementation of the algorithm is given by the following class:

```python
In [19]: class LogLikelihood(object):
    def __init__(self,Umatrix,Movieslist,likethreshold=3):
        self.Movieslist = Movieslist
        #calculate loglikelihood ratio for each pair
        self.nusers = len(Umatrix)
        self.Umatrix =Umatrix
        self.likethreshold = likethreshold
        self.likerange = range(self.likethreshold+1,5+1)
        self.dislikerange = range(1,self.likethreshold+1)
        self.loglikelihood_ratio()

    def calc_k(self,a,b):
        tmpk = [[0 for j in range(2)] for i in range(2)]
        for ratings in self.Umatrix:
            if ratings[a] in self.likerange and ratings[b] in self.likerange:
                tmpk[0][0] += 1
            if ratings[a] in self.likerange and ratings[b] in self.dislikerange:
                tmpk[0][1] += 1
            if ratings[a] in self.dislikerange and ratings[b] in self.likerange:
                tmpk[1][0] += 1
            if ratings[a] in self.dislikerange and ratings[b] in self.dislikerange:
                tmpk[1][1] += 1
        return tmpk

    def calc_llr(self,k_matrix):
        Hcols=Hrows=Htot=0.0
        if sum(k_matrix[0])+sum(k_matrix[1])==0:
            return 0.
        invN = 1.0/(sum(k_matrix[0])+sum(k_matrix[1]))
        for i in range(0,2):
            if((k_matrix[0][i]+k_matrix[1][i])!=0.0):
                Hcols += invN*(k_matrix[0][i]+k_matrix[1][i])*math.log((k_matrix[0][i]+k_matrix[1][i])*invN )#sum of row
            if((k_matrix[i][0]+k_matrix[i][1])!=0.0):
                Hrows += invN*(k_matrix[i][0]+k_matrix[i][1])*math.log((k_matrix[i][0]+k_matrix[i][1])*invN )#sum of col
            for j in range(0,2):
                if(k_matrix[i][j]!=0.0):
                    Htot +=invN*k_matrix[i][j]*math.log(invN*k_matrix[i][j])
        return 2.0*(Htot-Hcols-Hrows)/invN

    def loglikelihood_ratio(self):
        nitems = len(self.Movieslist)
        self.items_llr= pd.DataFrame(np.zeros((nitems,nitems))).astype(float)
        for i in xrange(nitems):
            for j in xrange(nitems):
                if(j>=i):
                    tmpk=self.calc_k(i,j)
                    self.items_llr.ix[i,j] = self.calc_llr(tmpk)
                else:
                    self.items_llr.ix[i,j] = self.items_llr.iat[j,i]

    def GetRecItems(self,u_vec,indxs=False):
        items_weight = np.dot(u_vec,self.items_llr)
        sortedweight = np.argsort(items_weight)
        seenindxs = [indx for indx in xrange(len(u_vec)) if u_vec[indx]>0]
        seenmovies = np.array(self.Movieslist)[seenindxs]
        #remove seen items
        recitems = np.array(self.Movieslist)[sortedweight]
        recitems = [m for m in recitems if m not in seenmovies]
        if indxs:
            items_weight[seenindxs]=-1
            recsvec = np.argsort(items_weight)[::-1][np.argsort(items_weight)>0]
            return recsvec
        return recitems[::-1]
```

The constructor takes as input the utility matrix, the movie titles list, and the `likethreshold` that is used to define if a user likes a movie or not (default 3). The function `loglikelihood_ratio` generates the matrix with all the LLR values for each pair of movies *i* and *j* calculating the matrix *k* (`calc_k`) and the corresponding LLR (`calc_llr`). The function `GetRecItems` returns the recommended movie list for the user with ratings given by `u_vec` (the method does not predict the rating values).

Hybrid recommendation systems

This is a class of methods that combine both CBF and CF in a single recommender to achieve better results. Several approaches have been tried and can be summarized in the following categories:

- **Weighted**: The CBF and CF predicted ratings are combined in to some weighted mean.

- **Mixed**: CF and CBF predicted movies are found separately and then merged in to a single list.

- **Switched**: Based on certain criteria, the CF predictions or CBF predictions are used.

- **Feature combination**: CF and CBF features are considered together to find the most similar users or items.

- **Feature augmentation**: Similar to feature combination, but the additional features are used to predict some ratings and then the main recommender uses these ratings to produce the recommendation list. For example, Content-Boosted Collaborative Filtering learns the ratings of unrated movies by a content-based model and then a collaborative approach is employed to define the recommendations.

As an example, we implement two hybrid feature combination methods merging an item's features CBF method with a user-based CF method. The first method employs a user-based CF to the expanded utility matrix that now also contains the average rating per genre per user. The Python class is as follows:

```
In [37]: class Hybrid_cbf_cf(object):
          def __init__(self,Movies,Movieslist,Umatrix):
              #calc user profiles:
              self.nfeatures = len(Movies[0])
              self.Movieslist = Movieslist
              self.Movies = Movies.astype(float)
              self.Umatrix_mfeats = np.zeros((len(Umatrix),len(Umatrix[0])+self.nfeatures))
              means = np.array([ Umatrix[i][Umatrix[i]>0].mean() for i in xrange(len(Umatrix))]).reshape(-1,1)
              diffs = np.array([ [Umatrix[i][j]-means[i] if Umatrix[i][j]>0 else 0.
                                 for j in xrange(len(Umatrix[i]))  ] for i in xrange(len(Umatrix))])
              self.Umatrix_mfeats[:,:len(Umatrix[0])] = Umatrix#diffs
              self.nmovies = len(Movies)
              #calc item features for each user
              for u in xrange(len(Umatrix)):
                  u_vec = Umatrix[u]
                  self.Umatrix_mfeats[u,len(Umatrix[0]):] = self.GetUserItemFeatures(u_vec)

          def GetUserItemFeatures(self,u_vec):
              mean_u = u_vec[u_vec>0].mean()
              #diff_u = u_vec-mean_u
              features_u = np.zeros(self.nfeatures).astype(float)
              cnts = np.zeros(self.nfeatures)
              for m in xrange(self.nmovies):
                  if u_vec[m]>0:#u has rated m
                      features_u += self.Movies[m]*u_vec[m]#self.Movies[m]*(diff_u[m])
                      cnts += self.Movies[m]
              #average:
              for m in xrange(self.nfeatures):
                  if cnts[m]>0:
                      features_u[m] = features_u[m]/float(cnts[m])
              return features_u

          def CalcRating(u_vec,r,neighs):
              rating = 0.
              den = 0.
              for j in xrange(len(neighs)):
                  rating += neighs[j][-1]*float(neighs[j][r]-neighs[j][neighs[j]>0][:-1].mean())
                  den += abs(neighs[j][-1])
              if den>0:
                  rating = np.round(u_vec[u_vec>0].mean()+(rating/den),0)
              else:
                  rating = np.round(u_vec[u_vec>0].mean(),0)
              if rating>5:
                  return 5.
              elif rating<1:
                  return 1.
              return rating
          #add similarity col
          nrows = len(self.Umatrix_mfeats)
          ncols = len(self.Umatrix_mfeats[0])
          data_sim = np.zeros((nrows,ncols+1))
          data_sim[:,:-1] = self.Umatrix_mfeats
          u_rec = np.zeros(len(u_vec))
          #calc similarities:
          mean = u_vec[u_vec>0].mean()
          u_vec_feats = u_vec#np.array([u_vec[i]-mean if u_vec[i]>0 else 0 for i in xrange(len(u_vec))])
          u_vec_feats = np.append(u_vec_feats,self.GetUserItemFeatures(u_vec))
```

```
for u in xrange(nrows):
    if np.array_equal(data_sim[u,:-1],u_vec)==False: #list(data_sim[u,:-1]) != list(u_vec):
        data_sim[u,ncols] = sim(data_sim[u,:-1],u_vec_feats)
    else:
        data_sim[u,ncols] = 0.
#order by similarity:
data_sim[:,:-1] = self.Umatrix_mfeats
u_rec = np.zeros(len(u_vec))
#calc similarities:
mean = u_vec[u_vec>0].mean()
u_vec_feats = u_vec#np.array([u_vec[i]-mean if u_vec[i]>0 else 0 for i in xrange(len(u_vec))])
u_vec_feats = np.append(u_vec_feats,self.GetUserItemFeatures(u_vec))

for u in xrange(nrows):
    if np.array_equal(data_sim[u,:-1],u_vec)==False: #list(data_sim[u,:-1]) != list(u_vec):
        data_sim[u,ncols] = sim(data_sim[u,:-1],u_vec_feats)
    else:
        data_sim[u,ncols] = 0.
#order by similarity:
data_sim =data_sim[data_sim[:,ncols].argsort()][::-1]
#find the K users for each item not rated:

for r in xrange(self.nmovies):
    if u_vec[r]==0:
        neighs = FindKNeighbours(r,data_sim,K)
        #calc the predicted rating
        u_rec[r] = CalcRating(u_vec,r,neighs)
return u_rec
```

The constructor generates the expanded utility matrix with the movies' genres average rating features associated to each user, `Umatrix_mfeats`. The function `CalcRatings` finds the K-NN using the Pearson correlation comparing the expanded feature vectors of the users. The second method applies and SVD factorization to the expanded utility matrix that contains the genre preferences for each user.

```
In [22]: class Hybrid_svd(object):
            def __init__(self,Movies,Movieslist,Umatrix,K,inp):
                #calc user profiles:
                self.nfeatures = len(Movies[0])
                self.Movieslist = Movieslist
                self.Movies = Movies.astype(float)

                R_tmp = copy.copy(Umatrix)
                R_tmp = R_tmp.astype(float)
                #imputation

                if inp != 'none':
                    R_tmp = imputation(inp,Umatrix)
                Umatrix_mfeats = np.zeros((len(Umatrix),len(Umatrix[0])+self.nfeatures))
                means = np.array([ Umatrix[i][Umatrix[i]>0].mean() for i in xrange(len(Umatrix))]).reshape(-1,1)
                diffs = np.array([ [float(Umatrix[i][j]-means[i])
                                 if Umatrix[i][j]>0 else float(R_tmp[i][j]-means[i]) for j in xrange(len(Umatrix[i]))  ]
                                 for i in xrange(len(Umatrix))])
                Umatrix_mfeats[:,:len(Umatrix[0])] = diffs#R_tmp
                self.nmovies = len(Movies)
                #calc item features for each user
                for u in xrange(len(Umatrix)):
                    u_vec = Umatrix[u]
                    Umatrix_mfeats[u,len(Umatrix[0]):] = self.GetUserItemFeatures(u_vec)

                #calc svd
                svd = TruncatedSVD(n_components=K, random_state=4)
                R_k = svd.fit_transform(Umatrix_mfeats)
                R_tmp = means+svd.inverse_transform(R_k)
                self.matrix = np.round(R_tmp[:,:self.nmovies],0)

            def GetUserItemFeatures(self,u_vec):
                mean_u = u_vec[u_vec>0].mean()
                diff_u = u_vec-mean_u
                features_u = np.zeros(self.nfeatures).astype(float)
                cnts = np.zeros(self.nfeatures)
                for m in xrange(self.nmovies):
                    if u_vec[m]>0:#u has rated m
                        features_u += self.Movies[m]*(diff_u[m])#self.Movies[m]*u_vec[m]
                        cnts += self.Movies[m]
                #average:
                for m in xrange(self.nfeatures):
                    if cnts[m]>0:
                        features_u[m] = features_u[m]/float(cnts[m])
                return features_u
```

As the SVD method, the ratings are subtracted with the user rating's average, and genre preferences are subtracted from the same user rating's average.

Evaluation of the recommendation systems

We have discussed all of the most relevant methods used in the commercial environment to date. The evaluation of a recommendation system can be executed offline (using only the data in the utility matrix) or online (using the utility matrix data and the new data provided in real time by each user using the website). The online evaluation procedures are discussed in *Chapter 7, Movie Recommendation System Web Application*, together with a proper online movie recommendation system website. In this section, we will evaluate the performances of the methods using two offline tests often used to evaluate recommendation systems: root mean square error on ratings and ranking accuracy. For all the evaluations in which k-fold cross-validation (see *Chapter 3, Supervised Machine Learning*) is applicable, a 5-fold cross-validation has been performed to obtain more objective results. The utility matrix has been divided in to 5 folds using the following function:

```
In [42]: def cross_validation(df,k):
             val_num = int(len(df)/float(k))
             print val_num
             df_trains = []
             df_vals = []
             for i in xrange(k):
                 start_val = (k-i-1)*val_num
                 end_val = start_val+val_num
                 df_trains.append(pd.concat([df[:start_val],df[end_val:]]))
                 df_vals.append(df[start_val:end_val])

             return df_trains,df_vals
```

Here df is a data frame object that stores the utility matrix and *k* is the number of folds. In the validation set, for each user ratings' vector u_vec, half of the ratings have been hidden so that the real value can be predicted.

```
In [23]: import random
         def HideRandomRatings(u_vec, ratiovals=0.5):
             u_test = np.zeros(len(u_vec))
             u_vals = np.zeros(len(u_vec))
             cnt = 0
             nratings = len(u_vec[u_vec>0])
             for i in xrange(len(u_vec)):
                 if u_vec[i]>0:
                     if bool(random.getrandbits(1)) or cnt>=int(nratings*ratiovals):
                         u_test[i]=u_vec[i]
                     else:#random choice to hide the rating:
                         cnt +=1
                         u_vals[i]=u_vec[i]
             return u_test,u_vals
```

`u_vals` stores the values to predict while `u_test` contains the ratings for testing the algorithms. Before we start to compare the different algorithms with the different measures, we load the utility matrix and the movie content matrix into data frames and split the data into 5 folds for cross-validation.

```
In [24]:  #load data
          df = pd.read_csv('data/utilitymatrix.csv')
          print df.head(4)
          df_movies = pd.read_csv('data/movies_content.csv')
          movies = df_movies.values[:,1:]
          print 'check:::',len(df.columns[1:]),'--',len(df_movies)
          movieslist = list(df.columns[1:])
          #k-fold cv 5 folds
          nfolds = 5
          df_trains,df_vals = cross_validation(df,nfolds)
```

`df_vals` contains the validation sets so the `HideRandomRatings` function presented in this section needs to be applied.

```
In [31]:  nmovies = len(df_vals[0].values[:,1:][0])
          s = []
          tests_vecs_folds = []
          for i in xrange(nfolds):
              u_vecs = df_vals[i].values[:,1:]
              vtests = np.empty((0,nmovies),float)
              vvals = np.empty((0,nmovies),float)
              for u_vec in u_vecs:
                  u_test,u_vals = HideRandomRatings(u_vec)
                  vvals = np.vstack([vvals,u_vals])
                  vtests = np.vstack([vtests,u_test])
              vals_vecs_folds.append(vvals)
              tests_vecs_folds.append(vtests)
```

The data available in the `movies` matrix, the `movieslist` list, and the data frames `df_trains`, `vals_vecs_folds`, `tests_vecs_folds` are now ready to be used for training and validating all the methods discussed in the previous sections. We can start evaluating the **root mean square error (RMSE)**.

Root mean square error (RMSE) evaluation

This validation technique is applicable only on CF methods and linear regression CBF since the predicted ratings are generated only by these algorithms. Given each rating *rij* in u_vals in the validation sets, the predicted rating $\hat{r}_{ij}$ is calculated using each method and the root mean square error is obtained:

$$RMSE = \sqrt{\frac{\sum\limits_{i,j \in u\_vals} \left(r_{ij} - \hat{r}_{ij} \right)^2}{N_{val}}}$$

Here, *Nval* is the number of ratings in the u_vals vectors. The presence of the square factor in this formula highly penalizes the large errors, so the methods with low RMSE (best values) are characterized by small errors spread over all the predicted ratings instead of large errors on few ratings, like the mean absolute error MAE=

$$\frac{\sum\limits_{i,j \in u\_vals} \left| r_{ij} - \hat{r}_{ij} \right|}{N_{val}}$$ would prefer.

The code to calculate the RMSE for the memory-based CF user-based and item-based methods is as follows:

```
In [43]: def SE(u_preds,u_vals):
             nratings = len(u_vals)
             se = 0.
             cnt = 0
             for i in xrange(nratings):
                 if u_vals[i]>0:
                     se +=  (u_vals[i]-u_preds[i])*(u_vals[i]-u_preds[i])
                     cnt += 1
             return se,cnt
```

```
In [40]: err_itembased = 0.
         cnt_itembased = 0
         err_userbased = 0.
         cnt_userbased = 0
         err_slopeone = 0.
         cnt_slopeone = 0
         err_cbfcf = 0.
         cnt_cbfcf = 0
         for i in xrange(nfolds):
             Umatrix = df_trains[i].values[:,1:]
             cfitembased = CF_itembased(Umatrix)
             cfslopeone = SlopeOne(Umatrix)
             cbfcf = Hybrid_cbf_cf(movies,movieslist,Umatrix)
             print 'fold:',i+1
             vec_vals = vals_vecs_folds[i]
             vec_tests = tests_vecs_folds[i]
             for j in xrange(len(vec_vals)):
                 u_vals = vec_vals[j]
                 u_test = vec_tests[j]
                 #cbfcf
                 u_preds = cbfcf.CalcRatings(u_test,5)
                 e,c =  SE(u_preds,u_vals)
                 err_cbfcf +=e
                 cnt_cbfcf +=c
                 #cf_userbased
                 u_preds = CF_userbased(u_test,5,Umatrix)
                 e,c =  SE(u_preds,u_vals)
                 err_userbased +=e
                 cnt_userbased +=c
                 #cf_itembased
                 u_preds = cfitembased.CalcRatings(u_test,5)
                 e,c =  SE(u_preds,u_vals)
                 err_itembased +=e
                 cnt_itembased +=c
                 #slope one
                 u_preds = cfslopeone.CalcRatings(u_test,5)
                 e,c =  SE(u_preds,u_vals)
                 err_slopeone +=e
                 cnt_slopeone +=c
         rmse_userbased = np.sqrt(err_userbased/float(cnt_userbased))
         rmse_itembased = np.sqrt(err_itembased/float(cnt_itembased))
         rmse_slopeone = np.sqrt(err_slopeone/float(cnt_slopeone))
         print 'user_userbased rmse:',rmse_userbased,'--',cnt_userbased
         print 'user_itembased rmse:',rmse_itembased,'--',cnt_itembased
         print 'slope one rmse:',rmse_slopeone,'--',cnt_slopeone

         rmse_cbfcf = np.sqrt(err_cbfcf/float(cnt_cbfcf))
         print 'cbfcf rmse:',rmse_cbfcf,'---',cnt_cbfcf
```

For each method, the SE function is called to compute the error for each fold and then the total RMSE of the folds is obtained.

Using 5 nearest-neighbors for item-based CF with slope one and 20 for user-based CF, the methods have the following errors:

Method	RMSE	Number of Predicted Ratings
CF user-based	1.01	39,972
CF item-based	1.03	39,972
Slope one	1.08	39,972
CF-CBF user-based	1.01	39,972

All have similar RMSE values but the best method is item-based Collaborative Filtering.

For the model-based methods, instead of not hidden validation ratings, u_test are included in the utility matrix for training and then the RMSE is calculated using the following script:

```
In [63]: err_svd = 0.
         cnt_svd = 0
         err_svd_em = 0.
         cnt_svd_em = 0
         err_als = 0.
         cnt_als = 0
         err_cbfreg = 0.
         cnt_cbfreg = 0
         for i in xrange(nfolds):
             Umatrix = df_trains[i].values[:,1:]
             print 'fold:',i+1
             teststartindx = len(Umatrix)
             vals_vecs = vals_vecs_folds[i]
             tests_vecs = tests_vecs_folds[i]
             for k in xrange(len(vals_vecs)):
                 u_vals = vals_vecs[k]
                 u_test = tests_vecs[k]
                 #add test vector to utility matrix
                 Umatrix = np.vstack([Umatrix,u_test])

             #svd_em_matrix = Hybrid_svd(movies,movieslist,Umatrix,20,'useraverage').matrix#SVD_EM(Umatrix,20,'useraverage',1)
             svd_matrix = SVD(Umatrix,20,'itemaverage')
             cbf_reg = CBF_regression(movies,Umatrix)
             #als_umatrix = SGD(Umatrix,20,50)#ALS(Umatrix,20,50)#NMF_alg(Umatrix,20,'itemaverage',0.001)
             #evaluate errors
             for indx in xrange(len(vals_vecs)):
                 #e,c = SE(als_umatrix[teststartindx+indx],vals_vecs[indx])
                 #err_als += e
                 #cnt_als += c
                 u_preds = cbf_reg.CalcRatings(Umatrix[teststartindx+indx])
                 e,c = SE(u_preds,vals_vecs[indx])
                 err_cbfreg +=e
                 cnt_cbfreg +=c

                 e,c = SE(svd_matrix[teststartindx+indx],vals_vecs[indx])
                 err_svd +=e
                 cnt_svd +=c
                 #e,c = SE(svd_em_matrix[teststartindx+indx],vals_vecs[indx])
                 #err_svd_em +=e
                 #cnt_svd_em +=c

         if cnt_svd==0: cnt_svd=1
         if cnt_svd_em==0: cnt_svd_em=1
         if cnt_als==0: cnt_als=1
         if cnt_cbfreg==0: cnt_cbfreg=1

         rmse_als = np.sqrt(err_als/float(cnt_als))
         rmse_svd = np.sqrt(err_svd/float(cnt_svd))
         rmse_svd_em = np.sqrt(err_svd_em/float(cnt_svd_em))
         rmse_cbfreg = np.sqrt(err_cbfreg/float(cnt_cbfreg))

         print 'svd rmse:',rmse_svd,'--',cnt_svd
         #print 'svd_em rmse:',rmse_svd_em,'--',cnt_svd_em
         #print 'als rmse:',rmse_als,'--',cnt_als
         print 'cbfreg rmse:',rmse_cbfreg,'--',cnt_cbfreg
```

The code calculates the RMSE only for CBF regression and SVD, and the reader can easily replicate the code to calculate the error for the other algorithms since most of the required code is just commented (SVD expect-maximization, SGD, ALS, and NMF). The results are shown in the following table (*K* dimension feature space):

Method	RMSE	Number Predicted Ratings
CBF linear regression (a= 0.01, l =0.0001, its=50)	1.09	39,972
SGD (K=20, 50 its, a =0.00001, l=0.001)	1.35	39,972
ALS (K=20, 50 its, l =0.001)	2.58	39,972
SVD (`imputation=useraverage`, *K*=20)	1.02	39,972
SVD EM (`imputation=itemaverage`, iterations=30,*K*=20)	1.03	39,972
HYBRID SVD (`imputation=useraverage`, *K*=20)	1.01	39,972
NMF (*K*=20 `imputation=useraverage`)	0.97	39,972

As expected, the ALS and SGD are the worst methods but they are discussed because they are instructive from a didactic point of view (they are also slow because the implementation is not as optimized as the methods from `sklearn` library).

All the others have similar results. However, just note that the hybrid methods have slightly better results than the corresponding SVD and CF user-based algorithms. Note that the movies to predict are chosen randomly so the results may vary.

Classification metrics

The rating error RMSE does not really indicate the quality of a method but is an academic measure that is not really used in a commercial environment. The goal of a website is to present content that is relevant to the user regardless of the exact rating the user gives. In order to evaluate the relevance of the recommended items, the `precision`, `recall`, and `f1` (see *Chapter 2, Unsupervised Machine Learning*) measures are used where the correct predictions are the items with ratings greater than 3. These measures are calculated on the first 50 items returned by each algorithm (if the algorithm return a recommended list or the 50 items with the highest predicted ratings for the other methods). The function that calculates the measures is as follows:

```
In [33]:  def ClassificationMetrica(vec_vals,vec_recs,likethreshold=3,shortlist=50,ratingsval=False,vec_test=None):
              #convert vals in indxs vec
              indxs_like = [i for i in xrange(len(vec_vals)) if vec_vals[i]>likethreshold]
              indxs_dislike = [i for i in xrange(len(vec_vals)) if vec_vals[i]<=likethreshold and vec_vals[i]>0]
              cnt = len(indxs_like)+len(indxs_dislike)
              indxs_rec = []
              if ratingsval:
                  #convert ratings into items's list
                  if vec_test==None:
                      raise 'Error no test vector'
                  indxs_rec = [i for i in xrange(len(vec_recs)) if vec_recs[i]>likethreshold and vec_test[i]<1][:shortlist]
              else:
                  #consider only the first slot of recs
                  indxs_rec = vec_recs[:shortlist]

              tp = len(set(indxs_rec).intersection(set(indxs_like)))
              fp = len(set(indxs_rec).intersection(set(indxs_dislike)))
              fn = len(set(indxs_like)^(set(indxs_rec).intersection(set(indxs_like))))
              precision = 0.
              if tp+fp>0:
                  precision = float(tp)/(tp+fp)
              recall = 0.
              if tp+fn>0:
                  recall = float(tp)/(tp+fn)
              f1 = 0.
              if recall+precision >0:
                  f1 = 2.*precision*recall/(precision+recall)

              return np.array([precision,recall,f1]),cnt
```

Here, Boolean `ratingsval` indicates if the method returns ratings or recommended list. We use the function `ClassificationMetrics` in the same way we compute the RMSE for all the methods, so the actual code to evaluate the measures is not shown (you can write it as an exercise). The following table summarizes the results for all the methods (*neighs* is number of nearest-neighbors, *K* dimension feature space):

Method	Precision	Recall	f1	Number of Predicted Ratings
CF user-based (*neighs*=20)	0.6	0.18	0.26	39,786
CBFCF user-based (*neighs*=20)	0.6	0.18	0.26	39,786
HYBRID SVD (*K*=20, imputation=useraverage)	0.54	0.12	0.18	39,786
CF item-based (*neighs*=5)	0.57	0.15	0.22	39,786
Slope one (*neighs*=5)	0.57	0.17	0.24	39,786
SVD EM (*K*=20, iterations=30, imputation=useraverage)	0.58	0.16	0.24	39,786
SVD (*K*=20, imputation=itemaverage)	0.53	0.12	0.18	39,786
CBF regression (a = 0.01, l =0.0001, iterations=50)	0.54	0.13	0.2	39,786
SGD (K=20, a =0.00001, l =0.001)	0.52	0.12	0.18	39,786
ALS (*K*=20, λ =0.001, iterations=50)	0.57	0.15	0.23	39,786
CBF average	0.56	0.12	0.19	39,786

Method	Precision	Recall	f1	Number of Predicted Ratings
LLR	0.63	0.3	0.39	39,786
NMF (*K*=20, λ =0.001, `imputation=ssss`)	0.53	0.13	0.19	39,786
Association rules	0.68	0.31	0.4	39,786

From the results you can see that the best method is association rules, and there is good precision also for the LLR, hybrid CBFCF user-based, and CF user-based methods. Note that the results may vary since the movies to predict have been randomly chosen.

Summary

In this chapter, we discussed the most commonly used recommendation system methods from Collaborative Filtering and content-based filtering to two simple hybrid algorithms. Note also that in the literature are present *modal* recommendation systems in which different data (user gender, demographics, views, locations, devices, and so on) are incorporated in to the same algorithm. These methods are more advanced and more different data is needed to use them.

In *Chapter 7, Movie Recommendation System Web Application,* we will implement a web recommendation system using the methods discussed in this chapter, but before that we will present the Django framework to build web applications in *Chapter 6, Getting Started with Django.*

6
Getting Started with Django

Django is an open source web framework employed in commercial environments because it is easy to use, stable, and flexible (it takes advantage of the multiple libraries available in Python).

In this chapter, we will focus on the features that we think are crucial for managing and analyzing data in the framework. We also explain the main parts relevant to building an essential web application, but further details and information can be found online at `https://docs.djangoproject.com` or other sources. We will introduce the main parts of the framework with the basic concepts of a web server application (settings, models, and commands), the basics of HTML and the shell interface, and the general ideas of a REST framework interface and how it is implemented in Django (serializers, REST calls, and swagger). After a brief introduction of the HTTP GET and POST method for transferring data over the Internet, we start installing and creating a new server in Django.

HTTP – the basics of the GET and POST methods

Hypertext Transfer Protocol (HTTP) allows a client (for example, the web browser) to interact with a server (our application). Given a URL of a server web page, the GET method is the way the client queries data from the server, specifying some parameters. This can be explained using the `curl` command, as follows:

```
curl -X GET url_path?name1=value1&name2=value2
```

After the ? symbol, the name/value pair specifies which data to query, and they are separated by a & symbol.

The way a client transfers data to the server is called POST, and the data is in the *body* of the call:

```
curl -X POST  -d @datafile.txt url_path
```

Now we can start discussing how to create a new server and an application using Django.

Installation and server creation

The Django library is installed by typing the following command in the Terminal:

```
sudo pip instal django
```

The command should install Django Version 1.7 or above (the author used version 1.7). In order to start a new app, we type the following command:

```
django-admin startproject test_server
```

It will generate a new folder test_app with the following tree of files:

```
└── test_server
    ├── manage.py
    └── test_server
        ├── __init__.py
        ├── settings.py
        ├── urls.py
        └── wsgi.py
```

We can see that, inside the folder, we have the manage.py file, which allows the programmer to run various actions, and another subfolder, test_app, with the following files:

- settings.py: This stores all the parameters' settings to configure the server
- urls.py: This collects all the URL paths available on your web application, and the actual functions behind the web pages are usually written in the views.py app file
- wsgi.py: This is a module to make a server communicate with a web application
- __init__.py: This file is used to define every folder as a package, to import modules internally

On our local machine, the server with a **Welcome to Django** page is deployed on `http://127.0.0.1:8080/` simply by typing the following command:

```
python manage.py runserver 8080
```

Here, `8080` is the port on which the server is started (if no port is specified, by default the server is started on `port 8000`). Now that the server is ready, we can create as many applications as we want by simply typing the following command:

```
python manage.py startapp nameapp
```

This will create a new folder, `nameapp`, inside the `test_app` folder at root:

```
├── manage.py
├── nameapp
│   ├── __init__.py
│   ├── admin.py
│   ├── migrations
│   ├── __init__.py
│   ├── models.py
│   ├── tests.py
│   └── views.py
└── test_server
    ├── __init__.py
    ├── settings.py
    ├── urls.py
    └── wsgi.py
```

We will discuss the contents of this folder and its functions after we explain the most important settings parameters. Note that for Django Version 1.9, the `nameapp` folder contains the `apps.py` file in order to configure `nameapp` without using the `settings.py` file.

Settings

The `settings.py` file stores all the configurations needed for the Django server to operate. The most important parameters to set are as follows:

- Apart from the common Django apps installed by default to manage a website, we will also install the REST framework:

```
INSTALLED_APPS = (
...
```

```
'rest_framework',
'rest_framework_swagger',
'nameapp',
)
```

The REST framework is an application that allows the Django app (`nameapp` in this case) to communicate through a REST API, and the REST Framework Swagger is just a web interactive interface to manage the REST APIs. These functionalities will be explained in the following sections. Also, note that each app created needs to be added in this field (in this case, `nameapp`).

- Different backend databases (**MySQL**, **Oracle**, **PostgreSQL**, and so on) can be used to store the data. In this case, we use **SQLite3** (the default option):

```
DATABASES = {
        'default': {
        'ENGINE': 'django.db.backends.sqlite3',
        'NAME': 'mydatabase',
        }
    }
```

The web pages are written in HTML, so a folder to store the HTML code is required. The `templates` folder is usually used to store the web pages layout:

```
TEMPLATE_DIRS = (
    os.path.join(BASE_DIR, 'templates'),
)
```

- To embellish a website, the CSS formatting and JavaScript code are usually stored in another folder, `static`, at the same level as the `server` folder. Then the settings need to be configured to take the files from the folder:

```
MEDIA_ROOT = os.path.join(BASE_DIR, 'static')
STATIC_URL = '/static/'
MEDIA_URL = ''
STATIC_ROOT = ''
STATICFILES_DIRS = ( os.path.join(BASE_DIR, "static"), )
```

- To set the URL of the website, the settings are configured to take the path from the file (in this case, `test_server/urls.py`):

```
ROOT_URLCONF = 'test_server.urls'
```

- It is possible to set up a file to store all the printout statements we want to put in the code for debugging purposes. We use the `logging` library and the following configuration:

```
LOGGING = {
    'version': 1,
```

```
        'disable_existing_loggers': True,
        'formatters': {
            'standard': {
                'format': '%(asctime)s %(levelname)s %(name)s
%(message)s'
            },
        },
        'handlers': {
            'default': {
                'level':'DEBUG',
                'class':'logging.handlers.RotatingFileHandler',
                'filename': 'test_server.log',
                'maxBytes': 1024*1024*5, # 5 MB
                'backupCount': 5,
                'formatter':'standard',
            },
        },
        'loggers': {
            '': {
                'handlers': ['default'],
                'level': 'DEBUG',
                'propagate': True
            },
        }
}
```

Here, the test_server.log file stores all the print statements defined using the logging library (for example, logging.debug('write something')).

Now that all the most important settings are configured, we can focus on developing a new app that creates a simple email address book. So we create the app as usual:

```
python manage.py startapp addresesapp
```

Now, we add the templates and static folder on the root test_server directory of the server:

```
├── addresesapp
│   ├── __init__.py
│   ├── admin.py
│   ├── migrations
│   ├── models.py
│   ├── tests.py
│   └── views.py
├── manage.py
└── test_server
```

```
├── __init__.py
├── __init__.pyc
├── settings.py
├── settings.pyc
├── static
├── templates
├── urls.py
└── wsgi.py
```

Note that the `nameapp` on the `INSTALLED_APPS` becomes `addressesapp`. In the following section, we will discuss the main features of how to implement the app. All the code can be found in the `chapter_6` folder of the author's GitHub repository (`https://github.com/ai2010/machine_learning_for_the_web/tree/master/chapter_6`).

Writing an app – most important features

To create a web application that stores e-mail addresses, we will need a table that stores the data and web pages that allow the end user to add, delete, and review the address book. Furthermore, we may want to transform the address book to read as a spreadsheet, or send the data to another app through the Internet. There are specific Django features to accomplish all these actions (`models`, `views`, `admin`, API REST-framework, and `commands`) and we will now discuss the way the data is stored.

Models

To create an e-mail address book, we need to store, in a table, the name of each contact with their e-mail address. A table in Django is called a model and it is defined in the `models.py` file:

```python
from django.db import models
from django.utils.translation import ugettext_lazy as _


class Person(models.Model):
    name = models.CharField(_('Name'), max_length=255, unique=True)
    mail = models.EmailField(max_length=255, blank=True)
    #display name on admin panel
    def __unicode__(self):
            return self.name
```

In Django, the columns of a table are the fields of the model, and can be of different types: integer, char, and so on. Note that Django automatically adds an incremental ID field to any new object. The unique option means that duplicate names cannot exist in the model, and blank states whether the field can be empty or not. The __unicode__ function is optional, and it is used to render each person as a string (we set the name string in this case).

Now that the model has been created, we need to apply it to the SQLite database:

```
python manage.py makemigrations
```

```
python manage.py migrate
```

makemigrations will transform the model changes to migration files (for folder migrations inside addressesapp), while migrate applies the change to the database schema. Note that in case multiple applications are used by the same website, then the command to generate migrations is python manage.py makemigrations 'appname'.

URL and views behind HTML web pages

Now that we know how to store data, we need to record contacts through a web page and show the contacts in another page. In the following section, the pages are described giving a brief overview of the main properties of HTML pages.

HTML pages

All the code explained in this section is stored in the folder template under the test_server folder.

The main page of the application allows the user to record a new contact, and it looks like the following screenshot:

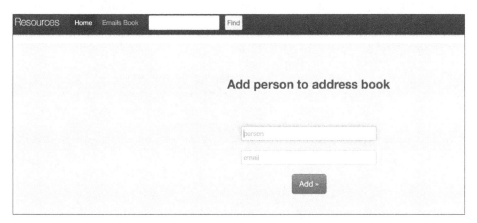

As you can see, the body of the page is specified by two boxes to be filled in with the person's name and their e-mail address, pressing **Add** to add them to the database. The HTML file, home.html, is as follows:

```
{% extends "addressesapp/base.html" %}

{% block content %}
        <form action="" method="POST">
            {% csrf_token %}
            <h2 align = Center>Add person to address book </h2>
            <p> <br><br></p>
            <p align = Center><input type="search" class="span3"
              placeholder="person" name="name" id="search"
              autofocus /> </p>
            <p align = Center><input type="search" class="span3"
              placeholder="email" name="email" id="search"
              autofocus /> </p>
            <p align = Center><button type="submit" class="btn
              btn-primary btn-large pull-center">Add
              &raquo;</button></p>
        </form>
{% endblock content %}
```

We used the POST form to submit the data collected by the two paragraph fields (specified by <p>...</p>) and activated by the **Add** button tag (&raquo: is to render the small arrows after the text). The title of the page, **Add person to address book**, is rendered by a header of type 2 (<h2>...</h2>). Note the csrt_token tag, which enables the cross-site forgery protection request (see more at https://www.squarefree.com/securitytips/web-developers.html#CSRF).

The style of the page (CSS and JavaScript files), as well as the page footer and the header bar with the **Home**, **Emails Book**, and **Find** buttons, are defined in the base.html file (see the template folder). The **Find** button is implemented as a form:

```
<form class="navbar-search pull-left" action="{% url 'get_contacts'
%}" method="GET">
            {% csrf_token %}
            <div style="overflow: hidden; padding-right: .5em;">
              <input type="text" name="term" style="width: 70%;" />
              <input type="submit" name="search" value="Find"
                size="30" style="float: right" />
            </div>
        </form>
```

The `div` tag has been used to define the text field and the **Find** button, which activates a GET call to the URL defined as `get_contacts` in the `urls.py` file (see the following section).

The other page to display is the address book:

```
{% extends "addressesapp/base.html" %}

{% block content %}
<h2 align = Center>Email address book</h2>
<P align=Center>[
{% for letter in alphabet %}
which is given by the book.html file:
{% extends "addressesapp/base.html" %}

{% block content %}
<h2 align = Center>Email address book</h2>
<P align=Center>[
{% for letter in alphabet %}
<a href="{% url 'addressesbook'  %}?letter={{letter}}" > {{letter}} </
a>
{% endfor %}
|<a href="addressesapp/book.html"> Index </a> ] </P>
<section id="gridSystem">
{% for contact in contacts %}
<div class="row show-grid">
    <p align = Center><strong> name: </strong>{{ contact.name }}
<strong>email:</strong> {{ contact.mail }}    
        <a class="right" href="{% url 'delete_person' contact.name
%}" >   delete </a>
```

```
        </p>
    </div>
    {% endfor %}
    </section>

    {% endblock content %}
```

Again, `base.html` is called to render the main header buttons, the footer, and the style. After a header (of type 2) containing **Email address book**, a `for` loop on the alphabet letters, `{% for letter in alphabet %}`, is performed to show only the contacts starting with the corresponding letter. This is achieved by calling the `addressesbook` URL with the letter to query `{{letter}}`. The list of contacts shown is then rendered, looping over the contacts list `{% for contact in contacts %}`: a paragraph tag displays the name, email, and a button to use to delete the person from the database. We will now discuss the implementation of the page actions (add, find, or delete person, and show address book).

URL declarations and views

We will now discuss the way `urls.py` and `views.py` work together with the HTML code of each page to perform the desired actions.

As we have seen, the two main pages of the application, home and address book, are associated with a URL, which in Django is declared in the `urls.py` file:

```
from django.conf.urls import patterns, include, url
from django.contrib import admin
from addressesapp.api import AddressesList


urlpatterns = patterns('',
    url(r'^docs/', include('rest_framework_swagger.urls')),
    url(r'^$', 'addressesapp.views.main'),
    url(r'^book/', 'addressesapp.views.addressesbook', name='addressesbo
ok'),
    url(r'^delete/(?P<name>.*)/', 'addressesapp.views.delete_person',
name='delete_person'),
    url(r'^book-search/', 'addressesapp.views.get_contacts', name='get_
contacts'),
    url(r'^addresses-list/', AddressesList.as_view(), name='addresses-
list'),
    url(r'^notfound/', 'addressesapp.views.notfound', name='notfound'),
    url(r'^admin/', include(admin.site.urls)),
)
```

Each URL is specified by a regex (an r in front of the URL string), so the main page is specified by http://127.0.0.1:8000/ (the ^ start symbol is followed by the $ end symbol) and its action (add record) is implemented in the main function of the views.py file:

```python
def main(request):
    context={}
    if request.method == 'POST':
        post_data = request.POST
        data = {}
        data['name'] = post_data.get('name', None)
        data['email'] = post_data.get('email', None)
        if data:
            return redirect('%s?%s' % (reverse('addressesapp.views.main'),
                            urllib.urlencode({'q': data})))
    elif request.method == 'GET':
        get_data = request.GET
        data= get_data.get('q',None)
        if not data:
            return render_to_response(
                'addressesapp/home.html', RequestContext(request,
context))
        data = literal_eval(get_data.get('q',None))
        print data
        if not data['name'] and not data['email']:
            return render_to_response(
                'addressesapp/home.html', RequestContext(request,
context))


        #add person to emails address book or update
        if Person.objects.filter(name=data['name']).exists():
            p = Person.objects.get(name=data['name'])
            p.mail=data['email']
            p.save()
        else:
            p = Person()
            p.name=data['name']
```

```
            p.mail=data['email']
            p.save()


    #restart page
    return render_to_response(
        'addressesapp/home.html', RequestContext(request,
            context))
```

Whenever the user posts a new contact to be store, the POST method redirects the call to a GET method. If the name and the email have been provided, a new object of the `Person` model will be added, or updated if it already exists. In this method, the same name but in capital letters will be considered a distinct name, so Andrea, ANDREA, and andrea will be three separate contacts. To change this, the reader can simply apply the lower function over the name field, so that the three andrea expressions will all refer to one andrea.

The find action in the `base.html` file is associated with the `http://127.0.0.1:8000/book-search/` URL, and the action is defined in the `get_contacts` function in `views.py`:

```
def get_contacts(request):
    logging.debug('here')
    if request.method == 'GET':
        get_data = request.GET
        data= get_data.get('term','')
        if data == '':
            return render_to_response(
                'addressesapp/nopersonfound.html',
                    RequestContext(request, {}))
        else:
            return redirect('%s?%s' %
        (reverse('addressesapp.views.addressesbook'),
    urllib.urlencode({'letter': data}))))
```

If the user specifies a non-empty string on the text header field, the function will redirect to the `addressesbook` function with the name to search (otherwise a not found page is displayed).

The header button **Emails book** is linked to the `http://127.0.0.1:8000/book/` URL, which shows the contacts according to the `addressesbook` function:

```python
def addressesbook(request):
    context = {}
    logging.debug('address book')
    get_data = request.GET
    letter = get_data.get('letter',None)
    if letter:
        contacts = Person.objects.filter(name__iregex=r"(^|\s)%s" % letter)
    else:
        contacts = Person.objects.all()
    #sorted alphabetically
    contacts = sort_lower(contacts,"name")#contacts.order_by("name")
    context['contacts']=contacts
    alphabetstring='ABCDEFGHIJKLMNOPQRSTUVWXYZ'
    context['alphabet']=[l for l in alphabetstring]
    return render_to_response(
        'addressesapp/book.html', RequestContext(request, context))
def sort_lower(lst, key_name):
    return sorted(lst, key=lambda item: getattr(item,
key_name).lower())
```

The letter field stores the name (in case of redirection from the **Find** header button) or the letter (in case of calling from the emails book page), and a lookup over the contacts in the `Person` model is performed. The retrieved contacts are then stored in the `contacts` context object, while the letters are stored in the `alphabet` context object. If no letter is specified, all the contacts in the database are returned. Note that the name can have both a capital and a lowercase first letter, so the usual `order_by` method will not sort the names in alphabetical order. Therefore, the function `sort_lower` will convert each name to lowercase and sort the contacts alphabetically.

The delete action is performed by the `delete_person` function and called by the `http://127.0.0.1:8000/delete/(?P<name>.*)/` URL. The `.*` indicates that all the characters are valid for forming a name (note that if we wanted only character numbers and whitespace, we should have `[a-zA-Z0-9 ]+`):

```
def delete_person(request,name):
    if Person.objects.filter(name=name).exists():
        p =  Person.objects.get(name=name)
        p.delete()

    context = {}
    contacts = Person.objects.all()
    #sorted alphabetically
    contacts = sort_lower(contacts,"name")#contacts.order_by("name")
    context['contacts']=contacts
    return render_to_response(
        'addressesapp/book.html', RequestContext(request, context))
```

The `name` query variable is searched on the `Person` table in the database and deleted. The function returns the emails book page with the remaining contacts.

In the same way, the not found URL activates the not found function, and you should now be able to understand how it works.

The admin URL refers to the Django interface (see following section) while the docs is the REST framework swagger discussed in the *RESTful application programming interfaces (APIs)* section of this book.

Admin

The admin panel is a user interface for managing the application, accessible through the browser. In the `admin.py` file, we can add the model just created with the following command:

```
from models import Person
admin.site.register(Person)
```

All the models can be accessed by a user interface at:

```
http://127.0.0.1:8000/admin/
```

At this link, the user name and password are required. We create that with the following command:

```
python manage.py createsuperuser
```

Then we type a username and password (in my case, andrea/a).

Now, we can explore the panel that follows:

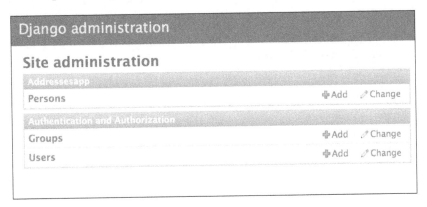

Clicking on **Persons**, we will see all Person objects shown by name (because the __unicode__ function in the model refers to the name field):

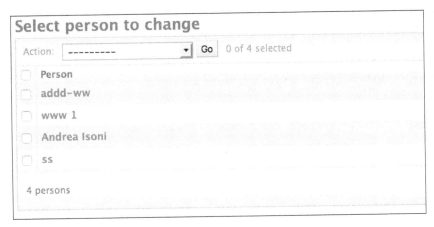

Shell interface

The Django framework also provides a shell to explore the created models and test them. To start it, we type the following in the terminal:

```
python manage.py shell
```

Now we can import the Person model and play with it:

```
In [1]: from addressesapp.models import Person
In [2]: newcontact = Person()
In [3]: newcontact.name = 'myfriend1'
In [4]: newcontact.mail = 'bla@.com'
In [5]: newcontact.save()
In [6]: Person.objects.all()
Out[6]: [<Person: ss>, <Person: Andrea Isoni>, <Person: www 1>,
<Person: addd-ww>, <Person: myfriend1>]
```

In these lines, we have created a new contact, myfriend1, and verified it has been added to the list of Person objects.

Commands

The Django framework also allows us to write custom commands through the manage.py module. For example, we would like to export the entire list of contacts into a CSV file. To achieve that, we create a commands folder inside a management folder (with __init__.py in each folder). The file implements the custom command to export the contacts list to CSV, extending the BaseCommand class:

```
from addressesapp.models import Person
from django.core.management.base import BaseCommand, CommandError
from optparse import make_option
import csv


class Command(BaseCommand):
    option_list = BaseCommand.option_list + (
                make_option('--output',
                            dest='output', type='string',
                            action='store',
```

```
                              help='output file'),
    )


    def person_data(self, person):
            return [person.name,person.mail]


    def handle(self, *args, **options):
        outputfile = options['output']
        contacts = Person.objects.all()

        header = ['Name','email']
        f = open(outputfile,'wb')
        writer = csv.writer(f, quoting=csv.QUOTE_NONNUMERIC)
        writer.writerow(header)
        for person in contacts:
            writer.writerow(self.person_data(person))
```

The command must define a `handler` function, which will perform the export operation. Type the following from the `test_server` folder:

```
python manage.py contacts_tocsv -output='contacts_list.csv'
```

RESTful application programming interfaces (APIs)

A RESTful API is an application programming interface that employs HTTP requests (such as GET and POST) to manage the data of an application. In this case, the API is used to obtain the address book through a `curl` call. In order to do that, we have defined the `rest_framework` app in the INSTALLED_APPS section of `settings.py`, and then the `api.py` file implements the API:

```
from rest_framework import viewsets, generics, views
from rest_framework.response import Response
from rest_framework.permissions import AllowAny
from rest_framework.pagination import PageNumberPagination
from addressesapp.serializers import AddressesSerializer
from addressesapp.models import Person


class LargeResultsSetPagination(PageNumberPagination):
```

```
    page_size = 1000
    page_size_query_param = 'page_size'
    max_page_size = 10000


class AddressesList(generics.ListAPIView):

    serializer_class = AddressesSerializer
    permission_classes = (AllowAny,)
    pagination_class = LargeResultsSetPagination

    def get_queryset(self):
        query = self.request.query_params.get
        if query('name'):
            return Person.objects.filter(name=query('name'))
        else:
            return Person.objects.all()
```

We have used the `ListAPIView` class to return all `Person` objects, or only the one that matches the `name` value. Since the returned list may be too large, we need to override the `PageNumberPagination` class to show more objects on the same page; the `LargeResultsSetPagination` class allows a maximum of 10,000 objects per page. This API needs to transform the `Person` objects to a JSON format object, which is performed by the `AddressesSerializer` serializer implemented in `serializers.py`:

```
from addressesapp.models import Person
from rest_framework import serializers


class AddressesSerializer(serializers.HyperlinkedModelSerializer):

    class Meta:
        model = Person
        fields = ('id', 'name', 'mail')
```

Now the address book can be retrieved using the `curl` command:

```
curl -X GET http://localhost:8000/addresses-list/
```

Note the forward slash at the end of the URL. In the same way, we can specify a name value to get their email:

```
curl -X GET http://localhost:8000/addresses-st/?name=name_value
```

Note that we can always specify the page query parameter, in case the number of contacts is too large (or change the pagination size value). In the `urls.py` file, we also defined the docs URL to be our Swagger RESTful API, which allows the user to explore and test the API using a browser:

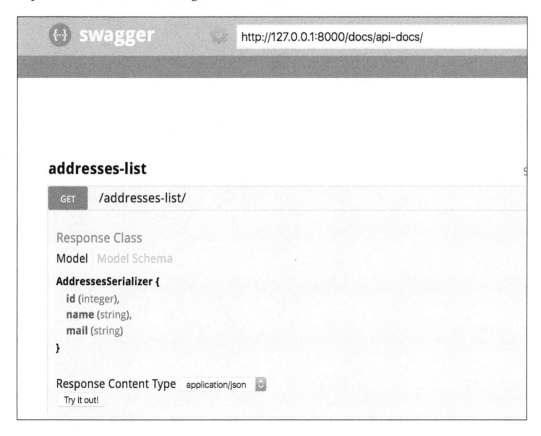

This is a user-friendly way to verify that the API is working as expected and the data is shown in the correct format.

Summary

In this chapter, we have discussed how to create a web application using the Django framework. The main features of Django, such as the `models`, `admin`, `views`, `commands`, `shell`, and the `RESTful API`, have been described, so the reader should now have the necessary knowledge to develop a web application in a real-life scenario.

We will use this knowledge, together with what we have learned in the preceding chapters, to build our movie recommendation engine and movie sentiment analysis application in the following two chapters.

7
Movie Recommendation System Web Application

The purpose of this chapter is to explain a real case example of the recommendation system in action, using the Django framework. We are going to implement a movie recommendation system in which each user that subscribes to the service will receive suggested movies based on his preferences as we have discussed in *Chapter 5, Recommendation systems*, also we are going to use the same data which consists of 603 movies rated more than 50 times by 942 users. In order to receive recommendations, each user has to rate a certain number of movies, so an information retrieval system (*Chapter 4, Web-mining techniques*) to search the movies to rate is implemented. The different parts of the Django application are going to be discussed: settings, models, user login/logout, commands, information retrieval system, recommendation systems, an admin interface and APIs (all the code is available on the GitHub of the author `chapter_7` folder at `https://github.com/ai2010/machine_learning_for_the_web/tree/master/chapter_7`). Since *Chapter 6, Basics of Django: a simple web framework* just introduced the main features of Django, whenever a new feature is employed a technical explanation is also provided. Now we can start describing the different settings and the initial setup to run the application.

Application setup

We create and start Django as usual:

```
django-admin startproject server_movierecsys
```

and from the `server_movierecsys` folder we start the application:

```
python manage.py startapp books_recsys_app
```

Now the `settings.py` needs to be configured. As we see in *Chapter 6, Basics of Django: a simple web framework* we set the installed apps, HTML templates, a layout formatting folder, and an SQLite database:

```
INSTALLED_APPS = (
    'django.contrib.admin',
    'django.contrib.auth',
    'django.contrib.contenttypes',
    'django.contrib.sessions',
    'django.contrib.messages',
    'django.contrib.staticfiles',
    'rest_framework',
    'rest_framework_swagger',
    'books_recsys_app',
)


TEMPLATE_DIRS = (
    os.path.join(BASE_DIR, 'templates'),
)
STATIC_URL = '/static/'
STATICFILES_DIRS = ( os.path.join(BASE_DIR, "static"), )
DATABASES = {
    'default': {
        'ENGINE': 'django.db.backends.sqlite3',
        'NAME': os.path.join(BASE_DIR, 'db.sqlite3'),
    }
}
```

Apart from the standard apps, and the rest framework (swagger), the `books_recsys_app` has been included in the installed apps list.

In this case, we need to load data persistently in the memory so that the user experience is improved by not calculating or retrieving data at each user request. To save data or the results of expensive calculations in the memory, we set up the cache system of Django in `settings.py`:

```
CACHES = {
    'default': {
        'BACKEND': 'django.core.cache.backends.filebased.
FileBasedCache',
        'LOCATION': '/var/tmp/django_cache',
        'TIMEOUT': None,
    }
}
```

We have chosen the **File Based Cache** cache type stored in `/var/tmp/django_cache` and a `None` timeout which means the data in the cache will never expire.

To use the admin interface, we set up the `superuser` account through the command:

```
python manage.py createsuperuser (admin/admin)
```

The application is live at `http://localhost:8000/` by typing:

```
python manage.py runserver
```

Models

In this application, we need to store the data related to each movie and the movies' ratings from each user of the website. We set up three models:

```python
class UserProfile(models.Model):
    user = models.ForeignKey(User, unique=True)
    array = jsonfield.JSONField()
    arrayratedmoviesindxs = jsonfield.JSONField()
    lastrecs = jsonfield.JSONField()

    def __unicode__(self):
            return self.user.username

    def save(self, *args, **kwargs):
        create = kwargs.pop('create', None)
        recsvec = kwargs.pop('recsvec', None)
        print 'create:',create
        if create==True:
            super(UserProfile, self).save(*args, **kwargs)
        elif recsvec!=None:
            self.lastrecs = json.dumps(recsvec.tolist())
            super(UserProfile, self).save(*args, **kwargs)
        else:
            nmovies = MovieData.objects.count()
            array = np.zeros(nmovies)
            ratedmovies = self.ratedmovies.all()
            self.arrayratedmoviesindxs = json.dumps([m.movieindx for m in ratedmovies])
            for m in ratedmovies:
                array[m.movieindx] = m.value
            self.array = json.dumps(array.tolist())
```

```
                    super(UserProfile, self).save(*args, **kwargs)

    class MovieRated(models.Model):
        user = models.ForeignKey(UserProfile, related_name='ratedmovies')
        movie = models.CharField(max_length=100)
        movieindx = models.IntegerField(default=-1)
        value = models.IntegerField()

    class MovieData(models.Model):
        title = models.CharField(max_length=100)
        array = jsonfield.JSONField()
        ndim = models.IntegerField(default=300)
        description = models.TextField()
```

The model `MovieData` stores the data for each movie: title, description, and vector representation (`ndim` is the dimension of the vector representation). `MovieRated` records each movie rated by the user logged in (each object `MovieRated` is associated with has a `UserProfile` that utilizes the website). The `UserProfile` model stores all the users that sign up to the website, so they can rate movies and receive recommendations. Each `UserProfile` extends the default Django user model by adding the `array` field, which stores all the movie's ratings from the `user`, and the `recsvec` field which stores his last recommendations: the `save` function is overridden to fill the `array` field with all the `MovieRated` objects associated with the user (if the `else` statement is `true`), and to fill the `lastrecs` field with the last recommendations (`else if` statement). Note that the `MovieRated` model has a `UserProfile` foreign key with the `related_name` equal to `ratedmovies`: in the `save` function of the `UserProfile` model, `self.ratedmovies.all()` refers to all the `RatedMovie` objects that have the same `UserProfile` value. The field `arrayratedmoviesindxs` on the `UserProfile` model records all the movies rated by the user and it is used by the API of the application.

To write these data structures on the database we need to run:

```
python manage.py makemigrations
python manage.py migrate
```

Commands

The commands used in this application are needed to load the data into the memory (cache) and make the user experience fast. Although the movie database is the same used in *Chapter 4, Web mining techniques* (that is 603 movies rated more than 50 times by 942 users), each movie needs a description to set up an information retrieval system on the movies to rate. The first command we develop takes all the movie titles in the utility matrix used in *Chapter 4, Web Mining Techniques* and collects the corresponding descriptions from **Open Movie Database (OMDb)** online service:

```python
from django.core.management.base import BaseCommand
import os
import optparse
import numpy as np
import json
import pandas as pd
import requests
class Command(BaseCommand):

    option_list = BaseCommand.option_list + (
            optparse.make_option('-i', '--input', dest='umatrixfile',
                                    type='string', action='store',
                                    help=('Input utility matrix')),
            optparse.make_option('-o', '--outputplots',
dest='plotsfile',
                                    type='string', action='store',
                                    help=('output file')),
            optparse.make_option('--om', '--outputumatrix',
dest='umatrixoutfile',
                                    type='string', action='store',
                                    help=('output file')),
        )


    def getplotfromomdb(self,col,df_moviesplots,df_movies,df_
utilitymatrix):
        string = col.split(';')[0]

        title=string[:-6].strip()
        year = string[-5:-1]
```

```
        plot = ' '.join(title.split(' ')).encode('ascii','ignore')+'.
    '

        url = "http://www.omdbapi.com/?t="+title+"&y="+year+"&plot=fu
ll&r=json"

        headers={"User-Agent": "Mozilla/5.0 (Windows NT 6.3; Win64;
x64) AppleWebKit/537.36 (KHTML, like Gecko) Chrome/37.0.2049.0
Safari/537.36"}
        r = requests.get(url,headers=headers)
        jsondata =  json.loads(r.content)
        if 'Plot' in jsondata:
            #store plot + title
            plot += jsondata['Plot'].encode('ascii','ignore')

        if plot!=None and plot!='' and plot!=np.nan and
len(plot)>3:#at least 3 letters to consider the movie
            df_moviesplots.loc[len(df_moviesplots)]=[string,plot]
            df_utilitymatrix[col] = df_movies[col]
            print len(df_utilitymatrix.columns)

        return df_moviesplots,df_utilitymatrix

    def handle(self, *args, **options):
        pathutilitymatrix = options['umatrixfile']
        df_movies = pd.read_csv(pathutilitymatrix)
        movieslist = list(df_movies.columns[1:])

        df_moviesplots = pd.DataFrame(columns=['title','plot'])
        df_utilitymatrix = pd.DataFrame()
        df_utilitymatrix['user'] = df_movies['user']

        for m in movieslist[:]:
            df_moviesplots,df_utilitymatrix=self.getplotfromomdb(m,df_
moviesplots,df_movies,df_utilitymatrix)

        outputfile = options['plotsfile']
        df_moviesplots.to_csv(outputfile, index=False)
        outumatrixfile = options['umatrixoutfile']
        df_utilitymatrix.to_csv(outumatrixfile, index=False)
```

The command syntax is:

```
python manage.py --input=utilitymatrix.csv --outputplots=plots.csv -
outputumatrix='umatrix.csv'
```

Each movie title contained in the `utilitymatrix` file is used by the `getplotfromomdb` function to retrieve the movie's description (`plot`) from the website `http://www.omdbapi.com/` using the requests in the Python module. The descriptions (and `titles`) of the movies are then saved in a CSV file (`outputplots`) together with the corresponding utility matrix (`outputumatrix`).

The other command will take the movie's descriptions and create an information retrieval system (**Term Frequency, Inverse Document Frequency (TF-IDF)** model) to allow the user to find movies typing some relevant words. This tf-idf model is then saved in the Django cache together with the initial recommendation systems models (**CF item-based** and **log-likelihood** ratio). The code is as follows:

```python
from django.core.management.base import BaseCommand
import os
import optparse
import numpy as np
import pandas as pd
import math
import json
import copy
from BeautifulSoup import BeautifulSoup
import nltk
from nltk.corpus import stopwords
from nltk.tokenize import WordPunctTokenizer
tknzr = WordPunctTokenizer()
#nltk.download('stopwords')
stoplist = stopwords.words('english')
from nltk.stem.porter import PorterStemmer
stemmer = PorterStemmer()
from sklearn.feature_extraction.text import TfidfVectorizer
from books_recsys_app.models import MovieData
from django.core.cache import cache


class Command(BaseCommand):

    option_list = BaseCommand.option_list + (
            optparse.make_option('-i', '--input', dest='input',
                                    type='string', action='store',
                                    help=('Input plots file')),
            optparse.make_option('--nmaxwords', '--nmaxwords',
dest='nmaxwords',
                                    type='int', action='store',
                                    help=('nmaxwords')),
            optparse.make_option('--umatrixfile', '--umatrixfile',
dest='umatrixfile',
```

```
                                    type='string', action='store',
                                    help=('umatrixfile')),
        )

    def PreprocessTfidf(self,texts,stoplist=[],stem=False):
        newtexts = []
        for i in xrange(len(texts)):
            text = texts[i]
            if stem:
                tmp = [w for w in tknzr.tokenize(text) if w not in
stoplist]
            else:
                tmp = [stemmer.stem(w) for w in [w for w in tknzr.
tokenize(text) if w not in stoplist]]
            newtexts.append(' '.join(tmp))
        return newtexts

    def handle(self, *args, **options):
        input_file = options['input']

        df = pd.read_csv(input_file)
        tot_textplots = df['plot'].tolist()
        tot_titles = df['title'].tolist()
        nmaxwords=options['nmaxwords']
        vectorizer = TfidfVectorizer(min_df=0,max_features=nmaxwords)
        processed_plots = self.PreprocessTfidf(tot_
textplots,stoplist,True)
        mod_tfidf = vectorizer.fit(processed_plots)
        vec_tfidf = mod_tfidf.transform(processed_plots)
        ndims = len(mod_tfidf.get_feature_names())
        nmovies = len(tot_titles[:])

        #delete all data
        MovieData.objects.all().delete()

        matr = np.empty([1,ndims])
        titles = []
        cnt=0
        for m in xrange(nmovies):
            moviedata = MovieData()
            moviedata.title=tot_titles[m]
            moviedata.description=tot_textplots[m]
            moviedata.ndim= ndims
            moviedata.array=json.dumps(vec_tfidf[m].toarray()[0].
tolist())
```

```
            moviedata.save()
            newrow = moviedata.array
            if cnt==0:
                matr[0]=newrow
            else:
                matr = np.vstack([matr, newrow])
            titles.append(moviedata.title)
            cnt+=1
        #cached
        cache.set('data', matr)
        cache.set('titles', titles)
        cache.set('model',mod_tfidf)


        #load the utility matrix
        umatrixfile = options['umatrixfile']
        df_umatrix = pd.read_csv(umatrixfile)
        Umatrix = df_umatrix.values[:,1:]
        cache.set('umatrix',Umatrix)
        #load rec methods...
        cf_itembased = CF_itembased(Umatrix)
        cache.set('cf_itembased',cf_itembased)
        llr = LogLikelihood(Umatrix,titles)
        cache.set('loglikelihood',llr)

from scipy.stats import pearsonr
from scipy.spatial.distance import cosine
def sim(x,y,metric='cos'):
    if metric == 'cos':
        return 1.-cosine(x,y)
    else:#correlation
        return pearsonr(x,y)[0]

class CF_itembased(object):
...
class LogLikelihood(object):
...
```

To run the command the syntax is:

```
python manage.py load_data --input=plots.csv --nmaxwords=30000
--umatrixfile=umatrix.csv
```

The input parameter takes the movie's descriptions obtained using the
`get_plotsfromtitles` command and creates a `tf-idf` model (see *Chapter 4,
Web-mining techniques*) using a maximum of words specified by the `nmaxwords`
parameter. The data of each movie is also saved in a `MovieData` object (title,
tf-idf representation, description, and `ndim` number of words of the tf-idf
vocabulary). Note that the first time the command is run the `stopwords` from
`nltk.download('stopwords')` (commented in the preceding code) need to be
downloaded.

The tf-idf model, the title's list, and the matrix of the tf-idf movies' representations,
are saved in the Django cache using the commands:

```
from django.core.cache import cache
...
cache.set('model',mod_tfidf)
cache.set('data', matr)
cache.set('titles', titles)
```

 Note that the cache Django module (`django.core.cache`) needs
to be loaded (at the beginning of the file) to be used.

In the same way, the utility matrix (`umatrixfile` parameter) is used to initialize
the two recommendation systems used by the application: item-based collaborative
filtering and log-likelihood ratio method. Both methods are not written in the
preceding code because they are essentially the same as the code described in
Chapter 5, Recommendation systems (the full code can be seen in the `chapter_7` folder
of the author's GitHub repository as usual). The methods and the utility matrix are
then loaded into the Django cache ready to use:

```
cache.set('umatrix',Umatrix)
    cache.set('cf_itembased',cf_itembased)
    cache.set('loglikelihood',llr)
```

Now the data (and models) can be used in the web pages just by calling the
corresponding name, as we will see in the following sections.

User sign up login/logout implementation

This application can recommend movies to different users that are registered on the website. To manage the registration process, we use the standard `User` Django module as we have seen in the *Models* sections. Each page of the website refers to the `base.html` page, which implements a top bar that allows the user to register or sign in (right side):

Clicking on one of the two buttons **sign in** or **sign up** will activate the code:

```
            <form class="navbar-search pull-right" action="{% url
'auth' %}" method="GET">
                {% csrf_token %}
                <div style="overflow: hidden; padding-right:
.5em;">
                    <input type="submit" name="auth_method"
value="sign up" size="30" style="float: right" />
                    <input type="submit" name="auth_method"
value="sign in" size="30" style="float: right" />
                </div>
            </form>
```

The two methods refer to the `urls.py`:

```
    url(r'^auth/', 'books_recsys_app.views.auth', name='auth')
```

This calls the `auth` function in the `views.py`:

```
def auth(request):
    if request.method == 'GET':
        data = request.GET
        auth_method = data.get('auth_method')
        if auth_method=='sign in':
            return render_to_response(
                'books_recsys_app/signin.html', RequestContext(request,
{}))
        else:
            return render_to_response(
                'books_recsys_app/createuser.html',
RequestContext(request, {}))
    elif request.method == 'POST':
        post_data = request.POST
```

```
         name = post_data.get('name', None)
         pwd = post_data.get('pwd', None)
         pwd1 = post_data.get('pwd1', None)
         create = post_data.get('create', None)#hidden input
         if name and pwd and create:
             if User.objects.filter(username=name).exists() or
pwd!=pwd1:
                 return render_to_response(
                     'books_recsys_app/userexistsorproblem.html',
RequestContext(request))
             user = User.objects.create_user(username=name,password=pwd)
             uprofile = UserProfile()
             uprofile.user = user
             uprofile.name = user.username
             uprofile.save(create=True)

             user = authenticate(username=name, password=pwd)
             login(request, user)
             return render_to_response(
                 'books_recsys_app/home.html', RequestContext(request))
         elif name and pwd:
              user = authenticate(username=name, password=pwd)
              if user:
                  login(request, user)
                  return render_to_response(
                      'books_recsys_app/home.html',
RequestContext(request))
              else:
                  #notfound
                  return render_to_response(
                      'books_recsys_app/nopersonfound.html',
                          RequestContext(request))
```

The function will redirect to the sign up page as shown in the following screenshot:

If you have already registered, it will take you to the sign in page as shown in the following screenshot:

The page allows the user to create a username and password and log in to the website. The data is then used to create a new object of the User Django model and the related `UserProfile` object (note that the `create` argument is `True` to save the object without associating an array of rated movies):

```
user = User.objects.create_user(username=name,password=pwd)
uprofile = UserProfile()
uprofile.user = user
uprofile.save(create=True)
user = authenticate(username=name, password=pwd)
```

The user is then logged in using the standard Django methods:

```
from django.contrib.auth import authenticate, login
...
login(request, user)
```

Hence, the website top bar looks like (username:**a**) as shown in the following screenshot:

Note that in cases where a user with the same name already exists (new sign up exception event) or where a user is not found (sign in exception event), both are implemented and the reader can look into the code to understand how these events are handled.

The **sign out** button refers to the `urls.py`:

```
url(r'^signout/','books_recsys_app.views.signout',name='signout')
```

This calls the `signout` function from `views.py`:

```
from django.contrib.auth import logout
...
def signout(request):
    logout(request)
    return render_to_response(
        'books_recsys_app/home.html', RequestContext(request))
```

The function uses the standard Django logout method and redirects to the home page (the **sign in** and **sign out** buttons will be shown again in the top bar). The user can now search for movies to rate using the information retrieval system (search engine) described in the next section.

Information retrieval system (movies query)

In order to rate movies, the user needs to search for them using the home page:

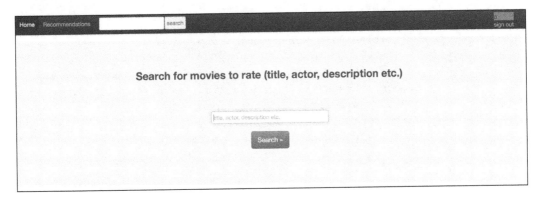

By Typing some relevant words in the text box, the page will call (through the `urls.py` corresponding *home* URL) the `home` function in the `views.py` file:

```python
def home(request):
    context={}
    if request.method == 'POST':
        post_data = request.POST
        data = {}
        data = post_data.get('data', None)
        if data:
            return redirect('%s?%s' % (reverse('books_recsys_app.
views.home'),
                                      urllib.urlencode({'q': data})))
    elif request.method == 'GET':
        get_data = request.GET
        data = get_data.get('q',None)
        titles = cache.get('titles')
        if titles==None:
            print 'load data...'
            texts = []
            mobjs = MovieData.objects.all()
            ndim = mobjs[0].ndim
            matr = np.empty([1,ndim])
            titles_list = []
            cnt=0
            for obj in mobjs[:]:
```

```
                    texts.append(obj.description)
                    newrow = np.array(obj.array)
                    #print 'enw:',newrow
                    if cnt==0:
                        matr[0]=newrow
                    else:
                        matr = np.vstack([matr, newrow])
                    titles_list.append(obj.title)
                    cnt+=1
                vectorizer = TfidfVectorizer(min_df=1,max_features=ndim)
                processedtexts = PreprocessTfidf(texts,stoplist,True)
                model = vectorizer.fit(processedtexts)
                cache.set('model',model)
                #cache.set('processedtexts',processedtexts)
                cache.set('data', matr)
                cache.set('titles', titles_list)
            else:
                print 'loaded',str(len(titles))

        Umatrix = cache.get('umatrix')
        if Umatrix==None:
            df_umatrix = pd.read_csv(umatrixpath)
            Umatrix = df_umatrix.values[:,1:]
            cache.set('umatrix',Umatrix)
            cf_itembased = CF_itembased(Umatrix)
            cache.set('cf_itembased',cf_itembased)
            cache.set('loglikelihood',LogLikelihood(Umatrix,moviesli
st))

        if not data:
            return render_to_response(
                'books_recsys_app/home.html', RequestContext(request,
context))


        #load all movies vectors/titles
        matr = cache.get('data')
        titles = cache.get('titles')
        model_tfidf = cache.get('model')
        #find movies similar to the query
        queryvec = model_tfidf.transform([data.lower().
encode('ascii','ignore')]).toarray()
        sims= cosine_similarity(queryvec,matr)[0]
        indxs_sims = list(sims.argsort()[::-1])
```

```
        titles_query = list(np.array(titles)[indxs_sims]
[:nmoviesperquery])

        context['movies']= zip(titles_query,indxs_
sims[:nmoviesperquery])
        context['rates']=[1,2,3,4,5]
        return render_to_response(
            'books_recsys_app/query_results.html',
                RequestContext(request, context))
```

The `data` parameter at the beginning of the function will store the typed query and the function will use it to transform it to a vector tf-idf representation using the model already loaded in memory by the `load_data` command:

```
        matr = cache.get('data')
        titles = cache.get('titles')
        model_tfidf = cache.get('model')
```

Also the matrix (key: `matr`) and the movies' titles (key: `titles`) are retrieved from the cache to return the list of movies similar to the query vector (see *Chapter 4, Web-mining techniques* for further details). Also note that in case the cache is empty, the models (and the other data) are created and loaded in memory directly from the first call of this function. For example, we can type `war` as a query and the website will return the most similar movies to this query (`query_results.html`):

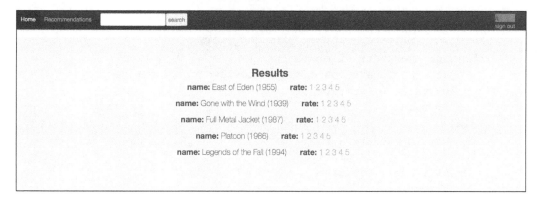

As we can see, we have five movies (at the beginning of the `views.py` file we can set the number of movies per query parameter: `nmoviesperquery`) and most of them are related to war. From this page we can rate the movies as we discuss in the following section.

Rating system

Each user (when logged in) can rate movies simply by clicking on the rate value (1 to 5) at the side of the movie title in the movies' results page (see preceding screenshot). This action will trigger the rate_movie function in the views.py file (through the corresponding URL in urls.py):

```
def rate_movie(request):
    data = request.GET
    rate = data.get("vote")
    movies,moviesindxs = zip(*literal_eval(data.get("movies")))
    movie = data.get("movie")
    movieindx = int(data.get("movieindx"))
    #save movie rate
    userprofile = None
    if request.user.is_superuser:
        return render_to_response(
            'books_recsys_app/superusersignin.html',
RequestContext(request))
    elif request.user.is_authenticated() :
        userprofile = UserProfile.objects.get(user=request.user)
    else:
        return render_to_response(
            'books_recsys_app/pleasesignin.html',
RequestContext(request))

    if MovieRated.objects.filter(movie=movie).
filter(user=userprofile).exists():
        mr = MovieRated.objects.get(movie=movie,user=userprofile)
        mr.value = int(rate)
        mr.save()
    else:
        mr = MovieRated()
        mr.user = userprofile
        mr.value = int(rate)
        mr.movie = movie
        mr.movieindx = movieindx
        mr.save()

    userprofile.save()
    #get back the remaining movies
    movies = RemoveFromList(movies,movie)
    moviesindxs = RemoveFromList(moviesindxs,movieindx)
    print movies
    context = {}
```

```
context["movies"] = zip(movies,moviesindxs)
context["rates"] = [1,2,3,4,5]
return render_to_response(
    'books_recsys_app/query_results.html',
        RequestContext(request, context))
```

The function will store the `rate` of the movie in an object of the `MovieRated` model, and the corresponding movies `rate` vector of the user is updated (through the `userprofile.save()`). The movies not rated are then sent back to the page `query_results.html`. Note that the user needs to be logged in to rate a movie or the exception event that will ask the user to sign in will be shown (page: `pleasesignin.html`).

Recommendation systems

This function will use the parameters set at the beginning of the `views.py` file:

```
nminimumrates=5
numrecs=5
recmethod = 'loglikelihood'
```

This defines the minimum number of movies to rate before obtaining recommendations, the number of recommendations to show to the user, and the recommendation system method respectively. To show recommendations the user can click on the **Recommendations** button on the top bar:

This action will trigger the `movies_recs` function in the `views.py` file (through the corresponding URL defined in the `urls.py` file):

```
def movies_recs(request):

    userprofile = None
    if request.user.is_superuser:
        return render_to_response(
            'books_recsys_app/superusersignin.html',
RequestContext(request))
    elif request.user.is_authenticated():
        userprofile = UserProfile.objects.get(user=request.user)
    else:
        return render_to_response(
            'books_recsys_app/pleasesignin.html',
RequestContext(request))
```

```
    ratedmovies=userprofile.ratedmovies.all()
    context = {}
    if len(ratedmovies)<nminimumrates:
        context['nrates'] = len(ratedmovies)
        context['nminimumrates']=nminimumrates
        return render_to_response(
            'books_recsys_app/underminimum.html',
RequestContext(request, context))

    u_vec = np.array(userprofile.array)
    Umatrix = cache.get('umatrix')
    movieslist = cache.get('titles')
    #recommendation...
    u_rec = None
    if recmethod == 'cf_userbased':
        u_rec = CF_userbased(u_vec,numrecs,Umatrix)
    elif recmethod == 'cf_itembased':
        cf_itembased = cache.get('cf_itembased')
        if cf_itembased == None:
            cf_itembased = CF_itembased(Umatrix)
        u_rec = cf_itembased.CalcRatings(u_vec,numrecs)
    elif recmethod == 'loglikelihood':
        llr = cache.get('loglikelihood')
        if llr == None:
            llr = LogLikelihood(Umatrix,movieslist)
        u_rec = llr.GetRecItems(u_vec,True)
    #save last recs
    userprofile.save(recsvec=u_rec)
    context['recs'] = list(np.array(movieslist)[list(u_rec)]
[:numrecs])
    return render_to_response(
        'books_recsys_app/recommendations.html',
            RequestContext(request, context))
```

The function will retrieve the rated movies vector from the corresponding `UserProfile` object and it will load the recommendation system method (specified by the `recmethod` parameter) from cache. The recommendations are first stored in the `userprofile` object and then returned to the `recommendations.html` page. For example, using the `cf_itembased` method:

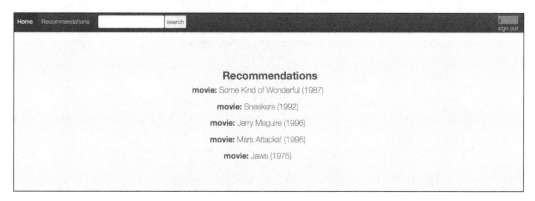

This is a sample result page after rating the five movies related to the word `war` (see preceding screenshot). The reader can play more with the parameters and the different algorithms to evaluate the differences.

Admin interface and API

In order to manage the data of the application, the admin interface and an API point can be set. From the admin panel we can see both the movie's data, and the user registered, writing the following `admin.py` file:

```
from django.contrib import admin
from books_recsys_app.models import MovieData,UserProfile

class MoviesAdmin(admin.ModelAdmin):
    list_display = ['title', 'description']

admin.site.register(UserProfile)
admin.site.register(MovieData,MoviesAdmin)
```

After setting the corresponding `admin` URL on the `urls.py` file:

```
url(r'^admin/', include(admin.site.urls))
```

We should see our admin panel (at `http://localhost:8000/admin/`) with the two models and the data within the models resembles the fields specified in the `admin.py` file:

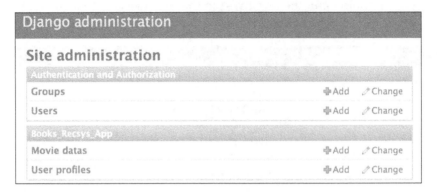

To set the API endpoint to retrieve the data for each registered user, first we need to write out `serializers.py` specifying which fields of the `UserProfile` model we want to employ:

```
from books_recsys_app.models import UserProfile
from rest_framework import serializers

class UsersSerializer(serializers.HyperlinkedModelSerializer):
    class Meta:
        model = UserProfile
        fields = ('name', 'arrayratedmoviesindxs','lastrecs')
```

In this case, we want to collect the ID of the movies, rated by the user, and his last recommended movie's ID. Then the API is set in the `api.py` file as follows:

```
from rest_framework import generics
from rest_framework.permissions import AllowAny
from rest_framework.pagination import PageNumberPagination
from books_recsys_app.serializers import UsersSerializer
from books_recsys_app.models import UserProfile

class LargeResultsSetPagination(PageNumberPagination):
    page_size = 1000
    page_size_query_param = 'page_size'
    max_page_size = 10000

class UsersList(generics.ListAPIView):

    serializer_class = UsersSerializer
```

```
    permission_classes = (AllowAny,)
    pagination_class = LargeResultsSetPagination

    def get_queryset(self):
        query = self.request.query_params.get
        if query('name'):
            return UserProfile.objects.filter(name=query('name'))
        else:
            return UserProfile.objects.all()
```

Note that a query parameter `name` is allowed in case we want to collect only the data for one particular user. After setting the corresponding URL in the `urls.py` file:

```
url(r'^users-list/',UsersList.as_view(),name='users-list')
```

The end point can be called through the `curl` command using the terminal:

```
curl -X GET localhost:8000/users-list/
```

It can also be called using the swagger interface for testing purposes (see *Chapter 6, Basics of Django: a simple web framework*).

Summary

We have just shown how to build an application to recommend movies using the Django framework. You now should have some degree of confidence in how to develop a professional web application using Python and the machine-learning algorithms that power it.

In the next chapter, an additional example on a movie's web sentiment reception will give you even more understanding to efficiently write your own machine-learning web application in Python.

8

Sentiment Analyser Application for Movie Reviews

In this chapter, we describe an application to determine the sentiment of movie reviews using algorithms and methods described throughout the book. In addition, the **Scrapy** library will be used to collect reviews from different websites through a search engine API (Bing search engine). The text and the title of the movie review is extracted using the newspaper library or following some pre-defined extraction rules of an HTML format page. The sentiment of each review is determined using a naive Bayes classifier on the most informative words (using the X^2 measure) in the same way as in *Chapter 4, Web Mining Techniques*. Also, the rank of each page related to each movie query is calculated for completeness using the PageRank algorithm discussed in *Chapter 4, Web Mining Techniques*. This chapter will discuss the code used to build the application, including the Django models and views and the Scrapy scraper is used to collect data from the web pages of the movie reviews. We start by giving an example of what the web application will be and explaining the search engine API used and how we include it in the application. We then describe how we collect the movie reviews, integrating the Scrapy library into Django, the models to store the data, and the main commands to manage the application. All the code discussed in this chapter is available in the GitHub repository of the author inside the `chapter_8` folder at `https://github.com/ai2010/machine_learning_for_the_web/tree/master/chapter_8`.

Application usage overview

The home web page is as follows:

The user can type in the movie name, if they want to know the review's sentiments and relevance. For example, we look for *Batman vs Superman Dawn of Justice* in the following screenshot:

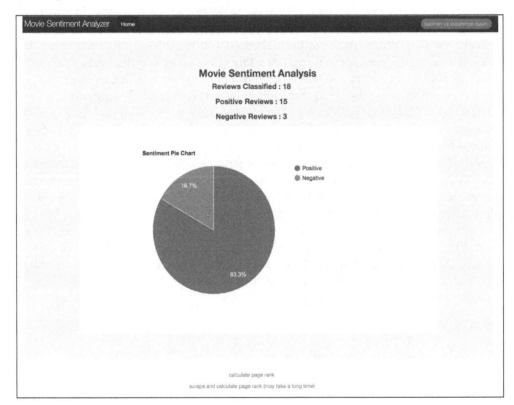

The application collects and scrapes 18 reviews from the Bing search engine and, using the Scrapy library, it analyzes their sentiment (15 positive and 3 negative). All data is stored in Django models, ready to be used to calculate the relevance of each page using the PageRank algorithm (the links at the bottom of the page as seen in the preceding screenshot). In this case, using the PageRank algorithm, we have the following:

This is a list of the most relevant pages to our movie review search, setting a depth parameter 2 on the scraping crawler (refer the following section for further details). Note that to have a good result on page relevance, you have to crawl thousands of pages (the preceding screenshot shows results for around 50 crawled pages).

To write the application, we start the server as usual (see *Chapter 6, Getting Started with Django*, and *Chapter 7, Movie Recommendation System Web Application*) and the main app in Django. First, we create a folder to store all our codes, `movie_reviews_analyzer_app`, and then we initialize Django using the following command:

```
mkdir  movie_reviews_analyzer_app
cd  movie_reviews_analyzer_app
django-admin startproject webmining_server
python manage.py startapp startapp pages
```

We set the settings in the `.py` file as we did in the *Settings* section of *Chapter 6, Getting Started with Django*, and the *Application Setup* section of *Chapter 7, Movie Recommendation System Web Application* (of course, in this case the name is `webmining_server` instead of `server_movierecsys`).

The sentiment analyzer application has the main views in the `.py` file in the main `webmining_server` folder instead of the `app` (pages) folder as we did previously (see *Chapter 6, Getting Started with Django*, and *Chapter 7, Movie Recommendation System Web Application*), because the functions now refer more to the general functioning of the server instead of the specific app (pages).

The last operation to make the web service operational is to create a `superuser` account and go live with the server:

`python manage.py createsuperuser (admin/admin)`

`python manage.py runserver`

Now that the structure of the application has been explained, we can discuss the different parts in more detail starting from the search engine API used to collect URLs.

Search engine choice and the application code

Since scraping directly from the most relevant search engines such as Google, Bing, Yahoo, and others is against their term of service, we need to take initial review pages from their REST API (using scraping services such as Crawlera, `http://crawlera.com/`, is also possible). We decided to use the Bing service, which allows 5,000 queries per month for free.

In order to do that, we register to the Microsoft Service to obtain the key needed to allow the search. Briefly, we followed these steps:

1. Register online on `https://datamarket.azure.com`.

2. In **My Account**, take the **Primary Account Key**.

3. Register a new application (under **DEVELOPERS | REGISTER**; put **Redirect URI**: `https://www.bing.com`)

After that, we can write a function that retrieves as many URLs relevant to our query as we want:

```
num_reviews = 30
def bing_api(query):
    keyBing = API_KEY          # get Bing key from: https://datamarket.
azure.com/account/keys
    credentialBing = 'Basic ' + (':%s' % keyBing).encode('base64')[:-
1] # the "-1" is to remove the trailing "\n" which encode adds
    searchString = '%27X'+query.replace(" ",'+')+'movie+review%27'
```

```
    top = 50#maximum allowed by Bing

    reviews_urls = []
    if num_reviews<top:
        offset = 0
        url = 'https://api.datamarket.azure.com/Bing/Search/Web?' + \
                'Query=%s&$top=%d&$skip=%d&$format=json' %
(searchString, num_reviews, offset)

        request = urllib2.Request(url)
        request.add_header('Authorization', credentialBing)
        requestOpener = urllib2.build_opener()
        response = requestOpener.open(request)
        results = json.load(response)
        reviews_urls = [ d['Url'] for d in results['d']['results']]
    else:
        nqueries = int(float(num_reviews)/top)+1
        for i in xrange(nqueries):
            offset = top*i
            if i==nqueries-1:
                top = num_reviews-offset
                url = 'https://api.datamarket.azure.com/Bing/Search/
Web?' + \
                    'Query=%s&$top=%d&$skip=%d&$format=json' %
(searchString, top, offset)

                request = urllib2.Request(url)
                request.add_header('Authorization', credentialBing)
                requestOpener = urllib2.build_opener()
                response = requestOpener.open(request)
            else:
                top=50
                url = 'https://api.datamarket.azure.com/Bing/Search/
Web?' + \
                    'Query=%s&$top=%d&$skip=%d&$format=json' %
(searchString, top, offset)

                request = urllib2.Request(url)
                request.add_header('Authorization', credentialBing)
                requestOpener = urllib2.build_opener()
                response = requestOpener.open(request)
            results = json.load(response)
            reviews_urls += [ d['Url'] for d in results['d']
['results']]
    return reviews_urls
```

The `API_KEY` parameter is taken from the Microsoft account, `query` is a string which specifies the movie name, and `num_reviews` = `30` is the number of URLs returned in total from the Bing API. With the list of URLs that contain the reviews, we can now set up a scraper to extract from each web page the title and the review text using Scrapy.

Scrapy setup and the application code

Scrapy is a Python library is used to extract content from web pages or to crawl pages linked to a given web page (see the *Web crawlers (or spiders)* section of *Chapter 4*, *Web Mining Techniques*, for more details). To install the library, type the following in the terminal:

```
sudo pip install Scrapy
```

Install the executable in the `bin` folder:

```
sudo easy_install scrapy
```

From the `movie_reviews_analyzer_app` folder, we initialize our Scrapy project as follows:

```
scrapy startproject scrapy_spider
```

This command will create the following tree inside the `scrapy_spider` folder:

```
├── __init__.py
├── items.py
├── pipelines.py
├── settings.py
├── spiders
│   ├── __init__.py
```

The `pipelines.py` and `items.py` files manage how the scraped data is stored and manipulated, and they will be discussed later in the *Spiders* and *Integrate Django with Scrapy* sections. The `settings.py` file sets the parameters each spider (or crawler) defined in the `spiders` folder uses to operate. In the following two sections, we describe the main parameters and spiders used in this application.

Scrapy settings

The `settings.py` file collects all the parameters used by each spider in the Scrapy project to scrape web pages. The main parameters are as follows:

- `DEPTH_LIMIT`: The number of subsequent pages crawled following an initial URL. The default is `0` and it means that no limit is set.

- `LOG_ENABLED`: To allow/deny Scrapy to log on the terminal while executing default is true.

- `ITEM_PIPELINES = {'scrapy_spider.pipelines.ReviewPipeline': 1000,}`: The path of the pipeline function to manipulate data extracted from each web page.

- `CONCURRENT_ITEMS = 200`: The number of concurrent items processed in the pipeline.

- `CONCURRENT_REQUESTS = 5000`: The maximum number of simultaneous requests handled by Scrapy.

- `CONCURRENT_REQUESTS_PER_DOMAIN = 3000`: The maximum number of simultaneous requests handled by Scrapy for each specified domain.

The larger the depth, more the pages are scraped and, consequently, the time needed to scrape increases. To speed up the process, you can set high value on the last three parameters. In this application (the `spiders` folder), we set two spiders: a scraper to extract data from each movie review URL (`movie_link_results.py`) and a crawler to generate a graph of webpages linked to the initial movie review URL (`recursive_link_results.py`).

Scraper

The scraper on `movie_link_results.py` looks as follows:

```
from newspaper import Article
from urlparse import urlparse
from scrapy.selector import Selector
from scrapy import Spider
from scrapy.spiders import BaseSpider,CrawlSpider, Rule
from scrapy.http import Request
from scrapy_spider import settings
from scrapy_spider.items import PageItem,SearchItem


unwanted_domains = ['youtube.com','www.youtube.com']
```

```
from nltk.corpus import stopwords
stopwords = set(stopwords.words('english'))


def CheckQueryinReview(keywords,title,content):
    content_list = map(lambda x:x.lower(),content.split(' '))
    title_list = map(lambda x:x.lower(),title.split(' '))
    words = content_list+title_list
    for k in keywords:
        if k in words:
            return True
    return False


class Search(Spider):
    name = 'scrapy_spider_reviews'

    def __init__(self,url_list,search_key):#specified by -a
        self.search_key = search_key
        self.keywords = [w.lower() for w in search_key.split(" ") if w
not in stopwords]
        self.start_urls =url_list.split(',')
        super(Search, self).__init__(url_list)

    def start_requests(self):
        for url in self.start_urls:
            yield Request(url=url, callback=self.parse_site,dont_
filter=True)

    def parse_site(self, response):
        ## Get the selector for xpath parsing or from newspaper

        def crop_emptyel(arr):
            return [u for u in arr if u!=' ']

        domain = urlparse(response.url).hostname
        a = Article(response.url)
        a.download()
```

```
        a.parse()
        title = a.title.encode('ascii','ignore').replace('\n','')
        sel = Selector(response)
        if title==None:
            title = sel.xpath('//title/text()').extract()
            if len(title)>0:
                title = title[0].encode('utf-8').strip().lower()


        content = a.text.encode('ascii','ignore').replace('\n','')
        if content == None:
            content = 'none'
        if len(crop_emptyel(sel.xpath('//div//article//p/text()').
extract()))>1:
                contents = crop_emptyel(sel.xpath('//div//article//p/
text()').extract())
                print 'divarticle'
            ….
            elif len(crop_emptyel(sel.xpath('/html/head/meta[@
name="description"]/@content').extract()))>0:
                contents = crop_emptyel(sel.xpath('/html/head/meta[@
name="description"]/@content').extract())
            content = ' '.join([c.encode('utf-8') for c in contents]).
strip().lower()


        #get search item
        search_item = SearchItem.django_model.objects.get(term=self.
search_key)
        #save item
        if not PageItem.django_model.objects.filter(url=response.url).
exists():
            if len(content) > 0:
                if CheckQueryinReview(self.keywords,title,content):
                    if domain not in unwanted_domains:
                        newpage = PageItem()
                        newpage['searchterm'] = search_item
                        newpage['title'] = title
                        newpage['content'] = content
```

```
                    newpage['url'] = response.url
                    newpage['depth'] = 0
                    newpage['review'] = True
                    #newpage.save()
                    return newpage
            else:
                return null
```

We can see that the `Spider` class from `scrapy` is inherited by the `Search` class and the following standard methods have to be defined to override the standard methods:

- `__init__`: The constructor of the spider needs to define the `start_urls` list that contains the URL to extract content from. In addition, we have custom variables such as `search_key` and `keywords` that store the information related to the query of the movie's title used on the search engine API.

- `start_requests`: This function is triggered when `spider` is called and it declares what to do for each URL in the `start_urls` list; for each URL, the custom `parse_site` function will be called (instead of the default `parse` function).

- `parse_site`: It is a custom function to parse data from each URL. To extract the title of the review and its text content, we used the newspaper library (`sudo pip install newspaper`) or, if it fails, we parse the HTML file directly using some defined rules to avoid the noise due to undesired tags (each rule structure is defined with the `sel.xpath` command). To achieve this result, we select some popular domains (`rottentomatoes`, `cnn`, and so on) and ensure the parsing is able to extract the content from these websites (not all the extraction rules are displayed in the preceding code but they can be found as usual in the GitHub file). The data is then stored in a page `Django` model using the related Scrapy item and the `ReviewPipeline` function (see the following section).

- `CheckQueryinReview`: This is a custom function to check whether the movie title (from the query) is contained in the content or title of each web page.

To run the spider, we need to type in the following command from the `scrapy_spider` (internal) folder:

```
scrapy crawl scrapy_spider_reviews -a url_list=listname -a search_
key=keyname
```

Pipelines

The pipelines define what to do when a new page is scraped by the spider. In the preceding case, the `parse_site` function returns a `PageItem` object, which triggers the following pipeline (`pipelines.py`):

```
class ReviewPipeline(object):

    def process_item(self, item, spider):
        #if spider.name == 'scrapy_spider_reviews':#not working
            item.save()
            return item
```

This class simply saves each item (a new page in the spider notation).

Crawler

As we showed in the overview (the preceding section), the relevance of the review is calculated using the PageRank algorithm after we have stored all the linked pages starting from the review's URL. The crawler `recursive_link_results.py` performs this operation:

```
#from scrapy.spider import Spider
from scrapy.selector import Selector
from scrapy.contrib.spiders import CrawlSpider, Rule
from scrapy.linkextractors import LinkExtractor
from scrapy.http import Request

from scrapy_spider.items import PageItem,LinkItem,SearchItem

class Search(CrawlSpider):

    name = 'scrapy_spider_recursive'

    def __init__(self,url_list,search_id):#specified by -a

        #REMARK is allowed_domains is not set then ALL are allowed!!!
        self.start_urls = url_list.split(',')
        self.search_id = int(search_id)

        #allow any link but the ones with different font
size(repetitions)
```

```
        self.rules = (

Rule(LinkExtractor(allow=(),deny=('fontSize=*','infoid=*','SortBy=*',
),unique=True), callback='parse_item', follow=True),
            )
        super(Search, self).__init__(url_list)


    def parse_item(self, response):
        sel = Selector(response)

        ## Get meta info from website
        title = sel.xpath('//title/text()').extract()
        if len(title)>0:
            title = title[0].encode('utf-8')

        contents = sel.xpath('/html/head/meta[@name="description"]/@
content').extract()
        content = ' '.join([c.encode('utf-8') for c in contents]).strip()

        fromurl = response.request.headers['Referer']
        tourl = response.url
        depth = response.request.meta['depth']

        #get search item
        search_item = SearchItem.django_model.objects.get(id=self.search_
id)
        #newpage
        if not PageItem.django_model.objects.filter(url=tourl).exists():
            newpage = PageItem()
            newpage['searchterm'] = search_item
            newpage['title'] = title
            newpage['content'] = content
            newpage['url'] = tourl
            newpage['depth'] = depth
```

```
        newpage.save()#cant use pipeline cause the execution can
finish here

        #get from_id,to_id
        from_page = PageItem.django_model.objects.get(url=fromurl)
        from_id = from_page.id
        to_page = PageItem.django_model.objects.get(url=tourl)
        to_id = to_page.id

        #newlink
        if not LinkItem.django_model.objects.filter(from_id=from_id).
filter(to_id=to_id).exists():
            newlink = LinkItem()
            newlink['searchterm'] = search_item
            newlink['from_id'] = from_id
            newlink['to_id'] = to_id
            newlink.save()
```

The CrawlSpider class from scrapy is inherited by the Search class, and the following standard methods have to be defined to override the standard methods (as for the spider case):

- __init__: The is a constructor of the class. The start_urls parameter defines the starting URL from which the spider will start to crawl until the DEPTH_LIMIT value is reached. The rules parameter sets the type of URL allowed/denied to scrape (in this case, the same page but with different font sizes is disregarded) and it defines the function to call to manipulate each retrieved page (parse_item). Also, a custom variable search_id is defined, which is needed to store the ID of the query within the other data.

- parse_item: This is a custom function called to store the important data from each retrieved page. A new Django item of the Page model (see the following section) from each page is created, which contains the title and content of the page (using the xpath HTML parser). To perform the PageRank algorithm, the connection from the page that links to each page and the page itself is saved as an object of the Link model using the related Scrapy item (see the following sections).

To run the crawler, we need to type the following from the (internal) scrapy_spider folder:

```
scrapy crawl scrapy_spider_recursive -a url_list=listname -a search_
id=keyname
```

Django models

The data collected using the spiders needs to be stored in a database. In Django, the database tables are called models and defined in the `models.py` file (within the `pages` folder). The content of this file is as follows:

```python
from django.db import models
from django.conf import settings
from django.utils.translation import ugettext_lazy as _


class SearchTerm(models.Model):
    term = models.CharField(_('search'), max_length=255)
    num_reviews = models.IntegerField(null=True,default=0)
    #display term on admin panel
    def __unicode__(self):
            return self.term


class Page(models.Model):
    searchterm = models.ForeignKey(SearchTerm, related_name='pages',null
=True,blank=True)
    url = models.URLField(_('url'), default='', blank=True)
    title = models.CharField(_('name'), max_length=255)
    depth = models.IntegerField(null=True,default=-1)
    html = models.TextField(_('html'),blank=True, default='')
    review = models.BooleanField(default=False)
    old_rank = models.FloatField(null=True,default=0)
    new_rank = models.FloatField(null=True,default=1)
    content = models.TextField(_('content'),blank=True, default='')
    sentiment = models.IntegerField(null=True,default=100)


class Link(models.Model):
    searchterm = models.ForeignKey(SearchTerm, related_name='links',null
=True,blank=True)
    from_id = models.IntegerField(null=True)
    to_id = models.IntegerField(null=True)
```

Each movie title typed on the home page of the application is stored in the `SearchTerm` model, while the data of each web page is collected in an object of the `Page` model. Apart from the content field (HTML, title, URL, content), the sentiment of the review and the depth in graph network are recorded (a Boolean also indicates if the web page is a movie review page or simply a linked page). The `Link` model stores all the graph links between pages, which are then used by the PageRank algorithm to calculate the relevance of the reviews web pages. Note that the `Page` model and the `Link` model are both linked to the related `SearchTerm` through a foreign key. As usual, to write these models as database tables, we type the following commands:

```
python manage.py makemigrations
python manage.py migrate
```

To populate these Django models, we need to make Scrapy interact with Django, and this is the subject of the following section.

Integrating Django with Scrapy

To make paths easy to call, we remove the external `scrapy_spider` folder so that inside the `movie_reviews_analyzer_app`, the `webmining_server` folder is at the same level as the `scrapy_spider` folder:

```
├── db.sqlite3
├── scrapy.cfg
├── scrapy_spider
│   ├── ...
│   ├── spiders
│   │   ...
└── webmining_server
```

We set the Django path into the Scrapy `settings.py` file:

```
# Setting up django's project full path.
import sys
sys.path.insert(0, BASE_DIR+'/webmining_server')
# Setting up django's settings module name.
os.environ['DJANGO_SETTINGS_MODULE'] = 'webmining_server.settings'
#import django to load models(otherwise AppRegistryNotReady: Models
aren't loaded yet):
import django
django.setup()
```

Now we can install the library that will allow managing Django models from Scrapy:

```
sudo pip install scrapy-djangoitem
```

In the `items.py` file, we write the links between Django models and Scrapy items as follows:

```
from scrapy_djangoitem import DjangoItem
from pages.models import Page,Link,SearchTerm


class SearchItem(DjangoItem):
    django_model = SearchTerm
class PageItem(DjangoItem):
    django_model = Page
class LinkItem(DjangoItem):
    django_model = Link
```

Each class inherits the `DjangoItem` class so that the original Django models declared with the `django_model` variable are automatically linked. The Scrapy project is now completed so we can continue our discussion explaining the Django codes that handle the data extracted by Scrapy and the Django commands needed to manage the applications.

Commands (sentiment analysis model and delete queries)

The application needs to manage some operations that are not allowed to the final user of the service, such as defining a sentiment analysis model and deleting a query of a movie in order to redo it instead of retrieving the existing data from memory. The following sections will explain the commands to perform these actions.

Sentiment analysis model loader

The final goal of this application is to determine the sentiment (positive or negative) of the movie reviews. To achieve that, a sentiment classifier must be built using some external data, and then it should be stored in memory (cache) to be used by each query request. This is the purpose of the `load_sentimentclassifier.py` command displayed hereafter:

```
import nltk.classify.util, nltk.metrics
from nltk.classify import NaiveBayesClassifier
from nltk.corpus import movie_reviews
```

```
from nltk.corpus import stopwords
from nltk.collocations import BigramCollocationFinder
from nltk.metrics import BigramAssocMeasures
from nltk.probability import FreqDist, ConditionalFreqDist
import collections
from django.core.management.base import BaseCommand, CommandError
from optparse import make_option
from django.core.cache import cache


stopwords = set(stopwords.words('english'))
method_selfeatures = 'best_words_features'


class Command(BaseCommand):
    option_list = BaseCommand.option_list + (
                make_option('-n', '--num_bestwords',
                            dest='num_bestwords', type='int',
                            action='store',
                            help=('number of words with high
information')),)


    def handle(self, *args, **options):
        num_bestwords = options['num_bestwords']
        self.bestwords = self.GetHighInformationWordsChi(num_bestwords)
        clf = self.train_clf(method_selfeatures)
        cache.set('clf',clf)
        cache.set('bestwords',self.bestwords)
```

At the beginning of the file, the variable method_selfeatures sets the method of feature selection (in this case, the features are the words in the reviews; see *Chapter 4, Web Mining Techniques,* for further details) used to train the classifier train_clf. The maximum number of best words (features) is defined by the input parameter num_bestwords. The classifier and the best features (bestwords) are then stored in the cache ready to be used by the application (using the cache module). The classifier and the methods to select the best words (features) are as follows:

```
    def train_clf(method):
        negidxs = movie_reviews.fileids('neg')
        posidxs = movie_reviews.fileids('pos')
```

```
        if method=='stopword_filtered_words_features':
            negfeatures = [(stopword_filtered_words_features(movie_
reviews.words(fileids=[file])), 'neg') for file in negidxs]
            posfeatures = [(stopword_filtered_words_features(movie_
reviews.words(fileids=[file])), 'pos') for file in posidxs]
        elif method=='best_words_features':
            negfeatures = [(best_words_features(movie_reviews.
words(fileids=[file])), 'neg') for file in negidxs]
            posfeatures = [(best_words_features(movie_reviews.
words(fileids=[file])), 'pos') for file in posidxs]
        elif method=='best_bigrams_words_features':
            negfeatures = [(best_bigrams_words_features(movie_reviews.
words(fileids=[file])), 'neg') for file in negidxs]
            posfeatures = [(best_bigrams_words_features(movie_reviews.
words(fileids=[file])), 'pos') for file in posidxs]


        trainfeatures = negfeatures + posfeatures
        clf = NaiveBayesClassifier.train(trainfeatures)
        return clf


    def stopword_filtered_words_features(self,words):
        return dict([(word, True) for word in words if word not in
stopwords])


    #eliminate Low Information Features
    def GetHighInformationWordsChi(self,num_bestwords):
        word_fd = FreqDist()
        label_word_fd = ConditionalFreqDist()

        for word in movie_reviews.words(categories=['pos']):
            word_fd[word.lower()] +=1
            label_word_fd['pos'][word.lower()] +=1

        for word in movie_reviews.words(categories=['neg']):
            word_fd[word.lower()] +=1
```

```
            label_word_fd['neg'][word.lower()] +=1


        pos_word_count = label_word_fd['pos'].N()
        neg_word_count = label_word_fd['neg'].N()
        total_word_count = pos_word_count + neg_word_count


        word_scores = {}
        for word, freq in word_fd.iteritems():
            pos_score = BigramAssocMeasures.chi_sq(label_word_fd['pos']
[word],
                (freq, pos_word_count), total_word_count)
            neg_score = BigramAssocMeasures.chi_sq(label_word_fd['neg']
[word],
                (freq, neg_word_count), total_word_count)
            word_scores[word] = pos_score + neg_score


        best = sorted(word_scores.iteritems(), key=lambda (w,s): s,
reverse=True)[:num_bestwords]
        bestwords = set([w for w, s in best])
        return bestwords


    def best_words_features(self,words):
        return dict([(word, True) for word in words if word in self.
bestwords])


    def best_bigrams_word_features(self,words,
measure=BigramAssocMeasures.chi_sq, nbigrams=200):
        bigram_finder = BigramCollocationFinder.from_words(words)
        bigrams = bigram_finder.nbest(measure, nbigrams)
        d = dict([(bigram, True) for bigram in bigrams])
        d.update(best_words_features(words))
        return d
```

Three methods are written to select words in the preceding code:

- `stopword_filtered_words_features`: Eliminates the `stopwords` using the **Natural Language Toolkit (NLTK)** list of conjunctions and considers the rest as relevant words

- `best_words_features`: Using the X^2 measure (`NLTK` library), the most informative words related to positive or negative reviews are selected (see *Chapter 4, Web Mining Techniques*, for further details)

- `best_bigrams_word_features`: Uses the X^2 measure (`NLTK` library) to find the 200 most informative bigrams from the set of words (see *Chapter 4, Web Mining Techniques*, for further details)

The chosen classifier is the Naive Bayes algorithm (see *Chapter 3, Supervised Machine Learning*) and the labeled text (positive, negative sentiment) is taken from the `NLTK.corpus` of `movie_reviews`. To install it, open a terminal in Python and install `movie_reviews` from `corpus`:

```
nltk.download()--> corpora/movie_reviews corpus
```

Deleting an already performed query

Since we can specify different parameters (such as the feature selection method, the number of best words, and so on), we may want to perform and store again the sentiment of the reviews with different values. The `delete_query` command is needed for this purpose and it is as follows:

```
from pages.models import Link,Page,SearchTerm
from django.core.management.base import BaseCommand, CommandError
from optparse import make_option


class Command(BaseCommand):
    option_list = BaseCommand.option_list + (
                make_option('-s', '--searchid',
                                dest='searchid', type='int',
                                action='store',
                                help=('id of the search term to delete')),)


    def handle(self, *args, **options):
        searchid = options['searchid']
        if searchid == None:
```

```
        print "please specify searchid: python manage.py
--searchid=--"

        #list
        for sobj in SearchTerm.objects.all():
            print 'id:',sobj.id,"  term:",sobj.term
    else:
        print 'delete...'
        search_obj = SearchTerm.objects.get(id=searchid)
        pages = search_obj.pages.all()
        pages.delete()
        links = search_obj.links.all()
        links.delete()
        search_obj.delete()
```

If we run the command without specifying the `searchid` (the ID of the query), the list of all the queries and related IDs will be shown. After that we can choose which query we want to delete by typing the following:

```
python manage.py delete_query --searchid=VALUE
```

We can use the cached sentiment analysis model to show the user the online sentiment of the chosen movie, as we explain in the following section.

Sentiment reviews analyser – Django views and HTML

Most of the code explained in this chapter (commands, Bing search engine, Scrapy, and Django models) is used in the function analyzer in `views.py` to power the home webpage shown in the *Application usage overview* section (after declaring the URL in the `urls.py` file as `url(r'^$','webmining_server.views.analyzer')`).

```
def analyzer(request):
    context = {}

    if request.method == 'POST':
        post_data = request.POST
        query = post_data.get('query', None)
        if query:
            return redirect('%s?%s' % (reverse('webmining_server.views.
analyzer'),
```

```
                              urllib.urlencode({'q': query})))
    elif request.method == 'GET':
        get_data = request.GET
        query = get_data.get('q')
        if not query:
            return render_to_response(
                'movie_reviews/home.html', RequestContext(request,
context))

        context['query'] = query
        stripped_query = query.strip().lower()
        urls = []

        if test_mode:
            urls = parse_bing_results()
        else:
            urls = bing_api(stripped_query)

        if len(urls)== 0:
            return render_to_response(
                'movie_reviews/noreviewsfound.html',
RequestContext(request, context))
        if not SearchTerm.objects.filter(term=stripped_query).exists():
            s = SearchTerm(term=stripped_query)
            s.save()
            try:
                #scrape
                cmd = 'cd ../scrapy_spider & scrapy crawl scrapy_spider_
reviews -a url_list=%s -a search_key=%s' %('\"'+str(','.join(urls[:num_
reviews]).encode('utf-8'))+'\"','\"'+str(stripped_query)+'\"')
                os.system(cmd)
            except:
                print 'error!'
                s.delete()
        else:
            #collect the pages already scraped
```

```
            s = SearchTerm.objects.get(term=stripped_query)


        #calc num pages
        pages = s.pages.all().filter(review=True)
        if len(pages) == 0:
            s.delete()
            return render_to_response(
                'movie_reviews/noreviewsfound.html',
RequestContext(request, context))


        s.num_reviews = len(pages)
        s.save()


        context['searchterm_id'] = int(s.id)


        #train classifier with nltk
        def train_clf(method):
            ...
        def stopword_filtered_words_features(words):
            ...
        #Eliminate Low Information Features
        def GetHighInformationWordsChi(num_bestwords):
            ...
        bestwords = cache.get('bestwords')
        if bestwords == None:
            bestwords = GetHighInformationWordsChi(num_bestwords)
        def best_words_features(words):
            ...
        def best_bigrams_words_features(words,
measure=BigramAssocMeasures.chi_sq, nbigrams=200):
            ...
        clf = cache.get('clf')
        if clf == None:
            clf = train_clf(method_selfeatures)


        cntpos = 0
```

```
cntneg = 0
for p in pages:
    words = p.content.split(" ")
    feats = best_words_features(words) #bigram_word_
features(words) #stopword_filtered_word_feats(words)
    #print feats
    str_sent = clf.classify(feats)
    if str_sent == 'pos':
        p.sentiment = 1
        cntpos +=1
    else:
        p.sentiment = -1
        cntneg +=1
    p.save()

context['reviews_classified'] = len(pages)
context['positive_count'] = cntpos
context['negative_count'] = cntneg
context['classified_information'] = True
return render_to_response(
'movie_reviews/home.html', RequestContext(request, context))
```

The inserted movie title is stored in the query variable and sent to the bing_api function to collect review's URL. The URL are then scraped calling Scrapy to find the review texts, which are processed using the clf classifier model and the selected most informative words (bestwords) retrieved from the cache (or the same model is generated again in case the cache is empty). The counts of the predicted sentiments of the reviews (positive_counts, negative_counts, and reviews_classified) are then sent back to the home.html (the templates folder) page, which uses the following Google pie chart code:

```
<h2 align = Center>Movie Reviews Sentiment Analysis</h2>
<div class="row">
<p align = Center><strong>Reviews Classified : {{ reviews_
classified }}</strong></p>
<p align = Center><strong>Positive Reviews : {{ positive_count
}}</strong></p>
<p align = Center><strong> Negative Reviews : {{ negative_
count }}</strong></p>
</div>
<section>
```

```
        <script type="text/javascript" src="https://www.google.com/
    jsapi"></script>
        <script type="text/javascript">
          google.load("visualization", "1", {packages:["corechart"]});
          google.setOnLoadCallback(drawChart);
          function drawChart() {
            var data = google.visualization.arrayToDataTable([
              ['Sentiment', 'Number'],
              ['Positive',      {{ positive_count }}],
              ['Negative',      {{ negative_count }}]
            ]);
            var options = { title: 'Sentiment Pie Chart'};
            var chart = new google.visualization.PieChart(document.
    getElementById('piechart'));
            chart.draw(data, options);
          }
        </script>
        <p align ="Center" id="piechart" style="width: 900px; height:
    500px;display: block; margin: 0 auto;text-align: center;" ></p>
        </div>
```

The function `drawChart` calls the Google `PieChart` visualization function, which takes as input the data (the positive and negative counts) to create the pie chart. To have more details about how the HTML code interacts with the Django views, refer to *Chapter 6, Getting Started with Django*, in the *URL and views behind html web pages* section. From the result page with the sentiment counts (see the *Application usage overview* section), the PagerRank relevance of the scraped reviews can be calculated using one of the two links at the bottom of the page. The Django code behind this operation is discussed in the following section.

PageRank: Django view and the algorithm code

To rank the importance of the online reviews, we have implemented the PageRank algorithm (see *Chapter 4, Web Mining Techniques*, in the *Ranking: PageRank algorithm* section) into the application. The `pgrank.py` file in the `pgrank` folder within the `webmining_server` folder implements the algorithm that follows:

```
from pages.models import Page,SearchTerm


num_iterations = 100000
eps=0.0001
```

```
D = 0.85


def pgrank(searchid):
    s = SearchTerm.objects.get(id=int(searchid))
    links = s.links.all()
    from_idxs = [i.from_id for i in links ]
    # Find the idxs that receive page rank
    links_received = []
    to_idxs = []
    for l in links:
        from_id = l.from_id
        to_id = l.to_id
        if from_id not in from_idxs: continue
        if to_id  not in from_idxs: continue
        links_received.append([from_id,to_id])
        if to_id  not in to_idxs: to_idxs.append(to_id)

    pages = s.pages.all()
    prev_ranks = dict()
    for node in from_idxs:
        ptmp  = Page.objects.get(id=node)
        prev_ranks[node] = ptmp.old_rank

    conv=1.
    cnt=0
    while conv>eps or cnt<num_iterations:
        next_ranks = dict()
        total = 0.0
        for (node,old_rank) in prev_ranks.items():
            total += old_rank
            next_ranks[node] = 0.0

        #find the outbound links and send the pagerank down to each of
them
        for (node, old_rank) in prev_ranks.items():
```

```
            give_idxs = []
            for (from_id, to_id) in links_received:
                if from_id != node: continue
                if to_id  not in to_idxs: continue
                give_idxs.append(to_id)
            if (len(give_idxs) < 1): continue
            amount = D*old_rank/len(give_idxs)
            for id in give_idxs:
                next_ranks[id] += amount
        tot = 0
        for (node,next_rank) in next_ranks.items():
            tot += next_rank
        const = (1-D)/ len(next_ranks)

        for node in next_ranks:
            next_ranks[node] += const

        tot = 0
        for (node,old_rank) in next_ranks.items():
            tot += next_rank

        difftot = 0
        for (node, old_rank) in prev_ranks.items():
            new_rank = next_ranks[node]
            diff = abs(old_rank-new_rank)
            difftot += diff
        conv= difftot/len(prev_ranks)
        cnt+=1
        prev_ranks = next_ranks

for (id,new_rank) in next_ranks.items():
    ptmp = Page.objects.get(id=id)
    url = ptmp.url

for (id,new_rank) in next_ranks.items():
```

```
        ptmp = Page.objects.get(id=id)
        ptmp.old_rank = ptmp.new_rank
        ptmp.new_rank = new_rank
        ptmp.save()
```

This code takes all the links stores associated with the given `SearchTerm` object and implements the PageRank score for each page *i* at time *t*, where *P(i)* is given by the recursive equation:

$$P(i)_t = \frac{(1-D)}{N} + D\sum_{j=1}^{N} A_{ji}P(j)_{t-1} \quad \forall i\ 1,...,N$$

Here, *N* is the total number of pages, and $A_{ij} = \frac{1}{N_j}$ (N_j is the number of out links of page *j*) if page *j* points to *i*; otherwise, *N* is 0. The parameter *D* is the so-called **damping factor** (set to 0.85 in the preceding code), and it represents the probability to follow the transition given by the transition matrix *A*. The equation is iterated until the convergence parameter `eps` is satisfied or the maximum number of iterations, `num_iterations`, is reached. The algorithm is called by clicking either **scrape and calculate page rank (may take a long time)** or **calculate page rank** links at the bottom of the `home.html` page after the sentiment of the movie reviews has been displayed. The link is linked to the function `pgrank_view` in the `views.py` (through the declared URL in `urls.py`: `url(r'^pg-rank/(?P<pk>\d+)/', 'webmining_server.views.pgrank_view', name='pgrank_view')`):

```python
def pgrank_view(request,pk):
    context = {}
    get_data = request.GET
    scrape = get_data.get('scrape','False')
    s = SearchTerm.objects.get(id=pk)

    if scrape == 'True':
        pages = s.pages.all().filter(review=True)
        urls = []
        for u in pages:
            urls.append(u.url)
        #crawl
```

```
        cmd = 'cd ../scrapy_spider & scrapy crawl scrapy_spider_recursive
-a url_list=%s -a search_id=%s' %('\"'+str(','.join(urls[:]).encode('utf-
8'))+'\"','\"'+str(pk)+'\"')

        os.system(cmd)


    links = s.links.all()
    if len(links)==0:
        context['no_links'] = True
        return render_to_response(
            'movie_reviews/pg-rank.html', RequestContext(request,
context))
    #calc pgranks
    pgrank(pk)
    #load pgranks in descending order of pagerank
    pages_ordered = s.pages.all().filter(review=True).order_by('-new_
rank')
    context['pages'] = pages_ordered

    return render_to_response(
        'movie_reviews/pg-rank.html', RequestContext(request, context))
```

This code calls the crawler to collect all the linked pages to the reviews and calculate the PageRank scores using the code discussed earlier. Then the scores are displayed in the pg-rank.html page (in descending order by page rank score) as we showed in the *Application usage overview* section of this chapter. Since this function can take a long time to process (to crawl thousands of pages), the command run_scrapelinks. py has been written to run the Scrapy crawler (the reader is invited to read or modify the script as they like as an exercise).

Admin and API

As the last part of the chapter, we describe briefly some possible admin management of the model and the implementation of an API endpoint to retrieve the data processed by the application. In the pages folder, we can set two admin interfaces in the admin.py file to check the data collected by the SearchTerm and Page models:

```
from django.contrib import admin
from django_markdown.admin import MarkdownField, AdminMarkdownWidget
```

```
from pages.models import SearchTerm,Page,Link


class SearchTermAdmin(admin.ModelAdmin):
    formfield_overrides = {MarkdownField: {'widget':
AdminMarkdownWidget}}
    list_display = ['id', 'term', 'num_reviews']
    ordering = ['-id']


class PageAdmin(admin.ModelAdmin):
    formfield_overrides = {MarkdownField: {'widget':
AdminMarkdownWidget}}
    list_display = ['id', 'searchterm', 'url','title','content']
    ordering = ['-id','-new_rank']


admin.site.register(SearchTerm,SearchTermAdmin)
admin.site.register(Page,PageAdmin)
admin.site.register(Link)
```

Note that both `SearchTermAdmin` and `PageAdmin` display objects with decreasing ID (and `new_rank` in the case of `PageAdmin`). The following screenshot is an example:

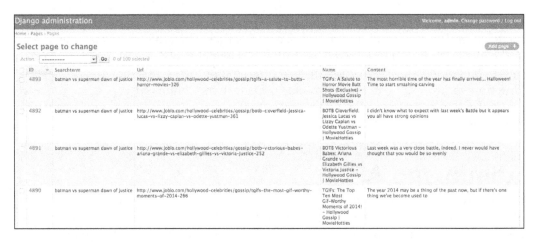

Note that although it is not necessary, the `Link` model has also been included in the admin interface (`admin.site.register(Link)`). More interestingly, we can set up an API endpoint to retrieve the sentiment counts related to a movie's title. In the `api.py` file inside the pages folder, we can have the following:

```
from rest_framework import views,generics
from rest_framework.permissions import AllowAny
from rest_framework.response import Response
from rest_framework.pagination import PageNumberPagination
from pages.serializers import SearchTermSerializer
from pages.models import SearchTerm,Page


class LargeResultsSetPagination(PageNumberPagination):
    page_size = 1000
    page_size_query_param = 'page_size'
    max_page_size = 10000


class SearchTermsList(generics.ListAPIView):

    serializer_class = SearchTermSerializer
    permission_classes = (AllowAny,)
    pagination_class = LargeResultsSetPagination

    def get_queryset(self):
        return SearchTerm.objects.all()


class PageCounts(views.APIView):

    permission_classes = (AllowAny,)
    def get(self,*args, **kwargs):
        searchid=self.kwargs['pk']
        reviewpages = Page.objects.filter(searchterm=searchid).
filter(review=True)
        npos = len([p for p in reviewpages if p.sentiment==1])
        nneg = len(reviewpages)-npos
        return Response({'npos':npos,'nneg':nneg})
```

The `PageCounts` class takes as input the ID of the search (the movie's title) and it returns the sentiments, that is, positive and negative counts, for the movie's reviews. To get the ID of `earchTerm` from a movie's title, you can either look at the admin interface or use the other API endpoint `SearchTermsList`; this simply returns the list of the movies' titles together with the associated ID. The serializer is set on the `serializers.py` file:

```
from pages.models import SearchTerm
from rest_framework import serializers


class SearchTermSerializer(serializers.HyperlinkedModelSerializer):
    class Meta:
        model = SearchTerm
        fields = ('id', 'term')
```

To call these endpoints, we can again use the swagger interface (see *Chapter 6, Getting Started with Django*) or use the `curl` command in the terminal to make these calls. For instance:

```
curl -X GET localhost:8000/search-list/
{"count":7,"next":null,"previous":null,"results":[{"id":24,"term":"the ma
rtian"},{"id":27,"term":"steve jobs"},{"id":29,"term":"suffragette"},{"i
d":39,"term":"southpaw"},{"id":40,"term":"vacation"},{"id":67,"term":"the
revenant"},{"id":68,"term":"batman vs superman dawn of justice"}]}
```

and

```
curl -X GET localhost:8000/pages-sentiment/68/
{"nneg":3,"npos":15}
```

Summary

In this chapter, we described a movie review sentiment analyzer web application to make you familiar with some of the algorithms and libraries we discussed in *Chapter 3, Supervised Machine Learning*, *Chapter 4, Web Mining Techniques*, and *Chapter 6, Getting Started with Django*.

This is the end of a journey: by reading this book and experimenting with the codes provided, you should have acquired significant practical knowledge about the most important machine learning algorithms used in the commercial environment nowadays.

You should be now ready to develop your own web applications and ideas using Python and some machine learning algorithms, learned by reading this book. Many challenging data-related problems are present in the real world today, waiting to be solved by people who can grasp and apply the material treated in this book, and you, who have arrived at this point, are certainly one of those people.

Index

A

ad.data file
  URL 28
admin
  API, implementing 263-266
  commands, writing 206, 207
  creating 204
  RESTful API 207-209
  shell interface, creating 206
agglomeration, linkage criteria
  average linkage 56
  complete linkage 56
  single linkage 56
  UPGMA 56
  Ward algorithm 56
agglomerative clustering 54
Alternating Least Square (ALS) 164, 165
app
  HTML web pages 197
  models, creating 197
  URL 197
  URL declarations 200-203
  views 200-203
  writing 196
array manipulations
  argsort method 18
  array_equal method 18
  concatenate method 18
  flatten method 18
  fromstring method 18
  random method 18
  reshape method 18
  shuffle method 18
  sort method 18
  tostring method 18

  transpose method 18
  unique method 18
array operations
  put method 22
  take method 22
arrays creation
  about 13
  Copy method 12
  Eye method 13
  Fill method 12
  identity method 12
  ones_like method 12
  ones method 12
  random submodule method 13
  Tolist method 12
  vstack method 13
  zeros_like method 12
  zeros method 12

B

batch gradient descent 75
Baum-Welch algorithm 111
BeautifulSoup 132
Boston's housing dataset
  URL 97
breadth-first algorithm 120

C

centroid methods
  about 50
  k-means 50, 51
classification
  about 4
  methods, comparing 96

G

Gaussian Naive Bayes 82-84
Gaussians clustering 46
generalized linear models
  about 75
  k-nearest neighbours (KNN) 80
  lasso regression 77
  linear regression 76
  logistic regression 77, 78
  probabilistic interpretation 78, 79
  ridge regression 76
GET method 191

H

hidden Markov model (HMM)
  about 107-112
  Python example 112-118
hierarchical methods 54-56
HTML web pages
  about 197
  creating 197-200
hybrid recommendation systems
  about 179, 182
  feature augmentation 179
  feature combination 179
  mixed 179
  switched 179
  weighted 179
Hypertext Transfer Protocol (HTTP)
  about 191
  GET method 191
  POST method 191

I

indexer 121
information retrieval models
  about 126
  Doc2Vec 128
  Latent Semantic Analysis (LSA) 127, 128
  TF-IDF 127
  Word2vec 128, 129
inverted index scheme 121

K

kernel function
  using 95, 96
k-means 41, 50, 51
k-means++ 50
k-means (Lloyd's algorithm) 50
k-medians clustering 50
k-nearest neighbours (KNN) 80

L

Laplace smoothing 82
lasso regression 77
Latent Dirichlet allocation (LDA)
  about 138
  example 142-144
  model 139-141
Latent Semantic Analysis (LSA) 126-128
learning recommendation system
  association rules 175-177
LIBLINEAR 41
libraries
  Django 42
  Natural Language Toolkit (NLTK) 41
  scikit-learn (sklearn) 41
  SciPy 41
  Scrapy 41
LIBSVM 41
linear algebra operations
  dot method 24
  inner method 24
  linalg method 25
linear regression 76
logistic regression 77, 78
log-likelihood ratio (LLR)
  about 177, 217
  recommendation system method 177-179

M

machine learning
  about 4
  concepts 2, 3
  example 5-7

W